D0891408

Praise for *Banned from California*

Foshee's life fascinates, and his tales crackle on the page. ... In this lively and moving biography, a vital contribution to the history of LGBTQ life and activism in 20th century America, veteran reporter and broadcaster Steele memorializes the life of Jim Foshee, who first fled Idaho for California at age 15 in 1954 and went on to witness and experience the front lines of the nascent gay liberation movement.

~ *Publishers Weekly,* **Booklife "Editor's Pick" for Outstanding Quality**

I was like, "Oh well, here I'm going to read about some guy—I don't know who he is—some gay guy." And you know what? I was captivated from the very beginning! It was really great! This kid had the gumption to go hitchhiking across states and get into all of these adventures—like how brave was he as a kid! He kept coming and going because every time he would go back home, they'd lock him up in a mental hospital, so he'd run away and go to California again. This kid did crazy stuff, I'm not kidding you. Amazing story!

~ **Lisa Pedersen, co-host of** *Out of Whack* **podcast**

Steele's excellent organization of his biography adds further insight, bringing the mid-century life of an American gay man into vivid relief and painting a detailed picture of an era when homosexuality was illegal in many parts of the country. ... Overall, Steele does an excellent job of presenting the story of an activist and making it clear why his story matters.

~ *Kirkus Reviews* **(starred review) for Exceptional Merit**

The book arrived on a Saturday, and I just sat down, and like bam! I was 50 pages in and was like, "Oh, I don't want to stop." And then I was reading it in bed, and I read it the next day, and I literally read it over three days. It is a fascinating story. I absolutely enjoyed reading it cover to cover. The book is an incredible read! ...

At 22 years old he was imprisoned. There is so much detail in those sections of the book of what prison life was like and working on a chain gang in Texas in 1960. And it's remarkable that he even lived to get out and tell the story.

~ **Daren Stehle, host of** *Think Queerly* **podcast**

A fascinating biography. Readers have a clear image of a boy, defiant and flawed, innocent and rebellious, a complicated protagonist reminiscent of Holden Caufield in J.D. Salinger's *The Catcher in the Rye.* ... A vivid story of the modern gay civil rights movement with court cases and uprisings long before the well-known Stonewall riots, providing readers more depth into this history.

~ **Nicholas Villanueva,** *Out Front Magazine*

It's a fabulous book about a gay-rights pioneer you've never heard of—but you should have heard of him. He chose to live his life as an openly gay man starting in the early 1950s when there were virtually no openly gay people. Jim spent most of the first part of his life in institutions from an orphanage when he was a toddler, to being in juvenile detention, to then being put in the state mental hospital where he spent years of his adolescence. Then he goes to prison in his early twenties in the State of Texas as an out effeminate gay man, as a queen let's say. It's a terrific book, and I highly recommend it!

~ **Adam Sank, host of** *The Adam Sank Show* **podcast**

This is the enlightening biographical tale of Jim Foshee, a 14-year-old runaway whose stories of "persecution, redemption and the gay civil rights movement" use the culture and history of homosexuality in America as a backdrop for his many travels. There are also many anecdotes of people Foshee met and places he traveled to—drag queens, hustlers, good cops and bad cops pass through his life. The book also chronicles his contributions to the gay community.

~ **Lynn Childs,** *Seattle Gay News*

Incredible! This story is amazing because you get a character, you get a person that could be me or you or you that's listening right now, and you kind of get to walk in his shoes and navigate life the way that he does with all of this adversity and all of these challenges surrounding him; and it's insane. It's really, really, really fascinating!

~ **Marko & Tony Critellis, co-hosts of** *Relationsh!t* **podcast**

Witness from the persecution—how one gay soul lived to tell. *Banned from California* is inspiring and edifying. It is handsomely assembled, has many vintage black-and-white pictures of locales and individuals and is written with economy and clarity. Not surprisingly, and though easy and comfortable to read, it is meticulously annotated. ~ **Dr. Lawrence D. Mass,** *Medium.com*

Very smooth and comfortable read. A fascinating adventure tale of a life with twists at every turn. Provocative and compelling. What an incredibly open and honest connection with a culture that gets far too little exposure on such an intimate and personal level. Jim's story is an adventure of a lifetime, but one that came with many struggles and enlightenments.

~ **Charles Pearson,** *eBay Reviews*

For more information visit the book's website: BannedCA.com

BANNED
from California

Banned from California

-Jim Foshee-
Persecution, Redemption, Liberation
… and the Gay Civil Rights Movement

Robert C. Steele

Wentworth-Schwartz Publishing Company, LRCS

Banned from California -Jim Foshee- Persecution, Redemption, Liberation … and the Gay Civil Rights Movement

Published by Wentworth-Schwartz Publishing Company, LRCS
www.BannedCA.com

Copyright © 2020 by Robert C. Steele
Second Edition

ISBN 978-1-7340108-0-0 (Paperback)
ISBN 978-1-7340108-1-7 (Hardcover)

Library of Congress Control Number: 2020906850

Publisher's Cataloging-in-Publication Data

Names: Steele, Robert C., author.

Title: Banned from California -Jim Foshee- Persecution, Redemption, Liberation … and the Gay Civil Rights Movement / Robert C. Steele.

Description: Includes bibliographical references and index. Wentworth-Schwartz Publishing Company, LRCS, 2020.

Identifiers: LCCN: 2020906850 | ISBN: 978-1-7340108-0-0

Subjects: LCSH Foshee, Jim. | Gay men--United States--Biography. | Gay activists--Biography. | Hollywood (Los Angeles, Calif.)--Biography. |

BISAC BIOGRAPHY & AUTOBIOGRAPHY / LGBT

Classification: LCC HQ75.8 .F67 .S84 2020
                      DDC 305.38/9664/092--dc23

For Additional Cataloging in Publication Data Block information visit:
https://lccn.loc.gov/2020906850

Printed in the United States of America

Wentworth-Schwartz Publishing Company, LRCS
For information see website www.BannedCA.com

Rev 12.19

Contents

Author's Note

In the 1990s I began work on this biography about the life of Jim Foshee.

I met Jim in 1973. We worked together in the gay liberation movement of the 1970s. Eventually we became friends, and he came to trust me with the stories and secrets of his life. Jim was a story teller who loved to talk about his life's adventures and misadventures.

I interviewed him on several occasions. The quotes included in this book come from those interviews, interviews of other individuals plus my own memories.

Accounts and facts covered in this book are supported by historical records; articles from old gay newspapers, newsletters, periodicals, and journals; government documents; letters; and various audio recordings.

Banned from California is Jim's means to speak about his life. His words are all placed in quotation marks.

Jim was born in 1939 and lived his life as an out gay person throughout the last half century of the 1900s. This biography details his life and times, which spanned more than six decades. He was flawed and complicated, yet he survived the obstacles in his life.

Jim Foshee noted during an interview: "This is my story. I can remember a lot of experiences, but at my age I can't recall them all perfectly. Most of my memories are very clear; a few are vague. After all, a lot of this happened a long time ago."

Robert C. Steele

Chapter 1

California Here I Come

Jim Foshee had been planning his escape for months. The year was 1954. The 15-year-old was determined to put 800 miles between himself and his family.

The sunshine of California beckoned. Jim recalled, "I learned that California was the place to be. The parishioners at my parents' churches always ranted and raved and claimed that California was the place where all the queers and fruits were located, so I figured that's the place for me!"

The Idaho winter Jim had experienced during the previous six months had been bitter cold with lots of snow. Now the late spring weather still remained chilly in the mornings and even colder at nights.

Jim lived with his family in the small town of Ketchum, Idaho. It was founded in the late 1880s as a smelting center for the local mining district. In the late-1930s the world-famous Sun Valley ski resort began its multi-million-dollar operations a couple of miles away. Ketchum received the overflow of tourists who were unable to afford a stay in the elegant rental accommodations at Sun Valley.

Jim earned a small amount of money doing chores at Ketchum's Sun Motel-Hotel, which his mother Fannie and her third husband owned. It looked like a large two-story ski lodge. The motel part was on the downstairs first floor where guests could drive up to the rooms facing the parking lot. The hotel part was upstairs and featured individual rooms and a bath at the end of a long hall. The Sun Motel-Hotel provided comfortable lodging at a reasonable price for people who didn't want to shell out lots of money at swanky Sun Valley.

"I saved my allowances and earnings from the lodge for my big adventure. The school year had just finished, and I was heading to sunny California!" Jim slipped out at dawn with his small suitcase, jacket and his saved money. The teenager was setting out on an adventure that would redefine his life and put him in the midst of the civil rights struggle of gay people across the United States of America spanning a half century.

Figure 1: Sun Motel-Hotel, Ketchum, Idaho.

Jim's gay journey started when he hitchhiked his way along the dusty highways of Utah and Nevada and through the desert of southern California. He thumbed his way into the Los Angeles metropolitan area and landed in Hollywood. For a star-struck teenage boy who knew he liked guys, he had arrived in the Land of OZ. However, the fun and excitement he anticipated didn't match reality. It didn't even come close.

"Hollywood wasn't quite what I had imagined. It seemed rundown. I wondered where all the glamorous people were. I just knew that I'd meet at least one or two movie stars. I thought they might even put me in the movies. But the stars were missing in action."

Jim spent his day visiting tourist sites. At night he hung around the Sunset Strip, that 1.5-mile stretch of Los Angeles in an unincorporated part of West Hollywood just east of Beverly Hills. This was the playground where Hollywood royalty went to blow off steam at restaurants and clubs such as Ciro's, Café Trocadero and Mocambo.

For teenagers and acting hopefuls, the Strip was more like The Boulevard of Broken Dreams, a place to wander and wait to be discovered. For mobsters such as Bugsy Siegel, Mickey Cohen and Meyer Lanskey it was a part of their West Coast money-making empire.

Jim's California adventure kicked off in earnest in front of a nightclub on the Sunset Strip called the Melody Room. There he spied Bunny emerging from the club swishing to the hilt. Bunny was a man who liked to dress like a woman at home and anywhere else thought to be safe. In drag Bunny looked like a splashy woman in her twenties. All of the homosexuals and crossdressers who knew Bunny referred to him as "her" and "she."

On this particular night Bunny was dressed in a conservative suit, having just conducted business inside the nightclub.

Figure 2: Melody Room nightclub where Jim met Bunny on the sidewalk in front. Sunset Blvd. & Larrabee Street on the Sunset Strip. 1955. [Bison Archives/HollywoodHistoricPhotos.com]

"I saw Bunny waiting for a taxicab, and I just knew this person was a gay kindred spirit."

Bunny worked at a department store near her home she shared with her partner Dutch. "That day I began learning that gay men never revealed their last names to other gay people, and oftentimes they hid behind monikers instead of using their real first names. I remember that Dutch's real name was pretty common like Bill or Mike or something like that."

Dutch worked as a computer expert making good wages. The computers Dutch worked on operated on vacuum tubes and punch cards, and they took up entire rooms at Dutch's work offices.

Bunny had lived in four or five different cities before ending up in downtown Los Angeles. She and Dutch lived in an area bounded by Main Street and Hill Street with Broadway running through the middle. According to Bunny, downtown LA was the heart of the gay scene in the city.

Bunny was from Louisiana and spoke with a Cajun accent that sounded almost foreign to Jim.

"Bunny was delighted with me, 'Oh, a little darlin'! You are so precious.' She expressed concern that I should have been at home at that hour of night. So, I announced that I was visiting from out of town. Bunny was wary, 'Oh no, you're a runaway. My dear, you never should be living out on these streets.'"

The two already were becoming trusted friends. Bunny took Jim under her wing, and Jim found in her a mentor.

Dutch was on a trip out of town, so Bunny made her own decision to take Jim off the streets and give him safe haven in her home.

During Jim's first day with Bunny she gave him a tour of the downtown area. Bunny and Jim walked a half dozen blocks or so from Bunny's apartment to a wide-open park called Pershing Square. It covered an entire city block. In all four directions Jim gazed at the unobstructed views of downtown's tall sky scrapers and businesses. Buried deep in the ground underneath the park was a three-level parking garage and bomb shelter.

"I'd never heard of such a thing in my life—a park located on top of a huge parking garage. As a young kid I couldn't help but marvel at the novelty of it all. We walked around the park, and I admired the

Figure 3: Pershing Square, downtown Los Angeles. 1954.
[Bison Archives/HollywoodHistoricPhotos.com]

beautiful flowers and bushes and trees growing around its outer edges. The middle of Pershing Square reminded me of a big football field with no bleachers or goal posts or markings. That's when I knew Los Angeles was going to be full of surprises."

Bunny taught Jim about the harsh realities of being gay in the United States during that era and explained the risks gay people faced, even in the heart of the gay community in Los Angeles.

"She would point out to me various men she knew and explain that every one of them could be arrested, lose their jobs and careers and be reduced to absolute nothingness. They could be thrown into prison for years for the felonies of homosexual acts. Their names could appear in newspapers, and they'd have no rights according to the law. I realized that at any moment the police could ruin my life."

This realization crystallized Jim's thinking. He decided the threat of being scorned by society was not going to force him to live in the shadows or live a double-life like so many gay people were required to do.

"Instead of fretting that the cops would get me, I figured why worry. It freed me to do what I wanted. I never thought about getting old. For all I knew I'd live forever. I was carefree."

"As we meandered around, Bunny pointed out gay bars in the area. We walked along Hill Street, and she told me about a homosexual organization located in a shabby old building that we passed by. I never imagined that such an organization ever would exist." The organization was ONE Incorporated. It was an influential group that sought to educate people about homosexuality through classes and periodicals that it published. It was a fleeting remark that day, but years later Jim's curiosity would lead him back to the group's office.

Bunny went to work in the daytime at a downtown department store while Jim walked all around the downtown area. He spent time in Pershing Square every day talking to all sorts of friendly people in the park. He also met gay people there and began searching for the man of his dreams.

Jim had been deprived of movies as a kid, but now all of a sudden here he was in downtown LA among theaters along Broadway that showed movies all day long. They were enchanting places with the smell of popcorn and captivating sounds from the screen. 1950s ushers escorted customers down the aisles with flashlights to direct them to their seats. Nobody talked. Jim felt like he was in a sacred place.

"I could spend the entire day at one theater pigging out on movies, three hits one after another for only fifty cents."

During the day there were respectable crowds on the streets, but nighttime laid bare the more seedy and run-down aspects of the downtown area. At first Jim was unfamiliar with the streets, and they scared him. Strange people were on those streets. A smell of danger seemed to permeate the air. But Jim was young, and it was obvious he did not have any money, so he learned he could wander around without anybody bothering him.

Bunny's rule was that Jim had to be back home before dark. She got home around 7:00 in the evenings. She would cook supper every night. Jim was not yet a good cook. Jim would clean the bathroom, straighten the house and then after dinner he would wash and dry dishes.

"After I finished drying dishes, I'd join Bunny in the living room. She'd relax and lounge around in women's clothes. She'd read the evening newspaper, and we'd listen to radio shows like *The Shadow* and *Arthur Godfrey's Talent Scouts* and *Our Miss Brooks*. This was a time when few households had a television set."

"Bunny had collected a few records, and we played some of them on her phonograph player. I'd play the Nat King Cole song *Unforgettable* and lie on her couch dreaming away to those wonderful lyrics."

Bunny would let Jim dress up in women's clothes alongside her in drag. She entertained Jim with lots of high-spirited merrymaking. She performed drag skits for Jim as she pantomimed to her Rae Bourbon albums, including *Let Me Tell You About My Operation* featuring skits about Rae's supposed sex change operation and *You're Stepping on My Eyelashes!* showcasing some of Rae's gay nightclub comedy skits.[1]

Figure 4: Rae Bourbon albums, 1950s. [author's collection]

Rae Bourbon was a man (Ray Bourbon) who had been a prolific entertainer in the pansy nightclubs of the 1920s and 1930s, which featured drag routines by female impersonators.[2] Rae then began recording and selling phonograph records of female impersonation routines.[3] Earlier in life, Ray had worked as a minor character actor and extra in Hollywood, and in one silent movie Ray died in the arms of Rudolph Valentino who kissed Ray on-screen.[4] Later in life, Rae performed with Mae West.

Bunny personally knew Rae Bourbon. Bunny and Rae had met inside the Melody Room nightclub, the same place where Jim had met Bunny on the street in front of the club. Bunny became a big fan of Rae and purchased some of the entertainer's records. Rae Bourbon's records made an initial early impression on Jim.

"Bunny told me that a lot of the bars and nightclubs that gay people patronized were owned by organized crime—and those included the Melody Room. I laughed at the rumors, but through the years I kept hearing the same claims about a lot of gay bars owned by mafioso types across the USA, so eventually I figured it had to be true."

Bunny and Jim would talk the evenings away. Jim told her about his dreams of finding an older mature husband. Bunny explained that if Jim wanted to succeed in a life of love, Jim would have to entice those men by being terribly effeminate. In the 1950s the game most homosexuals and crossdressers played was a reflection of heterosexual role models—one person was supposed to be masculine and the other one feminine.

"At bedtime I felt special turning in for the night sleeping in my own private bedroom under bunny's protection from the next room."

"Bunny's friend Trixie hung around a lot. She had a biting and sarcastic personality, and she constantly criticized Bunny's drag performances. But she owned a nice Nash Rambler that she used for driving Bunny around while Dutch was using their car in Montana visiting his parents and relatives."

Bunny was popular. On Friday night she and a couple of friends went out to a conservative gay bar where everybody minded themselves, dressed carefully in inconspicuous suits and ties, no flirting, no kissing, no makeup—do nothing that could attract the attention of undercover vice squad cops. Don't be an obvious queen.

The next night was quite a contrast. Bunny hosted a private drag party in her home. A dozen guys were inside the house dressed in drag—even Jim. It was his first time Jim watched a bunch of queens camping it up.

"I got the distinct impression that none of Bunny's close friends liked having me around and wished I'd just leave. But Bunny stuck by me and told them that she and I were like sisters and had fun in drag together—she thought I was adorable."

After more than a week staying with Bunny, Jim returned to her home one late afternoon to find Bunny arguing with a guy. Jim realized that Bunny's partner Dutch had returned. He was complaining about Jim being there, "I'm only gone two weeks, and you manage to drag home some stray kid. You've lost your senses—as if you ever had any."

Bunny tried to protest, but Dutch didn't budge, "He's going!"

∇

Jim's carefree life with Bunny was over. No more movies, parties, walks through downtown or long talks about gay life. Jim packed his suitcase and hit the streets.

"I'd messed up again. I was at a loss of what to do in Los Angeles now. I realized I'd better hightail it back home to Idaho. All of the money I'd spent going to the movies would have paid to get out of town and eat some food along the way."

He had no money for a hotel room, and the proprietors certainly would not rent to a 15-year-old.

He had hitchhiked into LA days earlier, and he would simply hitchhike back home now—if only he could figure out the maze of freeways that lead out of town. Jim decided that the big freeway entry lanes located downtown would be a good place to hitchhike. But the interchanges seemed to go on forever. If only he could manage to get out of LA, the rest of the trip would be easy to navigate.

Jim walked to a nearby park to pause a while to figure out what to do. "I saw a policeman, and all of a sudden I remembered that my mother always told me to trust the police, 'A policeman is always your best friend. They'll always help you.' I suddenly had this great idea. I walked up to him and asked where the police station was. The police had plenty of police cars running around the city. I told the officer that I'd like the police to give me a ride out of town, so I could hitchhike my way back home. He told me where the downtown LA police station was located. He even was nice enough to escort me there himself."

Inside the station the police realized that Jim was a runaway. He told them his name, and they told him to wait on one of the wooden benches. He smiled at his fine performance and change of luck.

"Before long two officers came down and met me. I was overjoyed about them helping me to get out of town. My mother was right."

In reality, these were juvenile detectives. The scene that played out next looked like a 1950s crime movie. The cops intended to get this unsuspecting runaway to start singing like a canary.

One detective had closely cropped hair—mean looking with the demeanor of a bulldog. The other guy was gentle and friendly and even got Jim a Coca-Cola to drink. One detective was nasty. The other was kind. Jim ignored the gruff guy and turned to the guy who was nice to him.

Both detectives threw questions at Jim one after another: What was he doing in the city? How long had he been there? He was a runaway, wasn't he?

Jim noticed the piece of paper lying on the table that read: All Points Bulletin—James "Jim" Foshee.

"They grilled me for what seemed like hours. I was a typical young teenager—not clever enough for them. They got me to admit that I really lived in Idaho and that I'd been in LA for a couple of weeks. And from there the game was all in the hands of my interrogators."

"Do you have any money?" "No."

"What have you been doing with your days here?" "Going to the movies."

"How did you get the money to get into the movies?" Jim couldn't get Bunny mixed up in this, "I've been staying with my uncle."

"Oh really. What's your uncle's name?" "Uncle Dutch."

"Where have you been living with Uncle Dutch?" "At a tall hotel across from Pershing Square."

"What room is it?" "I can't remember."

"Who's this Uncle Dutch? How old is he?" "In his twenties."

"Are you making money from guys to have sex with you?" "No. Not at all."

"So, you've been living with this Uncle Dutch. He really isn't your uncle, is he?" "Well, Dutch isn't exactly my uncle, but he is."

"This Dutch guy did things sexually to you, didn't he?" I played dumb and asked them what they meant. "He played with your dick, your pecker, your prick."

The detectives turned up the heat, informing Jim that if he refused to tell them where Dutch lived, they would take him next door to a room where they would hook him up to a machine. It would tell them exactly what they wanted to know and would prove if Jim was lying. Things were going to get rough. The detectives told Jim that if he refused to cooperate, he would not be going back home to Idaho. But if he revealed what he knew they would make sure he got back home safe and sound.

Jim explained that Dutch had gotten mad at him and made him leave his home, that Jim had walked around looking for a way to get out of Los Angeles and thought the police could help him.

The nice detective told Jim, "You don't owe anything to this guy. He stranded you in Los Angeles. He didn't even have the decency to give you a bus ticket back home." The detective told Jim that Dutch had treated him bad, and he claimed that he never would treat a boy the way Dutch treated Jim. By this time with Jim's delayed reaction, he started thinking the detective was correct—Dutch did do him wrong.

"Eventually the pressure and psychology wore me down. I wasn't the strongest person in the world."

Whenever the gruff detective asked questions, Jim would resist. But the nice officer was understanding and kept telling the gruff detective that Jim was a nice kid, that he was a good truthful boy. The detectives told Jim that as soon as he finished telling them the whole truth, they would take him home. They would not just merely take him to the edge of the LA metro area. They would put Jim on a train with a nice sleeping cabin to travel home in luxury. That sounded great to Jim.

The detectives brought in doughnuts as Jim explained to them where Dutch was located. They typed up a paper containing legalistic jargon and other technical words, which at that time Jim did not understand, such as "oral copulation" and "anal intercourse." They used no simple words like "homo" or "queer" or any other words Jim easily would recognize.

As soon as Jim signed the document the juvenile detectives put him and his suitcase into a police car and drove off.

"I was happy to be on my way to the train station and then home. But they drove me instead to Los Angeles's notorious juvenile hall. Obviously, we weren't at any train station. Hoping against hope I asked them where we were at. Maybe they had to stop along the way. They stated that we were at juvenile hall. They said this was where they put boys, and I'd have to stay there while they completed the paperwork. Well, I guessed that sort of made sense to me."

Guards locked up Jim in a large area with benches and a radio. Along the back were rooms with bunks. The doors to the outside all had small windows with bars.

When Jim walked in, the other kids saw him for what he was—an effeminate young teenager.

"They were the nastiest bunch of inner-city juvenile delinquents, real crooks and evil street kids. These were street punks—as dangerous and deadly as hardened criminals, and in fact many of them actually were already hardened criminals. I'd never been around people like them before. I was scared to death. They called me sissy and girl. They never hit me or hurt me, but they saw me as someone beneath them and someone to degrade."

The boys seemed to be going through a stage where they felt proud of being in prison—or at least as close as they had come to prison. The delinquents emulated the Bowery Boys whose movies roused the kids' bluster. The kids strutted around juvenile hall imitating the Bowery talk and bravado.

"To me these kids seemed like goofballs. I wasn't interested in kids my own age. I'd always been attracted to older guys. It wasn't that I disliked the guys, it was just that they were trashy young punks."

Even though the boys were only in their mid-teens, they already had accumulated plenty of street smarts. The juvenile delinquents had quite the vocabulary of cuss words, many that Jim had never heard before. Since his folks were very religious, he was not allowed to say darn, gee or golly, let alone hell or damn. So instead, he created substitute words like foot or shoot—his two main swear words at the time.

Guards constantly watched over the delinquents. All of the juveniles attended school in the lockup's classrooms, but they were always kept separate from older guys.

Jim felt lonely and out of place.

"These juvies 'talked shit' and claimed that you had to keep beating your meat until you came. They would look at each other's hands and laugh and say that if you jacked off, hair would grow on your palms. So I carefully checked my palms to make sure no hair was starting to grow."

"The showers were right across from my room. There was this older guy almost 17 years old who was getting ready to go to The Big

House as he called it. He was nude in the shower and had been nice to me. He wanted me to come and take care of him. He said he was going to have to go without it for a long time. So, I followed him to his room and gave him what he wanted. It was the only time I fooled around in juvenile hall."

The days dragged by. No officials came to see Jim, and no one told him what was going on. He was in limbo. He had not been charged with anything thus far.

"I didn't know anything about any rights. I figured I was kept in juvenile hall because I had committed a crime and that it was only a matter of time before I'd be charged. The authorities had told me that what I had done was wrong. I thought they could do anything to me they wanted."

Finally one day a public defender showed up and explained to Jim that he would be making a court appearance the next day. Up until then Jim had no idea what was happening. Jim asked if he was in trouble. The guy told Jim no. All Jim had to do was go to court and tell the judge about his time in LA. Then Jim would get out of juvenile hall and go home.

The next day a social worker took Jim to the large courthouse building. Jim waited in a side room and, just like the police interrogation, the scene that unfolded in court looked like a made-for-TV drama.

"I watched them open the door, and all of a sudden we were walking right into a large courtroom full of strangers. I didn't know if they were all there to view my case or were waiting for other cases. They immediately put me on the witness stand. The strangers in the courtroom audience kept staring at me."

The prosecutor began by asking Jim if he knew the difference between good and bad and telling the truth or not. Jim replied yes.

Sitting directly in front of Jim looking right into his face was Dutch, whose eyes were pleading, *"Oh, I'm so sorry."* Then Jim saw Bunny in back of Dutch dressed in a nice suit. She had tearful droopy eyes—like a poor basset hound.

"By this time, I'd concluded that the authorities had committed an injustice by lying to me and keeping me there all that time. I was mad."

The prosecutor asked Jim to tell the court what happened. He wanted Jim to identify the person in the courtroom that Jim had been staying with in LA. In his statement to the jury the prosecutor used words like oral copulation. Jim was slow in recalling what that phrase and others meant, but when the prosecutor spelled it out in plain English the courtroom audience was shocked.

"All of a sudden I realized what the court was trying to do. I couldn't let them do this to Dutch and Bunny. Dutch didn't belong in jail."

Jim let loose, "No! It didn't happen! The police made me say it!"

The courtroom erupted. The prosecutor turned to Jim, "What do you mean it didn't happen?"

Jim blurted out, "The police kept me in a room all night long and mistreated me! The police said if I told this story, they were going to send me home, and instead they put me in jail. I didn't do nothing. I didn't even go into that guy's house."

The audience leaned forward. Jim was embarrassed and started to cry. In later years court authorities mostly closed adolescent testimony from public view, but this was an era defined in part by public shaming in courtrooms across the country. There was no such thing as Miranda Rights at the time. And whether it was a police investigation, a criminal trial or a Congressional hearing, remaining silent or refusing to answer questions meant you must be guilty.

"I don't know where I got blaming the police for this mess and suffering. But as I saw it, it was true. My friends—as my mother referred to the police—had gotten me into this mess and caused this suffering."

The judge asked Jim, "Are you sure what you're saying?"

The prosecutor said, "Your honor, I don't understand this. We have a signed statement from this witness."

The judge turned to Jim again and asked, "Are you sure that nothing happened?"

Jim denied everything, "I only saw that guy the last day I was there. I never even talked to him. Nothing happened." The entire case had hinged on Jim's word about Dutch. The court had no other witnesses.

Dutch's defense attorney rose up, "Your Honor, I recommend dismissal of this case."

The judge was not ready to admit defeat and called a recess. As Jim was leaving the stand the judge told Jim's social worker, "I want to see this witness in my chambers." Jim and the social worker waited in the anteroom, and after a couple of minutes they went into the judge's office. The judge sat at his desk, livid, "Look son, we know this guy did it. I know you lied. You've cost the state a lot of money." Jim thought to heck with the state, it wasn't fair for the judge to put all the blame on him.

The judge spoke, "We could have sent this guy up for decades and gotten this child molester out of the way. Instead, he'll end up free. For the life of me I cannot figure out why you would want to protect this pervert."

The judge added, "Now we can go back into court, and we can just disregard your testimony."

Jim replied, "No, I won't!" Jim refused to back down.

His Honor blew his top, "This is a disgrace. You're a disgrace! You can never come back here! I ban you from the State of California! You stay at home with your parents, young man. What you need is strong discipline. If I hear that you dare come back to California, I'll send you to jail for good!"

"I never considered whether the judge in reality could ban me from the state. I didn't stop to think that he might be bluffing to get me to stay put at home with my parents and behave myself."

"I thought to myself that the judge was like so many straight people who just assumed that if you're 15 years old, you were preyed upon by some pervert. Now my anger was transferred toward the judge. I just wanted to go home and finally get this nightmare over."

Back in the courtroom the judge dismissed the case.

An officer of the court escorted Jim to Idaho. Court authorities worried that if they left Jim by himself, he might take off and get into more trouble. He and his escort traveled by train with their own two tiny bunks and ordered food delivered to their compartment. The escort knew nothing about Jim's case other than Jim was a runaway kid whom the officer was supposed to keep in his sights.

Jim's mother and her third husband Fred picked him up at the Shoshone, Idaho train station about 70 miles away from Ketchum and Sun Valley. They showed no sympathy. His stepfather was stern, but he left Jim's discipline to Jim's mother—the opposite way that Jim had been handled by his mother and her previous husband, Jim's first stepfather.

"Deep down, my mother always had known that I was homosexual or weird or different, but she wouldn't admit it since she was very religious. Homosexuality was against all she believed was right."

On the way home Jim's mother told him, "You'll learn not to do such foolish things." Los Angeles authorities had told his mother everything that had happened with the police and Dutch's trial. "She figured I'd gotten what I deserved."

"From that experience forward I learned to be wary of cops, but that didn't keep me from returning to California. That was the place for me."

Chapter 2

A Young Child

Jim made his acting debut in 1944 when he was five years old. He donned a little suit that his mother, Fannie, had given him and went to work for the Lord, putting on a good show as a young minister.

"I was imitating what I'd seen grown-ups do, like young kids often do. It was strictly imitative. I didn't know what I was talking about, but I did it because that's what was expected of me. I liked it because I was getting attention from my audiences."

Jim's father, "Charlie" Charles Daniel Foshee, served as a guest preacher in churches and revival tents all around the south and as far away as Ohio and California. Jim's mother, Fannie Sue Trummell accompanied her husband on the church circuit.

Jim's parents both had an extensive ancestral history in the USA's deep South (Alabama, Mississippi, the Carolinas, Virginia and British Colonial America going as far back as the 1600s). Many of the Foshees made their homes in Foshee, Alabama, an unincorporated community in southern Alabama. Foshees had immigrated to the USA from Europe, and because of those ancestral roots, the Foshees in America continued using the European pronunciation of Foshee (foe SHAY).

Jim's grandfather "Jim" James Mitchell Foshee moved to Texas as a young man where he met and married Charlie's mother Georgia Jones Foshee. They made their home in Dallas.

In 1911 Jim's mother, Fannie, was born in Mississippi. Her father, "J.E." James Elmer Trummell, was a farmer in Carroll County. After J.E.'s first wife died, he married 15-year-old Lillie Belle Brandon, Fannie's mother. Lillie Belle raised a total of nine children—four of

J.E.'s children from his first marriage plus five children born to Lillie Belle and J.E.

In the late 1920s Fannie worked in a steam laundry in San Angelo, Texas. One of her co-workers, Georgia, introduced Fannie to her son, Charlie Foshee. The two fell in love and married in 1930. Jim recalled, "My mother believed in the old school of thought that if a man proposed and if he was religious, he could do no wrong."

The following year the couple's first son, "Danny" Charles Daniel Foshee, Jr., was born in 1931 in Arkansas. Fannie tended home, taking care of baby Danny and her husband. Charlie worked as a laborer at odd jobs, and he preached. The couple left San Angelo and began to roam the U.S. riding the church circuit as itinerate preachers. In warm months they preached tent revivals. During cold months they preached inside buildings.

The couple was poor and living a hand-to-mouth existence. Verily, Charlie and Fannie were serving God wherever they were needed. The couple was a team, a two-person band in a sense, and their performances followed a rigid and predictable schedule wherever they went. While Charlie preached, Fannie accompanied him playing her accordion and singing.

Activities and church services began around 9:00 in the morning and shut down at 9:00 at night. Services started in mornings with religious hymns sung by the congregation. People would get up and testify and thank the Lord for the blessings they received. The minister preached the good news and condemned sin. Then everybody got on their hands and knees on the altar and prayed. Preachers like Charlie guided their flocks as the parishioners came "under the power" and spoke in tongues and danced—dancing was a sin unless done under the power of the Lord. Preachers seldom spoke in tongues or came under the power, instead guiding parishioners while they requested blessings from God.

A large afternoon meal followed mid-day services. The kids would play tag and other games while the grownups visited. Then everybody was treated to homemade ice cream.

Evening services resumed at about 5:00 with Charlie and Fannie repeating the day's earlier program all over again.

Lastly, the good minister appealed to the people to give money so the work of God could continue, but the parishioners were not rich.

The Great Depression had plunged the United States and the world into economic ruin. People had far less money to spend. Churches dealt with declining contributions that forced parishes to slash budgets for social programs and ministers' pay. Depending on the contributions raised, the church would split the take with the guest itinerate preachers—an earned honorarium. Fannie always was capable of meeting the family expenses with whatever money Charlie and she were able to pull in.

The church circuit took Jim's parents to the small towns of Palo Pinto County, Texas. There in 1933, 22-month-old Danny died of measles, leaving Charlie and Fannie childless. A little over a year later the couple was blessed with the birth of a baby daughter, "Ruthie" Eula Ruth Foshee. Ruthie was born at home in Young County, Texas on April 1, 1934.

Serving the Lord took Charlie and Fannie in 1935 to Oklahoma. By 1939 the couple was living in the Toledo, Ohio area. Fannie had suffered a couple of miscarriages after Ruthie's birth. Ruthie said her prayers every night asking God to bring her a baby brother.

Jim made his debut on March 6, 1939. "Jimmy" James David Foshee was born at home just like his sister, a common practice at the time—44% of births in the U.S. in 1940 occurred outside of a hospital.[5] Jimmy was the couple's second son and only living one.

"My mother claimed that I was born blind or became blind because the doctor used a solution to wash my eyes out, and it was too strong; so, I couldn't see. She told me the reason I regained my eyesight is that she took me to a faith healer, and he laid hands on me and supposedly cured me. She would always remind me that my cure was a great miracle."

A year after Jim's birth, church work took the family across the country to Montebello, California, a town east of Los Angeles that was being absorbed into the burgeoning LA metropolitan area. In the 1940 Census the couple listed Charlie's occupation as "preacher" and Fannie as not working outside the home.

The Great Depression was ending. The economy was making a comeback because the United States was beefing up its military in anticipation of possibly going to war with Nazi Germany and Imperial Japan.

Figure 5: Fannie, Ruthie, Jimmy & Charlie. Littlefield, Texas.

The Foshee family did not reap the rewards of an economy that was starting to boom again. Jimmy's and Ruthie's lives were about to be thrown into turmoil.

The family moved to the tiny town of Pine Hills, Alabama. Charlie fell ill. Doctors told him to slow down after being diagnosed with an enlarged heart after a bout with rheumatic fever. But Charlie had committed his life to God and continued preaching hard. On April 11, 1941, the Reverend Charles Daniel Foshee died.

"I was two years old when my father died. I don't remember a thing about him."

"In those days most people didn't go to hospitals. Unless they were wealthy, people couldn't afford it. When you got sick, you went to your room, and it may have taken months, but you eventually died."

Fannie was now faced with the difficult situation having to support Ruthie and Jimmy without a husband. Fannie strived to overcome her predicament.

Charlie had left no insurance. World War II had begun. Food and goods were rationed. Fannie would have to get herself a job in order to survive.

She and the kids moved to the Tuscaloosa, Alabama area.

Figure 6: Ruthie and Jimmy.

Fannie's mother, Lillie Belle, moved in and cared for the two grandchildren who adored the sweet funny lady. She cared for the children, prepared meals, took care of the house and helped her daughter with emotional support.

Fannie worked outside the house most days trying to make a halfway decent living to support the four of them the best she could manage.

Figure 7: Grandma Lillie Belle Trummell
in Salvation Army uniform.

After living together for a year and a half, Grandma Lillie Belle had to say goodbye to the kids. She moved out to live with one of her other daughters. Fannie was well known from her religious work with Charlie and had been given the chance to go back on the church circuit as a preacher with the Church of God. She could make decent money on the circuit, but she faced the difficult decision of what to do with her children. After praying, Fannie decided that the best thing for the children would be to place them in the Church of God Orphanage for homeless children in Cleveland, Tennessee.

The two children ended up living at the orphanage for three years. Upon entering, Ruthie was eight years old. She already had experienced the loss of her daddy, and now in the orphanage she was dealing with the emotional trauma of being alone in a strange place with neither parent.

Jimmy was about to turn three years old. "I really don't remember anything about entering the orphanage or how I initially dealt with it."

Figure 8: Jimmy at Church of God Orphanage, Cleveland, Tennessee.

Fannie preached the circuit at various week-long tent revivals around Tennessee, Alabama, Mississippi, Georgia, North Carolina, South Carolina—all over the South. Dressed in beautiful white suits with her accordion at her side, she was a rarity since very few women evangelists preached in the 1940s. She was in high demand across the South.

Fannie did not forget about her kids. She made sure she visited them once or twice a year. With the decent money she now made, she sent gifts and clothes. Jimmy received many books, so he started reading a lot at a very young age.

Ruthie and Jimmy were lucky in one aspect, because most of the other kids at the Church of God Orphanage were true orphans who had no one to love them and provide a home. But Ruthie and Jimmy were unlucky in a way, because they were split up—Jimmy lived on the boys' farm, and Ruthie lived at the girls' facility a couple of miles away in town.

"My sister used to come over and visit me at the boys' farm. I developed a close relationship with Ruthie. She was the one I depended on throughout my childhood because she would always look after me, sort of like my protector."

Figure 9: Church of God Orphanage, Cleveland, Tennessee. Mrs. Hayes (matron), Ruthie & Jimmy.

While most of the kids' caregivers at the orphanage were nice, some could be short tempered, impatient and unkind. The church ran the orphanage with a very firm hand but provided a stable life for the children it took in. "Since I don't remember a whole lot about the orphanage, it must not have been too terrible."

Ruthie and Jimmy became two of the best-dressed kids at the orphanage. It was during a visit one year that Fannie brought along the new little suit for 5-year-old Jimmy so he could preach the gospel. Charlie and Fannie believed that if you asked God, you could dedicate somebody's life to the Lord before they were born, thus they had dedicated Jimmy's life in service to the Lord as a future minister. It was at the orphanage that Jimmy would dress up in that suit, stand there and begin preaching to the kids.

After the two children had spent three years in the orphanage, Fannie was set to take them back to live with her in Hot Springs, New Mexico (later renamed Truth or Consequences, New Mexico). The town had numerous local hot springs and 40 different hot-spring spas.

In 1945, 11-year-old Ruthie with 6-year-old Jimmy in tow boarded a train in Tennessee to travel to their new home and life with their mother. The train was filled with soldiers and sailors who were returning home from World War II European battles. The servicemen all kept watch over the two children, proclaiming that they had fought for the children of America. Throughout that journey to Hot Springs the young men took care of Ruthie and Jimmy as though the two children were their own little brother and sister.

Fannie reunited with her two children at the Hot Springs train station, and they resumed their lives together. Living at Fannie's home seemed quiet to Jimmy in contrast to the usual hive of activity at the orphanage. The kids began to settle in together. Although Jimmy could not remember living with his mother before the orphanage, he was nonetheless beginning to get reacquainted with her. "She seemed to be a nice lady—a lot like some of the caregivers back at the orphanage."

Figure 10: Jimmy at Hot Springs, New Mexico.

The new home life was looking promising. "I was back with Ruthie and felt safe. I liked my mother too; but I couldn't remember much about her. I don't think I really was capable of bonding a lot with my mother, because by this time I'd already lived half of my life at the orphanage without my mother. I couldn't recall anything before the orphanage."

Chapter 3

Life with Fannie & Ross

Fannie Foshee always believed in the sanctity of marriage. She made it clear to her children that God intended for a person to marry only once in life.

Five years after her husband died, she changed her stated religious belief about marriage after meeting a part-time preacher named "Ross" John Ross Davis. He was a stern-looking man who wore wire-rimmed spectacles and bore a slight resemblance to President Harry S. Truman. Ross was the same age as Fannie, a couple of years younger than Charlie Foshee.

Figure 11: Ross Davis and Fannie, 1946.

Ross believed his true calling was spreading the word of the Lord and battling the influence of the devil on this mortal fallen world. He was unable to make a living preaching full time, so he worked at a regular job.

Within months after Ruth and Jim joined Fannie in Hot Springs, she and Ross married in April 1946. Fannie now believed her second marriage was part of God's plan for her and her children. Before they married, she already was involved in establishing her own church and had gained a reputation for herself as a faith-healer.

"Ruth and I didn't want her to marry Ross. I didn't remember my father, but my sister did. And we didn't want somebody else in our lives. We didn't need it—but my mother needed it, and that was the priority."

Ross moved into Fannie's house following their marriage. With Ross now a part of their lives, Fannie believed this marriage was a true blessing. After all, the children needed a father, and Jim needed a strong male role model.

"Ross had no sense of humor," Jim recalled. "He didn't want our friendship. He really didn't like the fact that my mother had two children. He was never a loving father and never paid us any attention unless he was disciplining us."

The discipline Ross metered out with the full support of Fannie amounted to beating Ruth and Jim with a variety of straps and switches every time he believed the two children came under the influence of the devil. This apparently happened so often that Jim, during one particular three-week period, ran away from home every day.

A beating or so-called discipline followed a simple pattern: Ross whipping Jim followed by Fannie trying to comfort Jim's hurt. Ross was the Man of the House and Fannie the subservient wife. The couple believed this to be true because, after all, such an arrangement was spelled out in the Bible. Ross made that point clear to Fannie on many occasions, and Fannie followed suit. Notwithstanding, this type of arrangement was part of Fannie's family history. This was how her father acted, severely whipping her and her siblings whenever he thought they needed it.

Ross and Fannie's church associates also believed that to spare the rod amounted to spoiling the child, as the old adage goes—or as these church people put it, giving the children a licking to blister them good when they needed something to think about.

"Ross didn't watch over us or pay us much attention, except when he punished us. To him everything was the devil's work. He was determined to make both of us into saints. He first started in on Ruth. She would do something wrong, and he would scream at her and beat her. She fought him and stood up to the abuse though. She was a little older than me, real stubborn and a tomboy. This kind of abuse was something new to us."

For weeks Ross and Fannie held nightly revivals. They insisted that Jim—the preachers' young son—go to all church services.

"Every night I was expected to show up dressed in my best clothes and sit in the front. After 10 or 20 minutes of that I was bored." Since the church lacked drinking water, Jim would tell his mother that he was thirsty and was going back to the parsonage where they lived. "Sometimes I'd just sneak off when they were praying."

Instead of going to the parsonage and returning to the revival, Jim started walking around exploring the town of Hot Springs and discovered a little Mexican movie theater three blocks from the parsonage. "I would slip out of church, and I'd hotfoot it down to the theater. I remember going by it, and for some reason this woman who was the cashier would let me in for free."

Jim got into a pattern of going there. The theater was completely Mexican. "I don't even know if Hot Springs had an Anglo movie theater." Jim would go inside, sit down and watch Mexican black and white westerns. "The characters all had big sombreros. They only spoke Spanish, so I couldn't understand a thing they said, but I could see enough in the action to understand what was going on." Jim would sit there in the dark and watch people living a different lifestyle, doing exciting things, riding horses and jumping off their horses. Jim felt a thrill from his new experiences at the movies.

Ross and Fannie had laid down the law that their children were forbidden to watch any movies. Movies were a tool of the devil. No films were good enough. They were all works of the devil, which meant the two kids were not allowed to even watch any Walt Disney movies or other children's movies.

Jim's mother and the church people around her had a healthy respect for books. Books had been around for centuries, and religious people believed they were good—they had an admiration for books. However, movies had existed for only about three decades by then, and the good religious people had not yet warmed up to the movies by the 1940s.

Jim's mother would buy him all of the kids' books he wanted. Jim was a voracious reader and read all sorts of stories like Robinson Crusoe, Huckleberry Fin, Tom Sawyer and adventure stories. "I guess she and Ross weren't that knowledgeable about these books. They didn't read Huckleberry Finn or Tarzan. They didn't know that Tarzan and Jane weren't married."

Even though Jim was absent from a revival, Ross was so distracted with the services that he often did not realize for an hour or two that Jim was missing. Since Ross was preaching, he was prevented from leaving until services were completed.

"After church it wouldn't take him long to come and drag me out of the theater. It happened all the time. He'd take me home and take a strap to me to beat the devil out of me. You have to understand, it wasn't me misbehaving—it was the devil that was doing all of this. But the more he beat me the more stubborn and resolved I was that I'd still go to the theater the next time I wanted to go." Fannie's prevailing attitude was that Ross's actions were morally right and fair—that it was the father's duty to discipline children.

After Ruth received one particular severe beating from Ross, she went to the Hot Springs Police Department and revealed to them what had been occurring. When the juvenile authorities examined the bloody marks over her body, they concluded that something very wrong was going on in that home. "At that time there must have been laws about overdoing a beating of a child, because as soon as Ruth went to the authorities, they summoned Ross to their offices for what was supposed to be a serious meeting; but Ross packed up and disappeared, and we just sat around in Hot Springs and waited until my mother heard from him."

$$\nabla$$

Ross had gone to Sunnyslope, Arizona, in the desert just north of Phoenix. It was another community in the U.S. that would get absorbed into an expanding metropolitan area a couple of decades later by getting annexed into the City of Phoenix. Ross was from the Phoenix area and had relatives there, including four children from his previous marriage.

Ross had found a job, and then he seized a serendipitous opportunity for him and Fannie to build a Church of God congregation in Sunnyslope. Ross sent for Fannie. She loaded up both kids and the family belongings and joined her husband in Arizona for the enthusiastic opportunity to build their own church in the desert community.

Sunnyslope was about a 15-minute drive from Phoenix. Its population was about a thousand people. The desert area was dry and considered to be a good place for people with tuberculosis or asthma in search of better health. The family lived in a big stone house on the edge of the community. "I'll never forget it, even though we only spent about a year there. The summers were so hot, and this stone house was so cool."

Figure 12: Jim, 10 years old. Sunnyslope, Arizona. January 1950.

"I remember that in the yard was a Saguaro cactus, and I made a lot of drawings of that cactus. But basically, you had to be very careful because I remember going Easter egg hunting outside our yard in the desert, and we were told to be careful when you picked up rocks because a rattlesnake might pop out. Now as I think about it, hiding Easter eggs in the desert was kind of stupid."

Jim's world extended as far as the back yard of the house, surrounded by primitive desert land, desert vegetation, cacti and desert creatures. He was no longer free in Sunnyslope to gallivant around and sneak off to movies. The two kids did get out by themselves though, but only when riding their school bus that passed by horse and cattle ranches and cotton farms along a 10-mile route to the town of Glendale where Jim attended first grade and Ruth the eighth grade.

Using his carpenter skills, Ross began constructing the new Church of God building and a parsonage for the preachers' family. They moved into the parsonage while the church was still being constructed. Fannie began assembling a congregation by going out in the town and using her refined street preaching skills to entice people into the new church.

Ross was finishing the construction of the church building when one day he fell off the church's new roof and broke his arm.

Ross and Fannie barely were making a decent living and were forced to work odd jobs to support themselves while they developed their mission. When Arizona cotton bolls were ready for harvest in the summer, Ross and Fannie picked cotton in the hot desert sun and brought Ruth and Jim along to help. Since Ross only had one working hand to pick cotton, Ruth was able during many days to pick more cotton with her two hands than Ross could with his one good hand, a rivalry that produced more cotton and more income. Nine-year-old Jim had a small pillowcase that he was able to fill with the cotton he had managed to pick during most days.

Ross' four children from his previous marriage lived in the town of Mesa in the eastern Phoenix metro area, but his kids never came around to visit. That was fine with Fannie who considered Ross' kids too grown up to be interacting much with Ruth and Jim.

In 1949, Ruth and Jim's half-sister was born in a Phoenix area hospital. "Anita" Anita Faye Davis was a frail, nervous little girl. Since there was a 10-year gap between her and Jim's ages, Jim wanted little to do with Anita. She was Ross' daughter, and in Jim's mind that tainted her.

The new Church of God in Sunnyslope was becoming quite successful. Ross wanted to be a preacher but was not a good public speaker, so Fannie became the main preacher at the church. She also played the piano and her accordion. Fannie, Ruth and Jim became a popular singing trio that entertained parishioners during church services. Fannie wore her beautiful white suits. She was very modest and believed that a woman who wore fancy clothes deserved all of the trashy comments she received from men, but if a woman behaved like a lady she would be treated with respect.

Things were going splendid in Sunnyslope—at least at church. Before Jim's mother went into the hospital to give birth to Jim's half-sister Anita, Ross tried to fondle Ruth. Jim was not aware of it at the time. "Ross didn't get away with it because Ruth was a feisty person and called Ross a dirty pervert." She didn't tell her mother, but she again turned in Ross to the authorities for child cruelty. The same pattern was repeating itself—Ross ran off again and got a job, and then Fannie traipsed after him with her kids in tow.

Following the family's year in Sunnyslope, Ross ended up in the northern panhandle of Idaho in the mining town of Kellogg about 100 miles south of Canada. Right after Fannie and her three kids arrived in Kellogg, Ruth went to the local police to give them advanced notice of what authorities in New Mexico and Arizona determined about the severe beatings Ross had inflicted.

The family lived on a farm outside of Kellogg. It had an underground storm cellar separate from the house. In case of bad weather, the family was able to stay underground in the protection of the cellar. Fannie used it to store potatoes and jars of food she canned as various fruits and vegetables became ripe for picking, including peaches, pears and tomatoes. She even made her own ketchup.

Jim was free from the confines of the isolating desert that surrounded his home back in Arizona, and now in Idaho he was able to explore again. Like most 10-year-olds, Jim was becoming more independent. First, he began walking everywhere but quickly caught on to the benefits of hitchhiking. He discovered it was a fast and easy way to get where he wanted to go—simply jut out his thumb and get a ride.

Jim would wake up on weekend mornings and decide things were boring. "I wouldn't tell anyone; I'd just go. I loved it. It was freedom.

I didn't have any money, but people would give me rides. We lived in the middle of nowhere, so the first ride of the day I usually got was from some farmer who was turning off from his ranch. I hitchhiked gobs of times."

At first Jim never traveled far, just to downtown Kellogg. Eventually he began exploring the other small towns near Kellogg. He would arrive in the nearby little town of Wallace and walk around the streets and look in the store windows. "I had a great sense of freedom, since I didn't need to wait for my folks to drive me. It was exciting."

Whenever Jim returned home, he would tell Fannie, "Oh, I was visiting a friend." Although he did not tell his mother each time he thumbed rides, she was aware that sometimes he was hitchhiking. A lot of the boys hitchhiked around the area. "I'm sure in her mind she didn't particularly like it, but there wasn't any perceived danger in those days. I don't ever remember getting yelled at or being grounded because I hitchhiked. After all, the Bible never said anything about hitchhiking being wrong."

"In the 1950s people didn't consider hitchhiking dangerous. Most of the people who picked me up were men, and they never bothered me in the least. I was just a kid, and the nice thing about being a kid at that time was that we didn't have the fear that someone was going to kidnap or murder us." Hitchhiking was cool. A lot of people were doing it. Jack Kerouac wrote about it in his book *On the Road*. Television featured stories about traveling the highways in the show *Route 66*. Even back during the Great Depression hitchhiking was the way a lot of people got around.

"I slowly realized I could be here today, gone tomorrow. As time went on, I became more and more mobile—and uncontrollable."

One day Jim's mother told him about a newspaper article she had read about kids in a town south of Kellogg who got picked up by a man who molested them. She told Jim to be careful because it was dangerous to hitchhike now. The child molester could be headed for Kellogg. She told Jim that he had better watch out for perverts—child molesters on the loose who put their hands on kids.

"That did it! I wanted some man to put his hands on me too. I only had this vague idea what a child molester would do because my mother didn't go into any great details. She merely said they do things to boys and tell them it's fun. And that just increased my curiosity."

"I thought, *'Well, he's out there somewhere, and maybe I can meet him.'* So, I set out looking for this child molester and decided that if I hitchhiked all around, the chances might be pretty good that I'd meet him. I spent about three days just thumbing every five or ten minutes, going this way and that way, traveling here and there. Whenever anybody came along, I hoped it would finally be him. It was kind of a game I was playing, because when the cars would stop and I'd get inside, I'd wonder if I was getting into his car. Then Mr. Child Molester would get to molest me and teach me about whatever it was that I knew I wanted to do. I wanted to see what it would be like to be molested. I just had a feeling that it would be a lot of fun."

"Of course, I never met Mr. Child Molester. I pursued it on and off for a couple of weeks or so, and then the story died down, and I just moved on I guess."

$$\nabla$$

Jim's sister Ruth had grown into a beautiful and popular young woman. The guys were looking at her. She was a wild blonde—15 years old but smart enough to know what men wanted from women.

"I guess she had tasted sex in her teens and decided that she liked it. Of course, she was doing all of this without my folks knowing it."

Ruth met a guy, and they decided to get married. Fannie planned a big church wedding. "Ruth's young age didn't seem unusual to my mother. In the first half of the 1900s, especially from the South where my mother was from, it wasn't uncommon for younger girls to get married. My mother's family thought that to get married and have babies was the only role a female had—and the sooner she did it the better."

Ruth had been dating her boyfriend for a year. One day a couple of weeks before the wedding Ruth disappeared, and everyone worried about her. Finally, she phoned Fannie and announced that she had met a new guy, and she didn't like the one she was planning to marry. The new guy wanted to marry her and take her away, so they eloped and were married in February 1950 by the Justice of the Peace in Superior, Montana.

"She married the guy basically to get away from Ross. So, in essence my stepfather got rid of her. He really didn't want to have the stepchildren he was stuck with."

Jim felt alone without his older sister.

Figure 13: Jim and Anita

Jim was a stubborn as ever having learned from Ruth how to push back when Ross started in. With Ruth out of the picture, Ross turned his attention to Jim. He became more demanding and took to beating Jim on a regular basis. He employed several methods. "He made sure he didn't cause me to bleed. He wouldn't punch me in the nose or burn me. He wouldn't hit me in the face. I suppose from his point of view he was just being a normal father. After he would beat me, my mother would come in and soothe me."

By this time, Ross' discipline had evolved into several sadistic methods of inflicting pain. "Ross was determined to beat the devil out of me. Sometimes he would tie me up with a strap, which is probably why I don't like S&M; the idea of it just doesn't seem fun to me. Anyway, I'd be helpless, and he'd literally beat me with a strap or belt—whatever he had."

There were rare times when Fannie thought Ross went too far and told him so. Ross then would revert to punishing Jim by cutting off his allowance and employing other typical punishments parents use.

It was not in Ross' nature to engage Jim as most parents or father figures are expected to do with children. He never asked Jim how school was going, let alone saying something encouraging or nice. Ross was not one for small talk, hobbies or sports. He was of German descent and came off as a stern, humorless, no-nonsense type of man whose sole focus was to complete tasks in a timely and efficient manner. One of those tasks was to reform Jim through physiological and physical torture with the intent of remaking him into someone else.

"I think if he'd lived in Germany during World War II, he would have made a good SS man for the Third Reich. One evening he took me down into the outside cellar and tied me to the post in the middle of it. My mother was visiting neighbors or probably doing some church work or something. He took his belt to me, and he took out a bottle of what I would later find out was ether. There's nothing more fowl smelling than ether. And he'd put it under my nose and laugh— he had this crazy laugh—then he'd stop and hit me with the belt again two or three times. Then he'd put the ether under my nose again. That's when I finally realized that he was really evil."

∇

A couple of years had passed since Ruth went away. Jim decided he was going away too. He stole some money from Ross. "I shouldn't have done it, but I felt good doing it to him—taking his money while he was in the shower." And off Jim went to Portland, Oregon on his first bus trip alone. He carried along his little pirate's chest piggy bank that he could open to retrieve money.

Portland was a few hours away from northern Idaho, but it was the nearest large city. Upon arriving at the Portland bus station Jim began exploring the nearby area and stumbled onto the theater district. The street seemed like it had nothing but theaters—everything from small movie houses featuring three hits for a dollar to big movie palaces that showed all of the new films. "It was wonderful. I was in seventh heaven. I'm eating all of this candy and popcorn and junk and watching the first English-speaking movies I'd ever seen."

The theaters would open about 9:00 or 10:00 in the morning. During the daytime Jim watched first-run films, including *Joan of Arc* and Walt Disney's *Cinderella*. As soon as one movie was over, Jim walked to the next one.

At night Jim had to find some place to stay. Motels would not rent rooms to kids. He only had the clothes on his back and no change of clothes—a lesson Jim learned—and on subsequent trips he always carried a suitcase with clean clothes.

Jim would sleep in one of the all-night theaters. "I remember there was this one dreadful movie about the Rose Bowl in Pasadena with this football player and a woman who hoped to be the Rose Queen; and I saw that thing over and over and over, because late at night the theaters quit having three features, and they would show one film repeatedly through the night."

It was difficult for Jim to fall asleep in the theaters, since the movies were noisy. He would curl up the best he could on a seat. "The ushers would come down the aisles with flashlights to show people to their seats, and I didn't want them to catch me sleeping. So, I had to be really careful. That was a time before the streets became dangerous. I could see other people in the theater, but I was too scared to talk to any of them. I would fall asleep, then I'd wake up, and the same movie would be on. In the mornings at 5:00 or 6:00 the theater would clear out, and the staff would clean it up."

Jim's fun lasted three or four days. One night when he entered a theater a cashier became suspicious and wondered why this boy was alone late at night. Two policemen entered the theater and took Jim to the lobby. They questioned him and determined he was a runaway kid, so they took him to the police station. They fed him good meals while he waited for Fannie to arrive in Portland to take him back home.

"When my mother and I got back home she was very tired from her trip. She said, 'You're in trouble. Your father's going to be very upset. Now you go upstairs and wait until he gets home' Well, she shouldn't have said that, because I was there about 10 minutes before

I walked out and ran away again." Jim did not get far. The local police found him the next day and took him back home. For a three-week period, he ran away every day. He was terrified of Ross. He did not want to have to see him. "I didn't want to be there with him and my mother. I just wanted to get away from them. I wanted to be with my older sister."

Jim was out of control. Every time he would be returned home, his mother would tell him Ross was going to take care of him. "I'd think, *'I'm not going to let him take care of me.'* And I'd leave again. It was a continuous running back and forth, running away from Ross to find any place to get away. They couldn't control me anymore."

∇

One night Ross was administering one of his beatings. "He had me get down on my hands and knees. He had this strap concoction with cuffs for my hands. He secured my hands around my back, then my feet and my hands were tied together so I couldn't fight. I was helpless." During this beating Jim fell off the bed. Ross got incensed and started choking him. Fannie usually would have stayed out of the discipline, but she happened to walk by the door, heard the commotion and opened the door. She thought Ross was being too excessive and asked him to please stop, but she ended up having to pull Ross off of his stepson.

During a house call at their home a physician examined Jim and told Fannie that if that incident had continued Jim could have wound up dead. "You'd think that my mother would have pressed charges, but she didn't want to. She and Ross were good God-fearing religious people and weren't supposed to have problems like that. And divorce was out of the question."

Fannie knew she had to do something—anything—to resolve the situation. Fannie realized that the latest episode was the closest she had come to a tragedy. Ross might do it next time, and Fannie did not want to see her son dead.

Jim had been unhappy around the house for a long time after Ruth left. The situation with Ross and Jim prodded Fannie to seek to remove Jim from the house one way or another. Fannie wrote a letter trying to get Jim into Boys Town, but the leaders there replied that they did not have the room—their spaces were for homeless boys without any guardians, not for boys with parents.

Fannie went to Idaho authorities and told them that Jim should be sent somewhere away from home.

As a first step a child psychologist talked with him, and after that Jim went to court. Fannie testified but said nothing about Ross beating Jim. In response to the psychologist's report, Fannie claimed she was unaware of Ross doing anything bad to Jim. The judge assumed that Jim was an incorrigible stubborn boy who ran away all of the time.

Court officials and Jim's folks told him about a wonderful place that had lawns and animals and boys who were Jim's age, making it seem like a fun summer camp. "It really wasn't my decision. Before I knew it, I'd been sentenced to a reform school. My crime: I was stubborn and ran away. I didn't do any dope or anything, but nonetheless the court determined that my parents couldn't handle me."

Chapter 4

Idaho Industrial Training School

IN 1952 state authorities placed 13-year-old Jim in the Idaho Industrial Training School, located in southeastern Idaho over 300 miles south of Kellogg and a couple of miles west of the small town of St. Anthony. The school was the only major juvenile institution in Idaho.

In 1905 the Idaho Industrial Reform School opened with the intention of changing the lives of hopeless juvenile delinquents. By the time Jim entered the reform school it had grown to almost 700 acres, 34 buildings and cottages, kitchens, a gymnasium with a swimming pool, a school and a library with over a thousand books.

"At first, I thought it seemed like a country club or summer camp, except that I'd been sent there. I'd been made a ward of the court, although I wasn't sure exactly what that meant."

Although the facility was basically a reform school, it didn't seem like one to Jim. It was more like a military school in the sense that the entire school was all spit and polish. Students were forced to march everywhere they went. In its controlled and disciplined environment, the staff employed harsh corporal punishment utilizing rubber paddles and leather straps. However, Jim was well behaved and never received any abuse or beatings.

"It really wasn't bad there. The main thing was that you couldn't run away." A large fence surrounded the Industrial Training School compound, but it had no guard towers, so some kids occasionally managed to "run" or escape.

The school provided control, training and education of juvenile delinquents who were placed at the school for offenses such as theft, truancy, incorrigibility and immorality. The school housed children who were minors or runaways—those with difficulties adjusting to school, those with parents unable to control them and those without proper parental care.

Boys outnumbered girls about four to one. Separate programs were designed for the boys and girls to build character and personality as future citizens so they could earn a living once they returned to society. Boys' programs emphasized industrial and manual training. Girls' programs concentrated on home economics and domestic sciences.

In many ways the Industrial Training School was self-supporting. The farm's hundreds of acres of fertile fields provided fresh fruits and vegetables to eat in the cafeterias while students learned gardening, irrigation, farming, livestock management, horticulture and greenhouse operations. Students also raised animals to eat, including ducks, geese, chickens and rabbits. Students raised herds of cattle for beef to eat, and they worked in the school's dairy to provide milk and butter.

The school taught trades at its various facilities—carpenter shop, blacksmith shop, tailor shop, shoe shop, steam laundry, sewing room, kitchens, dining rooms, cold storage units, granaries, and root cellars to store vegetables. Vocational training included agriculture, blacksmithing, carpentry, brick laying, laundering, painting, plastering, printing, shoemaking, stone cutting, cement work, baking, horticulture, equipment operation and cooking.[6]

Students would spend a half-day attending classroom schooling and the other half-day in vocational training. Each company of students slept in one of the cottage dormitories on bunk beds. "We were required to make our beds and split a corner with the sheets. All of us ate in a dining room where big metal pitchers sat on long dining tables."

"I had lots of adventures there—a lot of fun things happened. I lived there with kids about my age, and I made a lot of friends."

Every student had small chores to do. Since Jim and the other kids in his dormitory were younger children, the school did not train them for actual job skills. Primarily, those boys' chores were to clean the dormitory together. The dormitories had bedspreads that hung to the floor called counter panes. Some boys would get under the bedspreads and explore each other's bodies. "At our ages, we were mainly experimenting, just groping around and showing each other what we were playing with. There never was any true sex. I had crushes on some boys, but once we got together under the bedsheets, I didn't quite know what to do with them."

The school kept the younger boys separated from the older juvenile delinquents—mid-teens to 20-year-olds. Jim would see them all the time in the dining room, since his Company D was comprised of young teens sitting at tables near the older guys.

"I liked living at the reform school. It seemed like the old orphanage—what little of the orphanage I could remember. It was a big relief being away from my mother and Ross and not having to suffer."

Jim felt protected under the staff members' understanding and caring. The house fathers had the ability to get the young kids to conform to the rules by telling the boys the way things had to be done. They were not overly friendly, yet they provided the boys with a masculine presence and positive role models.

Upon Jim's completion of his sentence under less than a year, the state released him and sent him home. "I really didn't want to go back home. Anywhere was better than home."

$$\nabla$$

Some things had changed at home in the year Jim had been gone. Grandma Lillie Belle was again living with the family. Jim adored the funny lady. A couple of Jim's aunts were visiting their sister Fannie. Between the two aunts, Fannie, Jim's half-sister Anita and Grandma Lillie Belle, it now seemed like the women of the house were the ones in charge.

When Jim's two aunts left and returned home, things settled down. However, Lillie Belle had changed. She was in her sixties and becoming senile. Her mental maturity and thoughts started reverting back to her childhood.

A couple of days after Jim's aunts departed, Grandma Lillie Belle disappeared. After a few hours worrying, Fannie received a call from her from a bus station about 60 miles from Kellogg. Grandma had gotten on a bus and run off to meet some man. A few weeks previously Lillie Belle had placed her name in a correspondence ad without Fannie's knowledge and received a reply from a man after she had sent him a picture of herself—an old picture showing Lillie Belle about 40 years younger than she was now. He told her he would meet her at that town's bus station. Even though she never had met the man, she announced to Fannie over the phone that she was going to marry him. She had it all planned.

"My mother was absolutely dumbfounded and declared, 'I'm going to meet this man.' So she and Ross and my little half-sister Anita and I all jumped in the car. We all had to go save Grandma!"

When the family arrived at the bus station, Ross and Anita stayed in the car while Fannie took Jim with her into the station in search of Grandma.

"And there she was—sort of looking like Betty Davis in the movie *Whatever Happened to Baby Jane*. She had on this terrible cheap black wig that looked like something you'd order from the back pages of a comic book." Lillie Belle was wearing rouge on her cheeks—two huge bright red dots. She hadn't worn makeup since she was a young lady in the 1920s. She had painted her lips in a bright red bee stung look popularized by silent film star May Murray, where lipstick covered the middle part of the lips while the corner of the lips remained uncovered. She was wearing a dress many years out of style, reminiscent of a 1920s flapper-type dress that she had kept for years since she was young. "And she was reeking of cheap perfume. I guess she forgot that ladies put on only a little amount."

Fannie asked Lillie Belle what she was doing there, and she replied that she was waiting for her boyfriend. "Suddenly I realized that in her mind she was just this young girl."

Fannie kept calm. She told Lillie Belle everything was okay, that they all could meet him and have coffee and visit together since everybody already was there. Lillie Belle thought that was okay, good.

Lillie Belle had a picture that the man had sent her, so as soon as he got off the bus, they knew who he was. "He was expecting this fairly young woman. And it was sad, it was funny, but it was so sad."

The four of them sat at a table. The grownups had coffee, and Jim drank a Coca-Cola.

"I'm just sort of sitting there flabbergasted with all that was going on. The guy's talking to Grandma, and it's obvious he's not going to take her with him." The gentleman tried to explain that he didn't think it would work, but Lillie Belle refused to accept no for an answer. She had determined that this was her long last chance. Her husband—Jim's grandfather—had died years before.

"She looked so lonely. It was pathetic."

"The guy finally said he had to catch his bus and said he would write her again. Of course, we knew he wouldn't. The guy was really nice about it."

So, the family returned back home with Lillie Belle who rode in the back seat with Jim. Lille Belle was unhappy with the turn of events, acting like a young girl crying, protesting and questioning Fannie why she wasn't supposed to seek out the happiness she attempted to find.

∇

Throughout the next few days it was apparent that nothing had changed at home except Jim's grandmother. "Ross made it obvious he disliked me, turning his nose up, ignoring me. So after a couple of days in that negative atmosphere, I reverted to the only solution I knew—running away. I couldn't stay home. I just could not stay home." Jim never got far. Fannie and the court threw up their hands, and after a couple of months being back home, the state returned Jim to the Idaho Industrial Training School—once again to be reformed.

"I kept thinking it wouldn't be bad at all going back there."

Since Jim was older, he was placed with older juvenile delinquents in a different company, cottage and dorm. The boys told him that since he was back in the reform school, he really was under the system now, and he could be there forever.

Jim served his previous term with the younger boys who didn't do a lot of physical work other than keeping their dormitory clean. But the school required the older boys to perform outside physical labor. Jim ended up working in the greenhouses.

"During my first term at the training school, I didn't have any interactions with these older boys. But with my new term that changed. It all started the first night back when I was temporarily placed under initial first-day medical observation. They put me in this big room where they had all these beds, and it's where boys stayed who had medical problems, broken bones and whatnot. I had this big room practically all to myself."

"During that night there was just one other guy there. He was about 18, and he was a Blackfoot Indian. One thing about the Indians in there, they had none of the trepidations and inhibitions that some of the White guys had. They talked a lot about screwing guys— 'cornholing' as all the guys in the company called it. I just felt compelled to go over to him. He was wrapped up in a bunch of sheets. Then all of a sudden, he told me to get into bed with him, so I crawled into his bed. We slipped off my nightclothes, and right there—my first experience with anal sex. I'd heard about anal sex, and that's what he wanted. It hurt like hell. I didn't know anything about lubricants, let alone the proper way to lubricate myself for anal sex so it wouldn't hurt. After he was done, he went to sleep, and I crawled out of his bed and went back to my own."

Then other guys also began to take advantage of this situation. Jim felt that telling the boys no would not have prevented their sexual advances. "If I'd been older around their ages, I probably would have been at the bottom of the pecking order and bullied by them, but since I was young, they just looked at it like they were taking something from a defenseless younger guy. But I liked it. I didn't have any problems with them. It was there that I really learned about my sexual orientation."

A few short weeks later the staff discovered that many of the teenagers were having sex with Jim. The house fathers thought Jim was at fault and told him that he was a bad influence on the older juvenile delinquents. After that, Jim's standing at the training school deteriorated. "Let me just say that things did not work out at all. The reform school decided that this kid had to go because I had a problem. And I did have problems. My gayness at that time was coming to the forefront, and I didn't fully comprehend what all was happening."

The training school's medical staff concluded that Jim was mentally ill with severe social maladjustment problems, and they instituted procedures to transfer him out of the Idaho Industrial Training School and into Idaho's state mental hospital in accordance with Chapter 47, Idaho Industrial Training School, Article 1: Government of School:

> "49.36. Transfer of insane patients. Whenever, in the opinion of the medical superintendent of said institution, inmate thereof is insane, he shall make an affidavit setting forth the fact and file the same with the board of directors of said institution, and such board of directors shall summon one or both of the medical superintendents of the Idaho insane asylum, located at Blackfoot and the northern Idaho insane asylum located at Orofino to examine such alleged case of insanity and report his or their findings thereon to such board of directors, and the board is hereby authorized, in its discretion, in case such physician or physicians report such inmate to be insane, to make an order transferring such inmate to the Idaho insane asylum at Blackfoot, when such person shall have been committed to said sanitarium from one of the counties within the jurisdiction of the said Idaho insane asylum at Blackfoot."

Fannie traveled the 300 miles from Kellogg to Blackfoot, Idaho to meet with the superintendent of the Idaho state mental institution, State Hospital South. It was located at Blackfoot about 60 miles south of the Idaho Industrial Training School. The superintendent explained to Fannie that in his professional opinion the best course of action to help Jim was to admit him to the state hospital by Judicial Order from the county through a petition signed by Fannie. He told her that the Idaho Industrial Training School was more successful with masculine boys, but the mental hospital was better suited to deal more effectively with Jim's diagnosed sexual deviation and sociopathic personality.

"Everyone decided to send me there. This was one of the lowest points in my life. It was either go to the hospital or die—and to me it didn't much matter."

Chapter 5

To the Hospital

14-year-old Jim was placed in the Idaho State Hospital South on October 8, 1953. "From then through the rest of my teenage years, I lived mainly at that mental institution."

Figure 14: Entrance, South Idaho Sanitarium (later named State Hospital South).
[Courtesy Idaho State Archives]

The hospital opened in the 1880s as the South Idaho Sanitarium. For decades the Idaho insane asylum's aid to patients was limited to warehousing people diagnosed with mental illness problems and relying on more barbaric practices for treatment such as frontal lobotomies and electro-convulsive therapy.

"I know that people pretty much view mental hospitals as snake pits. Films and articles reveal sadistic guards abusing patients placed there. But that never happened to me. Through all the years I spent at the hospital everybody was kind to me. All of the psychiatrists and social workers were nice. As I look back on it, I have to say I was never mistreated at the state hospital—disciplined yes—but never mistreated. I had plenty of friends at the hospital. The nurses loved me and would give me cards at Christmastime and on my birthday."

By the time Jim entered the mental hospital in the 1950s a new era was dawning in the fields of psychology and psychiatry. Leading-edge breakthroughs in new effective medicines and drug therapies improved the mental health of many patients. Now the hospital was able to treat patients with the goal of returning many of them back to normal lives outside the institution.

The hospital complex sat on large open grounds. Many patients were housed in open wards and were free to walk around. Open-ward patients were aware when the dining hall served food and had the freedom to walk there and eat their meals whenever they wanted. The grounds had no guards and no locked gates.

In addition to the main large hospital administration building, other various buildings were scattered around the nice big campus. It all looked and felt as though it was a respectable college instead of a mental institution.

Figure 15: Main administration building, Idaho State Hospital South.
[Courtesy Idaho State Archives]

Jim lived in one of the open wards with other patients who were all dealing with minor mental problems including those who could not adjust or suffered from severe depression.

"The building I lived in looked like a house. There were a lot of wonderful student nurses who were training and practicing there, and they were very nice. There was a 'mother' who was the administrator in charge of us. She was this big heavy-set Mormon lady with about ten kids of her own. In the ward with me were 10 to 15 other kids. I had a room by myself that I didn't have to share with anybody."

The hospital's violent patients were all locked up in an isolated ward in the hospital complex. Jim and other patients only saw the maniacal ones when guards were escorting them to a doctor or other appointments.

"The mental hospital's schoolroom was the place where I got most of my education throughout my teenage years."

The hospital had a large recreation room where patients could watch movies, attend dances and enjoy some live entertainment. The hospital even had a small soda shop. "I spent a lot of time there socializing. We had freedom. We never had to march in unison like we did back at the reform school. We could even get permission from the hospital staff to go downtown on occasions."

Jim sang with the hospital's orchestra during patient dances. The staff encouraged Jim by telling him that he had talent. "I always felt that I was a big hit. I rehearsed beforehand, and then I'd get on stage and do cover versions of Elvis and other singers while the patients were dancing together. The dance floor was filled with the usual patients, and some couples looked pretty odd. The staff would bring all sorts of patients to the dances, but I really didn't interact with most of them."

$$\nabla$$

Jim settled in at the hospital, but things back home changed drastically. "With my older sister Ruth gone and now me out of the way, you'd think that Ross would have calmed down. But one night he went crazy and flipped out."

Fannie, Lillie Belle and Anita were in the house. Ross was angry. When he went outside Fannie locked the door and wouldn't let him back in. He tried to enter through the front windows, but they were locked. "He was screaming that he was going to kill the three of them huddled there in the house. He was so violent."

Fannie sneaked out the back door and ran a few houses down the next street to summon Fred Hoffer to help. Fred was a friendly occasional part-time minister who Ross and Fannie met in church and liked. They had invited Fred a few times to their house to visit. He was a strong man due to years working in the mines and forests as a full-time miner and logger.

Fred accompanied Fannie back to her house to diffuse the situation. He went around to the front door. "Ross was just fuming. Fred told Ross, 'Brother, now you don't want to harm your wife and your baby.' And Ross turned on him. So, Fred put his big arms around Ross and gave him a bear hug until he calmed down. Because of all the ruckus, neighbors called the police, and Ross ended up getting hauled off to jail."

Because of her religious convictions, Fannie never imagined leaving Ross—until now. She moved from Kellogg down to the south central town of Twin Falls where a sister and other relatives lived. She filed for divorce, but Ross fought back pushing the case to a trial in attempt to gain full custody of his daughter Anita. Both Jim and Ruth offered to return home to testify, but Fannie told them that she did not want to put the kids through that ordeal.

The divorce was finalized on April 2, 1954, and Ross moved back to the Phoenix area.

The day after the divorce Fannie and Fred Hoffer got married in Twin Falls. They moved about 70 miles north, and they lived in the towns of Ketchum and Hailey for almost two decades. Frederick Benjamin Hoffer was two years older than Fannie. He was only a couple of months younger than Fannie's first husband Charlie Foshee.

"For years my mother wouldn't leave Ross because her religious denomination, the Church of God, didn't believe in divorce. So, when she divorced Ross and married Fred, she solved her predicament in the way many religious people resolve an awkward religious obstacle—she simply chose another church that conformed to her new beliefs. In this case she switched to the Assembly of God, because it recognized divorce as a legitimate option."

"I should have been ecstatic at the turn of events getting Ross out of our lives, but I was consumed with resentment. My mother wouldn't get a divorce when my sister Ruth was being abused. She wouldn't get a divorce for my life being screwed up. But she certainly got a divorce when she herself was threatened."

Chapter 6

Return to California

"I was at the mental hospital for a few months, and then the medical staff began trying to push me out of the hospital, wanting me to go on a trial home visit for a few weeks."

So, Jim went to Ketchum to the home of Fannie and her husband.

"Things weren't so bad with my new stepfather, my mother's third husband. Fred actually was a good guy. I look back on him with no bad memories at all. He tried. He really tried hard to be friendly to me. He tried to be a father to me. But by that time it was too late—I was unreachable."

Jim spent a couple of weeks at home as the summertime season approached, but he was bored. "I hated Ketchum. Idaho was dull. People would sit around worrying about day-to-day mundane things. The small towns and small minds of Idaho just couldn't compete with the excitement of living in Los Angeles and Hollywood and the Sunset Strip."

It was time for another adventure to the Golden State.

"There always would be a ride over the next horizon. During this hitchhiking trip, radio stations were playing a song about riding the highways, *(Get Your Kicks On) Route 66*, another Nat King Cole tune. I really loved his music. Most people I knew in LA liked his songs and his voice; but most people I knew in Idaho didn't like his music or him. They wondered what in the world I saw in the guy. This demonstrated to me two divergent attitudes in two different parts of the country."

During Jim's second trip to California he decided he would live there for a long while. In his mind this was a brave and defiant move.

"It was only a year earlier that the judge in LA had banned me from California. I didn't think about questioning whether California could actually enforce the ban against me or not. I was leery about going back to Los Angeles. I worried that they might be waiting for me in LA or especially on the California state line where officials stopped vehicles and asked people what produce and plants they were bringing into the state. What if they had a list?"

This time Jim decided to go to San Diego. He hung around the downtown area. The weather was foggy and chilly in the mornings, but each afternoon it turned sunny and warm.

"I idolized the sailors walking down Broadway in downtown. I was absolutely fascinated by the way they wore their white uniforms and strutted around—it was obvious they were proud of themselves. A lot of them kept entering and leaving a locker club called the Seven Seas, which was opened 24 hours a day. I'd go right up to the guys and strike up conversations."

A group of three sailors came out of the Seven Seas, and Jim started talking with them. They served on the same ship. He walked with them a half dozen blocks down to San Diego Bay and the piers. At the ferry landing the sailors chipped in and bought Jim a ticket to ride the ferry with them across the bay to Coronado Island.

"I became sort of a mascot to the sailors, and they let me wear a navy hat. I was wearing a t-shirt that on the back said: Don't be Ashamed ... Even the Sun Goes Down."

"On the island we all ate hamburgers and swam in the ocean along the large long beach there. In late afternoon the sailors had to go back aboard their ship tied up at Naval Air Station North Island. They gave me money to take the ferry back across the bay to downtown, but since I was already on Coronado Island, I figured why not spend an extra day or two there? I'd never been on an island before. I slept a couple of nights in bushes on the lawns of large expensive homes across the street from the beach and drifted off to sleep with the sounds of the surf in the background."

"I spent my daytime sightseeing. I walked all around the big upscale Hotel del Coronado pretending my parents were vacationing there. One elderly couple I was talking with on the hotel's sun deck bought me lunch to eat with them on the outside dining area."

Jim liked San Diego and thought it was a nice place, but he concluded within a week that Los Angeles and Hollywood had all of the real fun and excitement. Besides, there would be plenty of sailors nearby in Long Beach. It was dawning on Jim that the LA area had millions of people there, and the police didn't have time to stop and check everyone to see who might be on their lists. He would just have to make sure he never got into trouble. So back to Los Angeles he went.

$$\nabla$$

"In those days people couldn't get into certain places and towns. If you got in trouble or were homeless, wandering through town, hitchhiking, whatever, the authorities had two choices: They simply could drive you to the edge of town and say, 'Never come back or we'll throw your ass in jail,' or they could go ahead and arrest you, put you on work details or something and make life so miserable for you that you'd never come back. At that time those things were pretty common across the country."

In the 1950s, homosexual acts were illegal in all of the states across the country. Even the American Civil Liberties Union asserted that civil rights did not pertain to homosexuals.

"At that time whether a person was lesbian, homosexual male, bisexual or transgendered, many generally referred to themselves as gay." For the most part they were invisible to society, viewed as perverts lurking in the shadows ready to pounce on or seduce unsuspecting heterosexual men, women and boys—a subversive enemy from within.

"I didn't have any knowledge of legality. I was only a kid. Even most adults didn't know what their rights were. The common citizen never thought about having any legal rights. There was little public suing and standing up to the government. That was the way things were in the 1950s. The authorities were God. You did what they said. If the cops didn't like you, they'd strike you or beat you. I learned not to trust the police. The vice squad was always on the lookout for us homosexuals. We'd hear all of the time about gay people's experiences with police lying in court. And if you were convicted of sodomy, you could spend years in prison."

In the early 1950s during the McCarthy era, U.S. Senator Joseph McCarthy embarked on a highly-publicized quest to rid the government of communists and homosexuals. In the U.S. House of Representatives, the House Un-American Activities Committee also investigated communists and homosexuals. President Dwight D. Eisenhower issued an executive order declaring that sexual perversion was grounds for homosexuals to be removed from their government jobs. Thousands of homosexuals were fired as security risks. The "lavender scare" had hit America.

"I witnessed the Los Angeles area being strictly segregated in the 1950s and 1960s. I lived primarily in the Hollywood area. Hollywood and the coastal areas to the west were lily-White. Hispanics stayed in East Los Angeles, and Blacks stayed in South Central Los Angeles and Watts. If the police found a carload of Blacks or Hispanics in Hollywood, the cops would chase them out. It was like there was an imaginary dividing line. They couldn't rent apartments in Hollywood. They just were not welcomed in Hollywood."

The only place Jim could visit his "Spanish" friends was in the Main Street area of downtown where they lived. Being Hispanic deterred them from risking a trip into the Hollywood area. Roommates and buddies Juan and Bruno would invite Jim to stay overnight at their apartment. Juan worked at a lawn maintenance landscaping company. Bruno would watch his favorite TV program every day, *The Jack LaLanne Show*, so he could learn bodybuilding techniques and fitness tips. He would exercise and lift weights in the living room in front of the TV. Bruno worked hard to keep up sexy looks because he made his living as a rough-trade hustler selling sex. He was the first hustler Jim ever had met.

Juan and Bruno lived a half dozen blocks from where Bunny had lived when Jim made his first escape to LA the previous year. Jim went to Bunny's old house in search of her, but she no longer lived there. "I never saw Bunny again, but her warm care and advice helped guide me through my early life."

Although there were gay bars on downtown Main Street, Jim and his friends were only teenagers—too young to get inside. Try as they might, none of the downtown friends ever had any success sneaking into any Main Street bars. The security guards manning the bar entrances were eagle-eyed and unyielding.

"Juan told me about a cool new meeting place that opened for business called Cooper Do-nuts on downtown Main Street between two gay bars—the Waldorf and Harold's. It was open all night long, and everybody was welcomed to come and be themselves—including gays, lesbians, crossdressers and guys wearing makeup. So, Juan and other teenage friends and I started going there."

"After I returned to Idaho in springtime, Juan wrote a letter telling me that I'd just missed something big. The police had raided Cooper Do-nuts right after I left town, and the gays there revolted and rose up against the cops. Juan said everybody poured out of the donut shop, and instead of throwing rocks and bottles at the cops, he said the crowd threw donuts and coffee and trash—typical of the gay crowd there. The cops retreated to their cars and got backups and shut down the street for a full day."

The LA metropolitan area was huge and sprawling and difficult to get around. Jim would have been stranded constantly, except he walked all of the time—for miles and miles. He was too proud to ask anybody for money to ride a streetcar or bus anywhere, so he usually walked long treks back and forth between downtown Los Angeles, Santa Monica and Hollywood.

Often he walked or hitchhiked as far west as he could—to the beachfront. There was always a load of fun at beach parties happening at the popular gay beach area on the Santa Monica shoreline. Parties or not, a lot of cruising always was going on at the beaches. At Muscle Beach, guys exercised and lifted weights, and scores of beach bums surfed the waves up and down the coastline. It was against this backdrop that Jim felt that LA was where he belonged.

"Throughout the 1950s and 1960s, I always ended up back in Los Angeles. There was something about LA. It could be bad for me at times. Nothing ever seemed to go a hundred percent right. But I met a lot of guys, and I always had fun."

Sometimes Jim would sleep inside and sometimes outside. He lived life in the margins of LA's madding commotion. When he had enough, he would spend a couple of days and nights up in the quiet hills overlooking the city.

Figure 16: Teenage Jim.

"I experienced what hunger and starvation felt like. One time another guy and I lived on two packages of stale doughnuts for a week. But through all my times in LA, I persisted and survived."

Jim was so young that no one would hire him. So, he had no place to live. "Nowadays you'd call it homeless or on the streets. But that's the way we lived and survived. If you were a young gay person, you couldn't get a job. Even a job cleaning some lousy hamburger joint was hard to get."

"When older sexy guys would come up to me, they didn't exactly pay me for sex in hard cold cash. They would take me out to dinner or breakfast, and I would get a place to sleep for the night. I had the one thing that people wanted. They certainly didn't want me because I was a knowledgeable conversationalist. It was all sex. They wanted young, and they wanted beauty."

Whenever Jim and his friends would hear about two guys in their crowd having sex together, they would frown, "Oh Mary, that's like incest with a sister." They would hear of masculine bodyguards and bodybuilders sleeping with each other, and they thought that was quite strange.

"In the straight world it was a masculine guy and a feminine woman. We all assumed, why shouldn't it be the same with gay relationships? Few butch guys I knew even admitted to being homosexual—they called themselves 'bisexual' or 'straight'—and that's what my friends and I actually believed."

"Everyone assumed in the 1950s that the only true gay people were effeminate queens and masculine dykes. They were the ones we saw standing out front and taking the brunt of the oppression while the less obvious homosexuals often slipped by. I realized that our situation in life wasn't right and that we should have the right to live just like anyone else. We knew we were living in a hostile society, so everyone had to survive by their wits."

Some of the less obvious homosexuals in Hollywood slipped by thanks to a studio system that protected its box office stars from the gossip rags. Rock Hudson was one of them. The studio system realized that the gossip rags were determined to out Rock Hudson, so they arranged a sham marriage to protect their money-making interests.

Jim was unafraid of being openly gay, unlike most homosexuals in the 1950s. He knew the risks and was willing to take them rather than live a double life of deception. He didn't think twice about going to known gay hangouts or gay parties. He had no qualms about talking to another man in a sexual manner, even if that man could be an undercover vice cop. The police could arrest someone for being gay at any time or anywhere. Getting arrested for being gay was the price homosexuals paid for being openly gay in America in the 1950s. The struggle in this context was more poignant and courageous because after all, these obviously queer men did not have Rock Hudson's money, connections or a Hollywood system to protect them from the law and the court of public opinion.

Jim's desire during those years was to live in a city where gay people flourished and to attempt finding the man of his dreams. He was not politically aware. "The guys in my crowd never thought of any such thing as gay politics. Up until the 1950s there weren't any politicians who were friendly to the gay community. We saw no one outwardly agitating for homosexual rights because people, including politicians, just would have laughed."

Jim found himself in the midst of the dawning of the unprecedented bold 1950s homosexual movement starting to slowly build momentum across the country, mostly in big cities such as LA, New York and Chicago. Jim unwittingly was a part of that movement. He did not and could not grasp how his defiance and courage like so many thousands of other gay people at the time would usher in the major civil rights movement in America for gay equality.

Chapter 7

Touched by the Homophiles

During Jim's second visit to Los Angeles he met a guy from San Jose who had lived in LA for more than a decade. He told Jim about a gay mafia. No, they didn't have guns as the mafia did, but they had good lawyers like high-profile mobsters. Then a couple of other guys told Jim more about the group. No, it wasn't the mafia. It was a secret syndicate watching out for gay people. Jim was intrigued. What did it all mean? He was intent on finding out more about this nebulous group.

"Finally, one guy I met knew a lot about the group. He confirmed that the group was real, and I remember he wrote down the name for me: 'Mattasheen Society.' The group's name actually was spelled 'Mattachine'—'The Mattachine Society.' I guess he was trying to spell it the way it was pronounced. And that's how information spread in those times—by word of mouth and rumor—and not a hundred percent correct. But the arrival of the gay press changed all of that."

Jim began reading up about the Mattachine Society in a magazine that an older guy showed him—*ONE* magazine. The name of the magazine was boldly printed on its monthly covers: *ONE The Homosexual Viewpoint*. It was the first enduring gay publication in the USA. It essentially marked the true beginning of the gay press. It was written and printed in Los Angeles starting in 1953 and distributed across the country throughout the 1950s and 1960s.

In addition to *ONE*, Jim also read other homosexual publications that later began publishing in the mid-1950s. Following *ONE*'s lead, these newer publications shied away from any explicit material and offered respectable content.

In 1955 *Mattachine Review* began publishing. It featured landmark studies and somewhat bland 'don't-stir-up-trouble' type of articles. *The Ladder* was a lesbian magazine that began publishing in Los Angeles in 1956. In 1958 the ONE Institute *Quarterly of Homophile Studies* began publishing scholarly articles concerning homosexuality. "I would read these three publications whenever a free copy was lying around, but I didn't go out of my way to purchase them like I did with *ONE*. *Mattachine Review* was boring as all daylight in my limited teenage opinion. At that young age I wasn't interested enough in lesbian literature to spend my money on *The Ladder*. And the *Quarterly of Homophile Studies* was too highbrow and academic for my young tastes."

The emergence of the gay press coincided with another landmark publication that tapped into the simmering long overdue sexual revolution of straight America. Its champion was publisher Hugh Hefner and his monthly magazine *Playboy*.

For gay America, the sexual revolution was still in the shadows, a subculture with its own clubs, code words, customs and now publications. Most of straight America was ignorant of what was happening in gay circles at the time. Straight America was coming to terms with its own sexual revolution with different rules and publications. Heterosexual men satisfied their sexual fantasies with *Playboy* magazine, Marilyn Monroe's tits, edgy Hollywood movies and pin-up girls. It was out in the open. However, gay men were restricted to clandestinely look elsewhere—in muscle magazines like *Physique Pictorial*.

"I'd see guys posing in these magazines under the guise of muscles and health. The magazines were full of advertising for healthy products. But interspersed were all those pictures of gorgeous men wearing only their tiny briefs. You couldn't see what they had between their legs, but you sure could fantasize."

At that time nudist magazines were also available. They were the only publications showing full frontals of people without clothes. Jim did not find them sensuous at all. To him the nudist publications contained a heterosexual family-life slant, and he could not relate to that.

The most popular magazine read by the gay people Jim knew was *ONE* magazine. *ONE* was a monthly publication about the size of

Reader's Digest containing two or three dozen pages per issue. By 1957 about 3,000 monthly copies were printed and sold through subscriptions and sold at newsstands.[7] Briefly in 1955 *ONE*'s press run rose to 7,500 monthly copies.[8]

"I could buy copies of *ONE* at a couple of newsstands right out on the sidewalks in Hollywood. I remember that *ONE* was discreetly displayed on the top shelf behind the vendor, and he had to grab it and hand it over in a paper sack. The name "*ONE*" in large bold letters was placed right up there prominently on the rack. But the rest of the nameplate 'The Homosexual Viewpoint' was always covered up by other publications put in front of it."

Copies of *ONE* were mailed out across the country and then further circulated among friends. It began reaching more and more isolated homosexuals. It was something gay people read at home or in other safe places; no one read it out in the open or on public transportation.

Jim basically read *ONE* for the news. He learned what was happening across the country and around the world. Serious articles told of police harassment and misconduct, raids of gay bars and gays being entrapped, persecuted and arrested. It also printed feature articles, fiction and essays. It was unpretentious and easy to understand. It was not lewd—it contained neither pornography nor explicit sexual content. It did not print photos. It ran very few ads.

It printed letters to the editor. Jim especially liked reading people's responses about various issues and being able to hear gay voices from across the country using this forum to speak out. The letters to the editor were written by homosexuals who used either assumed names or fake names or first names only. In the 1950s no readers were brazened enough to risk revealing their real names in a nationwide homosexual publication.

ONE positioned itself into the forefront of the emerging movement. *ONE*'s radical publishing venture operated on a shoestring budget, yet it awakened homosexuals nationwide, advocating a new sense that defined who homosexuals were— citizens deserving equal treatment under the law. It was written by a seemingly large professional staff of gay men and lesbians. However, readers were unaware that in order to make the staff appear larger than it actually was, some writers would pen three or four columns under

Figure 17: Core ONE Incorporated staff, publishers of *ONE* magazine. (left to right) Don Slater, W. Dorr Legg and Jim Kepner. Circa 1957-1958. [Courtesy of ONE Archives at the USC Libraries]

various names. Although some *ONE* writers bravely used their own true names in bylines, most articles were written under pseudonyms.

"To me it seemed puzzling that even though few heterosexuals were interested in *ONE*, many of the straight people who paid attention to it were scared by the magazine. Now instead of finding a communist under every bed, they were finding a queer there."

ONE magazine enlightened readers that there was a gay history. Often when Jim read in *ONE* about homosexuals or crossdressers in history, the information would stimulate his interest, and he would look up more information about those people. Jim became aware that many gay people in history were not weirdos, but rather had accomplished some great things. Prior to *ONE*, word-of-mouth was the method available to gay people for passing along any facts about gay people in history.

"I thought the magazine ran compelling feature articles, but the poetry it printed left a lot to be desired in my opinion. Still, *ONE* was the best thing we had in the 1950s. In its own way, *ONE* was extremely important. Once I discovered the magazine, I had the tie I was looking for. It kept me informed and gave me all of my gay knowledge. I felt liberated reading it. I was young, and my hormones were flowing, and I needed this connection with other gay people out there. It made me more aware."

Jim thought he learned more from *ONE* than he ever did from the mainstream press. He wasn't surprised whenever he read another negative mainstream story about homosexuals. Censorship and homophobia were the norm in the 1950s. When he read about violations of gay people, he expected it based on all he and his friends had seen and experienced first-hand. There may have been some people out there who were crazy or had low morals, but despite what the press-at-large claimed, Jim knew that most of those stories did not apply to him or the gay people he knew. "The mainstream press was always telling us we all were sick. Whenever another negative article appeared in the press, we would dismiss it, 'What do they know? They're not gay.'"

Although Jim only was able to purchase *ONE* magazine when he was in California, he would usually take copies with him back to Idaho.

$$\nabla$$

The federal government gave *ONE* a difficult time for daring to push open viewpoints by homosexuals. Jim and many other gay people in LA eventually became aware of a commonly-known series of events between *ONE* and the federal government.

In a fateful article published in the November 1955 edition of *ONE*,[9] Chuck Roland (under the pseudonym David L. Freeman) wrote an article hinting that FBI Director J. Edgar Hoover was in an intimate relationship with his assistant and closest personal friend, FBI Associate Director Clyde Tolson. General rumor and common knowledge insinuated that Hoover and Tolson—who rode to and from work together, dined together and vacationed together—were an intimate couple.

Chuck Rowland wrote in his *ONE* article that homosexuals "occupy key positions with oil companies or the FBI (it's true!)."

Hoover and Tolson were alarmed. The FBI perceived the *ONE* article as slanderous. Tolson noted, "I think we should take this crowd on and make them put up or shut up." Hoover officially concurred. Tolson determined that the FBI should open an investigation.[10] FBI headquarters instructed the FBI Los Angeles office by air-tel to interview the article's writer.

FBI agents visited the ONE Incorporated offices in attempt to identify and locate "David L. Freeman," but they were unaware that the author listed on the article was a pseudonym used by Chuck Rowland. Agents interviewed the person who happened to be there in the ONE office, W. Dorr Legg (William Lambert), Chairman of the Board of ONE Inc. Agents investigating the article wanted to know what the ONE Inc. staff knew. Dorr Legg was sarcastic to the agents, refused to furnish any information and directed agents to ONE Inc.'s lawyer.

The FBI commenced a plan of action to coordinate with the Los Angeles Police Department and County Sheriff's Office to determine if ONE Inc. was properly registered under California law to do business. They also referred the magazine to the U.S. Department of Justice for an opinion concerning any possible obscenity in *ONE*'s November 1955 edition.

Additionally, they contacted U.S. postal authorities for pertinent information regarding *ONE* and its mailability through the U.S. Post Office.[11] However, the U.S. Post Office was already ahead of the FBI. The previous year, in *ONE*'s second year of publication, the U.S. government notified ONE Inc. that the Post Office had impounded the magazine's October 1954 issue, refusing to deliver it through the mail, calling the magazine obscene and filthy.

The federal government maneuver was a major blow to the magazine.

ONE Inc. attorney Eric Julber filed a lawsuit against the postmaster's ruling before the U.S. District Court in LA and lost. The judge ruled that the Post Office was proper in refusing to transmit *ONE* through the mails because the magazine was calculated to stimulate the lust of homosexual readers. ONE Inc. appealed to the U.S. Ninth Circuit Court of Appeals and again lost. The court ruled that articles in the magazine were nothing more than cheap pornography, morally depraving and debasing.[12]

After these two legal setbacks, ONE members were dejected and dispirited, but ONE Inc.'s attorney prevailed upon members of ONE to let him attempt to appeal the case to the U.S. Supreme Court. ONE's pessimistic members okayed the attorney's plan of action.

In January 1958, four years after the postmaster issued his ruling, the U.S. Supreme Court, without hearing oral arguments, ruled unanimously in ONE's favor.[13] The high court reversed the lower courts' opinions, essentially ruling that *ONE* magazine's discussion of homosexuality was not obscene, but an exercise of free speech—homosexuals had the same right to freedom of the press as anybody else in the USA. Gay publications could be disseminated legally through the U.S. Post Office. The Post Office and the FBI backed off.

"All the gay people I knew in LA talked about the Supreme Court ruling. I was surprised that the government was letting us say what we wanted in our own homosexual publications."

This was the first legal victory for homosexuals in the U.S. Supreme Court. The landmark decision made it possible for subsequent gay publications to exist, which allowed the equal-rights-for-homosexuals movement to develop and advance. *ONE* magazine fought and won that crucial initial battle.

$$\nabla$$

"It's through *ONE* magazine that I began learning about the Mattachine Society."

Figure 18: Mattachine Christmas party in Los Angeles 1952-1953. Sitting at top: Harry Hay. Sitting at lower left corner back of head & facing away from camera: Konrad Stevens. Sitting on floor: Dale Jennings, Rudi Gernreich, Stan Witt, Bob Hull, Chuck Rowland (in glasses) and Paul Bernard. Photographer: Jim Gruber. [J. Gruber Papers, James C. Hormel LGBTQIA Center, San Francisco History Center, San Francisco Public Library]

Figure 19: Mattachine Society early members: (clockwise from lower right)
Bob Hull, Jim Gruber, Chuck Rowland, Konrad Stevens, unknown. [Courtesy The Tangent Group]

In November 1950 a group of men met together in Los Angeles and formed an organization for homosexuals. Many historians recognize this as the true beginning of the modern gay civil rights movement. In the USA a few small short-lived organizations already had attempted to address intolerance and oppression of homosexuals, but the authorities raided them and shut them down. Other short-lived homosexual organizations that escaped government notice existed only for a few months before fading away with no significant impact.

"I understood that the Mattachine Society had been a very secretive organization. When it first formed, it was too dangerous to let everybody know it existed—people were afraid of becoming targets that authorities could entrap." In response to that risk, Mattachine organizers utilized secret cells modeled on Communist Party strategies and tactics, which some members were familiar with being former Communist Party members. They applied an amount of Marxist social theory in launching their battle to alter the plight of homosexuals and keep the police off their backs.

During the Mattachine Society's first two years only a handful of people knew the person next to them. No one knew all of the people in Mattachine. "That way, I suppose, if you got arrested you weren't able to tell the police about others." Mattachine members feared being busted and raided by police if they were not extra careful. And for good reason. In 1924 a gay rights organization in Chicago called the Society for Human Rights lasted only a few months before the authorities arrested members, effectively abolishing the group. Mattachine activists were determined that their new organization would not succumb to that same fate.

The organization began its outreach by hosting regularly scheduled discussion groups where homosexuals could talk about their lives and problems, discover how much they had in common, create a bond and replace the prevailing cynical attitude among homosexuals with a healthier positive outlook. "Back then most gay guys had kind of a bitchy back-biting way of speaking to each other. I guess that pretty much revealed how we unconsciously pigeonholed ourselves."

The Mattachine Society worked toward instilling a new gay consciousness among homosexuals and began challenging anti-gay discrimination.

The U.S. civil rights movement was gaining significant momentum in 1950 when the Mattachine Society was founded

For gay activists, the movement had to start with changing the narrative. Activists in the 1950s shunned the term "homosexual" because it was both a legal term associated with criminality and a medical term associated with pathological sickness. Some activists also shunned the word "gay" because they thought it was too colloquial for serious discussion.[14] ONE Incorporated, *ONE* magazine and the Mattachine Society chose to strategically use the term "homophile" from the Greek root's homo (the same) and philos (love). They reasoned that "homophile" emphasized the emotional attraction instead of concentrating on the sexual aspect of "homosexual." In subsequent decades the term "homophile" was dropped because the word "gay" became widely accepted as the standard word most people commonly used.

"Gay" had been used back to at least the 1800s when Oscar Wilde was popular and "gay"; although it is uncertain whether Oscar Wilde specifically was referring to his sexuality. People researching the etymology of "gay" have offered various assessments that trace the word further back in history to other countries and languages.

"I remember in the 1950s that I thought the word 'gay' was cool to use, but that put off some older guys I dated. They thought we were ruining a good code word by popularly using 'gay' and that before long guys would be afraid to ask anybody if they were 'gay' because everybody else would have learned what 'gay' meant."

As for the name Mattachine Society, the word "Mattachine" was the name of a medieval group of French performers who traveled to villages throughout the countryside. They performed incognito behind masks and costumes and acted out the social injustices of the day—just as many gay people in the 1950s hid incognito.

"In the mid-1950s I heard about the famous local story that most gay guys in LA were familiar with, and I realized there was hope for us homosexuals." During the Mattachine Society's second year, one of its co-founders was targeted by police—Dale Jennings—a former World War II army sergeant who had served on Guadalcanal island.

Figure 20: Dale Jennings. [Courtesy The Tangent Group]

Dale said he was walking through a park and had just finished using the restroom; and as he left, a rough-looking character struck up a conversation and followed him home. Inside Dale's home the guy revealed himself to be a cop, handcuffed Dale and arrested him for lewd conduct.

In the middle of the night Dale called his friend, Mattachine co-founder Harry Hay, who bailed him out of jail. Dale wanted to fight the charge. Members of the Mattachine Society knew of cases where police targeted gays, entrapped them, hauled them into court and managed to get them convicted of lewd conduct. It did not take a lot of effort or any real evidence to make a charge stick—it was a cop's word against a defendant's, and entrapped homosexuals made no serious efforts to fight back in court.

For Dale Jennings' case, the Mattachine Society mounted an aggressive legal defense initiative, raising enough money to hire an assertive competent lawyer instead of relying on a bland uninterested court-appointed attorney who inevitably would end up losing the case.

At his 1952 trial Dale brashly admitted he was a homosexual but denied he engaged in any lewd conduct. Harry Hay noted that Dale's lawyer caught the police officer in a lie as he was testifying on the witness stand.[15] Officers contradicted themselves. A hung jury could not reach a unanimous decision, voting 11-1 (11 jurors voting for acquittal and one juror voting to find Dale guilty). It just was not worth the City of LA's time and money to proceed further, so the city moved for the court to dismiss the case. The news of the victory rapidly spread by word-of-mouth among homosexuals, and Dale Jennings became an underground hero. The following year *ONE* magazine published and printed detailed information about the Dale Jennings case to set the record straight.[16]

Word continued to spread about the case. As a result of this legal victory, more gays joined the Mattachine Society, and the group was able to begin stepping out of the cloak of secrecy and operate in the open. There was safety in numbers. Members no longer had to meet in cell groups. Gay leaders became unafraid to publicly express their views and speak truth to power.

The group sent questionnaires to candidates for political office inquiring about their views on reforming laws that affected homosexuals and on eliminating police harassment of homosexuals. They pushed the legal system to affirm the rights of homosexuals to congregate in gay bars. They challenged legislators to explain in clear and specific terms the definition of "lewd conduct," a catch-all term that police used to harass and persecute gay people. The law had been vague enough to permit the police and courts to apply their own interpretation. Mattachine maintained that merely asking another consenting adult to engage in a private homosexual relationship was not and should not be considered a crime. After all, the criminal justice system certainly did not consider it a crime when two heterosexuals talked about having sex.

The Mattachine Society continued to grow in terms of numbers and influence. Chapters began forming in other major cities across the USA: San Francisco, New York, Boston, Philadelphia, Chicago, Denver, Detroit, Phoenix and the District of Columbia. The group began holding annual nationwide conventions for members in various cities to meet together.

ONE Incorporated added an educational division named the ONE Institute of Homophile Studies and opened an office where people could stop in. Located at 232 South Hill Street in downtown LA, ONE Inc. evolved into what some historians refer to as the first gay center in the USA.

Jim considered himself a beneficiary of ONE. "I wasn't involved in any kind of activism when I was younger, but after reading *ONE* magazine and learning a lot about the Mattachine Society, I sort of wanted to be involved in a gay organization. I stopped and made contact with ONE. But it was obvious they didn't want me around. I thought, *'Okay, they don't like my type. I guess I'm not intellectual enough for them.'"*

"A couple of years later I became friends with an interracial Black/White couple. The Black guy in the relationship was Bailey Whitaker. He was a school teacher who taught special education classes for kids with learning disabilities. He and I would play our favorite music on the bar's jukebox—Nat King Cole and Johnny Mathis songs."

"It turned out that Bailey had been involved with both ONE Incorporated and *ONE* magazine. In fact, Bailey was the person who named *ONE* magazine—after a quote by the Victorian writer Thomas Carlyle who wrote, 'A mystic bond of brotherhood makes all men one.' I remember that my friends would always wonder about a guy's sexuality by asking, 'Is he one?' I don't remember my friends usually asking, 'Is he gay?' We usually asked, 'Is he one?' So, the name *ONE* seemed sensible to me."

Figure 21: Partners W. Dorr Legg & Bailey Whitaker stand beside each other on the left. Three other friends stand beside each other on the right. [Courtesy of ONE Archives at the USC Libraries]

Bailey Whitaker was a formidable force in the success of *ONE* magazine. Under his pseudonym Guy Rousseau, he was one of ONE Inc.'s founding members who voted to incorporate in 1952[17] as a California non-profit body.[18] His partner had been Dorr Legg, Chairman of the Board of ONE Inc. Bailey served as *ONE* magazine's first circulation manager and found sales representatives across the USA who might want to earn good commissions by selling *ONE* magazine. He also encouraged more people to subscribe by providing mail-in subscription cards inserted inside the magazine.[19]

"I told Baily about ONE turning me away. He explained that of course they did—the groups couldn't have anything to do with me then because I was under 21." The homophile groups had a firm rule that members did not talk to anyone who was underage. Both ONE and Mattachine did everything they could to prevent opening themselves to any potential charges of influencing minors. They refused to interact with anyone under 21. They even cancelled *ONE* magazine subscriptions of anyone discovered to be under 21.

"Bailey was a mentor and teacher in the same way that Bunny had been years earlier. They both taught me things I needed to know in order to survive as a homosexual. Bailey and I kept in contact and remained friends throughout his life."

Chapter 8

From Home Visits to California

During his teenage years, Jim essentially lived three different lives: 1) life in the mental hospital, 2) life at home with his family and with kids in schools, and 3) the life he loved best, adventures out on his own on the West Coast.

"One night before bedtime in the mental hospital I overheard one nurse tell another, 'There's nothing wrong with that kid.' I wasn't crazy. I didn't talk to myself. I was just a teenager."

The staff's biggest concern was that Jim could slip into becoming institutionalized at the hospital for the long-term. Jim's therapists tried various techniques to reintegrate him into society. It did not work for a long time, but it did prompt Jim to begin considering his future. The staff's goal was to encourage Jim to eventually begin taking his own steps to permanently return to society.

"After a couple years at the hospital the staff had me go to a school in town away from the hospital. Then I'd return to the hospital at night. It didn't take long for the other kids in school to find out that I was living at the nuthouse. Things just didn't work out. People in town were wary of us patients."

The staff tried to figure out why Jim ran away from home so frequently. "Frankly, staff members were nicer than my own family. The people at the mental hospital looked good compared to what I had at my mother's place. Things weren't bad at the hospital. I had plenty of friends, and the nurses were nice to me."

"After a few months living again in the hospital, the staff started in on me again. They tried to get me to return back home, like they were pushing me out again. They kept it up wanting me to try another home visit—another kind of conditional release. This time though they made me feel better and more secure by promising me that I could return to the hospital whenever I wanted."

Every time the hospital staff sent Jim home to live with his family, things never quite worked out, and he would return to the hospital. It seemed to be an unbreakable cycle.

"My main problem was that I was uncontrollable at home. I didn't want to be there. The minute I got home I couldn't wait to get back to the hospital where my real friends lived—where the people who really cared for me were at."

When Jim returned to his family, they would be living at a new location—Fred, Fannie and Anita had settled into a new home. At a new school the kids assumed Jim was just like they were. "Deep down I realized I was alienated from these kids—and from all the people I knew in Idaho. I couldn't be truthful and tell people who I really was. Not only was I gay and doing things in California, but I was living most of my life in a mental institution."

Back at home Fannie and Fred had a close connection and truly were in love with each other. Fred treated his step-daughter Anita as his own. After the couple got married, they moved from Twin Falls to Hailey, Idaho—a dozen miles from Sun Valley ski resort—and a little over 100 miles from the state mental hospital.

Figure 22: Fred, Anita & Fannie in the Idaho high mountains of
Salmon National Forest north of Ketchum & Sun Valley.

Figure 23: Sun Motel-Hotel, Ketchum, Idaho on old US 93 Highway, now Highway 75.
"Spacious lobby, steam heat, restful accommodations, room phones, TV in lobby." [Post Card]

Fred and Fannie decided to own their own business together rather than work as preachers. They invested in the Sun Motel-Hotel in Ketchum and moved there to live at their business. Fred utilized his construction skills to refurbish the inside walls and front office. He also built a sturdy second story deck and walkway around the outside, so second-floor guests could reach their vehicles as first-story guests could, which minimized foot traffic through the hotel lobby.

Figure 24: Sun Motel-Hotel, Ketchum, Idaho, with new second story deck & walkway.

Fred and Fannie had little business knowledge and zero experience in the hospitality industry. They were unprepared for the type of guests who rented their rooms—the unwashed public, unshaven, smokers, swearing and men bringing women into their rooms.

"My mother and Fred weren't turning a profit. During many months they lost money. Let's just say that my mother lacked a lot of finesse when she dealt with guests. She didn't really have a good grasp about operating a business for profit. A lot of people who wanted to rent rooms would declare that they just got married. That was an oddly common claim. So, my mother started asking for the marriage licenses of those couples—not a smart move when you're losing money."

Figure 25: A fellow employee & Jim both worked at the
Sun Motel-Hotel in Ketchum, Idaho on old US 93 Highway, now Highway 75.

After the upscale Sun Valley Lodge opened at the Sun Valley ski resort, corporations began buying up prime real estate in Ketchum to build super hotels. Fred and Fannie and all other lodgers were charging about $9. The super hotels were charging $50 a night. The locals were flabbergasted, insisting that nobody would pay that outrageous amount of money for lodging in Ketchum. Unfortunately, that was the wave of the future. Ketchum's old hotels began going out of business or recasting themselves as large nationwide motel chains.

The summer off-season caused too many vacancies and a lack of profits. Fred and Fannie were able to hang on to the Sun Motel-Hotel for three or four years. When they were about to lose the Sun, they finally gave up the business and moved back to Hailey.

"I was uncomfortable at my mother's place, so I ended up running away for more adventures in California. Essentially, I'd be off on these 3-month or 6-month sabbaticals, if that's what you want to call them. I would live by my wits until I ended up with absolutely no money. Then I'd hitchhike back to Idaho and return to the mental institution."

Chapter 9

Hooray for Hollywood

In California Jim entertained himself by walking around Los Angeles. He met a wide variety of characters there, unlike Idaho where everybody seemed to be alike. "I met more important people in a month in LA than I would meet in 20 years in most places."

Jim was young, and guys would try to pick him up from their cars. "The attention was wonderful, although it did get a little old."

"My life as a young kid at home was pretty dreary, and there was no excitement. It mostly was filled with religion. But in LA I could live in a fantasy world watching movies. They were fun. They were exciting and different. And everybody paid attention to the movies. I wanted to be in them. Even as a kid I subconsciously realized that movies are the only form of immortality you can have. You can build a fancy building or a bridge or you can be a politician. You can write a book, but in time the book falls apart, then becomes relegated to the basement of a library, and then people forget about it and don't read it anymore. In a movie an actor achieves a sort of immortality."

During Jim's many trips to Hollywood, he attempted to get himself discovered. He dreamed of making it big, but then reality set in. He was just another teenager like so many hundreds of other people who arrive in Hollywood seeking to become a star. "It was a wonderful vision at that time because the studio bosses were still around. I figured I'd be under contract in no time. If it was good enough for Judy Garland and Mickey Rooney and all those other wonderful stars, why wouldn't it be good enough for me?"

Hollywood of the movies was a world away from the actual city of Hollywood where Jim walked the streets. So many beautiful people were around plumping gas or working in restaurants waiting for their big break. In order to make it, an aspiring actor needed to get an audition, and in order to get an audition the actor needed an agent. And agents only took on aspiring actors they believed could make them a lot of money.

People needed more than just desire to break into the movies. It was necessary to meet the right people. If a person hung around the right places it was possible to meet influential people who worked in the movie industry. Jim met a succession of guys claiming they were an agent or producer or scriptwriter or casting director or character actor or whatever. Some of them were real, but most were not.

"I never met any A-1 stars. I wasn't quite on the 'A' circuit. You had to be at least 21 years old and be able to go into the really sleek bars where you could meet these industry guys. I didn't have that slick blonde Harvard-educated look. And I was too effeminate. They were generally looking for masculine guys, although I didn't realize that at the time."

Too often the guys Jim met had no real connections inside the movie industry. "Their claims to me were nothing more than a scam to score sex. All a guy would have to say to me was, 'Hey boy, you ought to be in show business, and I'm just the person who can set you up.' Usually it was just a come-on to get me to sleep with them. But who knew, I might end up getting immortality out of this. It was worth trying, so I would go to bed with them."

Jim met a lot of the guys at parties. A lot of them were older guys seeking young good-looking guys to bed. "I was living hand-to-mouth. I knew that all I had to do was meet up with the right person. I figured the sex was just what you had to do to become a star—the old casting couch. People might think the casting couch doesn't exist or that it's only for women, but they don't know what they're talking about. Even though it's fashionable to pretend that these major male stars get there wholly on their own talent, a lot of good-looking successful male stars in Hollywood experience the casting couch first-hand. There are so many people out there who want to be in the movies. If a Hollywood operative said, 'This is what you have to do,' and you said, 'I'm too good for that,' the reply would be, 'Fine, so sell gasoline, I can go next door and find 20 guys who think it's worth it.' Your career would be over before it ever began."

"I did get to see the studios, and I actually auditioned reading a script one time. Most of the time it was all just a come-on. The only one who didn't realize it was a sham was me."

Jim hung around with two different groups of kids. Since they were not old enough to get into the bars, they had their own gathering places. In downtown Los Angeles Jim and other gay teenagers hung out at Cooper Do-nuts on Main Street. In Hollywood Jim and friends would meet at Coffee Dan's on Hollywood Boulevard and Highland Avenue. Both places were open 24 hours a day. Both establishments catered to a large gay crowd at night. Jim and the other teenagers were fascinated by all sorts of people who would show up at these two places—the under-21-crowd, transvestites, beat wannabes, rough trade and older chicken hawks looking for young guys.

The trend at the time was wearing teased hair. Cashmere sweaters were the rage. Jim and his friends would cruise and rate the various people who patronized these spots. "We would speculate about what they might do for a living. One night at Coffee Dan's a guy came in, and somebody said that he was a movie producer. My eyes lit up, 'Oh, really!' We played it cool. We didn't rush up to these guys. We sort of sat there and pretended like we could have cared less. The men would come in and choose us. In reality, if one of these Hollywood operatives would have come into Coffee Dan's and announced that he was looking for someone to be in a movie he would have been stampeded."

"This particular guy approached me and said he was a producer. By this time, I pretty well had it with so many film business imposters. He told me he thought I would be perfect for a role he had in mind. He explained that it was a juvenile film about gangs and alienation. Producers needed a guy in the movie who was not butch but plays a sissy. I thought, *'Honey, that's me!'* Maybe this was it. My true potential finally would be seen in the movies."

Jim told the guy that yes, he certainly could play the part. So, the guy had Jim go with him to his apartment. "He nonchalantly handed me the script as if it was no big deal. The movie script looked strange with all sorts of instructions in it. I couldn't seem to get a sense of the character I was reading. He helped by giving me some direction and instructions—the character should be read this way or that way. So, I would read the part again. He was really raising my self-confidence, and I realized that this actually could turn into something."

"He casually sat down and then put his arm around me—and I thought, *'There goes the movie career. It'll never happen.'* I realized what he really wanted. He just had a smoother approach. But just in case, I did it with him anyway."

"Humphry Bogart and Dustin Hoffman certainly weren't beautiful. A lot of the actors were very short and just ordinary. But there's something about how the camera saw them that just made them special. The guy told me that the camera has to love you or else you'll never be seen. That's what all these movie stars have in common, no matter how short or bald or ugly or fat or whatever, the camera likes them. I thought, *'How can they say the camera doesn't like me?'* I figured that if I passed a screen test, I could be a big deal. According to the statistics though, I'd probably end up as a fading celeb or some vanishing star that everybody would forget."

Jim encountered one legitimate brush with true Hollywood fame. A friend of his had a date coming to pick him up. Jim's friend was flighty and had a tendency to flake out. He was not thrilled about going on that particular date, so he asked Jim to fill in for him. An older ordinary gentleman showed up. He wore no suit or tie. He didn't make much of an impression, but Jim liked him. The guy was invited to a dinner and wanted Jim to accompany him. "We ended up at some sort of Greek ambassador's residence. The ambassador also had sent somebody to the USO to invite a couple of servicemen. I don't know if he offered them money or what."

Jim sat at the large table eating a Greek dinner along with his date, the ambassador, his assistant and the two servicemen. It was Jim's first time eating lamb, and he was surprised how exquisite it tasted. During the dinner Jim learned that his date was an important producer-director.

After dinner Jim's date played a new record and asked what Jim thought of it. "I told him it sounded very European, but I was thinking there was no way it would ever make it to the top 40. I was very impressed by who and what he was, and we ended up spending the night together. Later I would see his movie, which would win an academy award. The song that he had me listen to that night ended up being played all across the country."

Rumors circulated about certain actors who were popular, beautiful and supposedly gay. Many of Jim's acquaintances claimed to have slept with every known homosexual actor in town and with everybody who was anybody. Jim did not. "I did meet some small character actors and a few grips and technicians, and I had sex with them. I never had sex or dated or even met any big-name actors everyone was talking about. Gay guys would play this game of one-upmanship about whom they slept with, 'Well I can top that. I slept with so and so.' Thinking back on it now, it was so silly and innocent."

"It seemed like half of the gay guys in Hollywood, especially the younger ones, were all claiming to have slept with poor old Tab Hunter. He was one of the most beautiful actors around. He made hearts throb. He was absolutely perfect, a beautiful blonde with a perfect body and just a hunk to end all hunks. The rumor was that he was gay, and everybody was claiming they were going to bed with him. I realized that even if the rumors of him being gay were true, it would be impossible for him to be that promiscuous."

During one of Jim's trips to San Francisco after turning 21, he went to an offbeat bar hidden away in the basement of a building. "I'm sitting there, and in walks Montgomery Clift. And the whole place buzzed. He was one of the most beautiful, gifted actors of the 1950s. I loved him in *A Place in the Sun* with Elizabeth Taylor. An even better film of his was *Red River* with John Wayne, where I think he looked his finest."

That night in the bar Montgomery Clift was a mess. He was on a downward slide, taking pills and drinking heavily. It was about 1961, four or five years after his 1956 car accident when he crashed into a telephone pole and sustained injuries so severe that he needed plastic surgery to reconstruct his face. Elizabeth Taylor knew Monty and loved him as a best friend. He had just left a party at her home, and she rushed to the accident site and was credited for helping to save his life.

Montgomery Clift sat at the San Francisco bar with no one around him and no one with him. "Everybody in the bar was like, *'Will it be me?'* People were walking past him, but everyone was very discrete about it. No one ran up to him and asked for his autograph. Everyone was sort of flexing there, and he had his pick of anybody in that bar, just because of who he was. I didn't say anything to him. That would have been rude. What would I have said to him? You just don't walk up to someone and say, 'I love your movies.' That would be silly. There were certain things everybody knew you just didn't do. After an hour or so one of the guys there left the bar with Montgomery Clift."

The public would soon learn about Montgomery Clift's profound dissatisfaction after having made it earlier in Hollywood. He died of a heart attack in 1966 at the age of 45.

"Anyway, I was getting nowhere in the movie business. Every person ends up one day realizing that not all dreams come true. Either a person has great talent and opportunity, or they don't. If a person has talent, Hollywood can use it, and everybody makes lots of money. If a person doesn't have the necessary talent, Hollywood will use them in other ways. The public doesn't see the thousands and thousands of lost dreams or the dissatisfaction of people who are supposed to have made it. I came to the reality that a dream come true doesn't automatically solve problems, and often it can create a host of new ones."

Chapter 10

The Star Cafe

Springtime in Idaho ushered in an enchanting awakening each year—a place with waterfalls in full force as farmers redirected water for new crops. Each springtime, Idaho's mental hospital grounds underwent a beautiful transformation as flowers blossomed, trees grew new buds, and grass turned into lush green carpets.

Jim's joyful spring at the hospital came to a hapless halt when the staff again decided that he should attempt another home visit. "Here I was being pushed out again."

The hospital sent Jim back home to his mother. Fannie and her third husband Fred had moved back to the old mining town of Hailey.

"On my way from the mental hospital to Hailey, I considered dressing in female clothes and begin passing as a girl. There was one problem. My mother just wouldn't understand it at all, and it would be impossible to pass by her every morning and afternoon in girl's clothes."

Fred and Fannie lived in a large Victorian home on a corner lot. "It reminded me of the house in the movie *Psycho*. It had turrets or towers with roofs going way up. The paint was peeling, and it just seemed strange. The house was beautiful inside and had a round grand staircase inside the large entryway."

Fred resumed part-time work as a minister. Fannie raised rabbits in the back yard and sold them to the local butcher.

Jim attended a combined junior high & high school. He knew better than to inform anyone that he was freshly discharged from a mental hospital.

Since Jim was effeminate, guys his age were reluctant to associate with him. Jim did make one true friend in Hailey. She was kind and friendly to him. She looked nice and had fine tastes in clothes. She was fun to be around, but Jim found her compulsively worried about gaining more weight.

She had an older brother who worked at a gasoline station. He had graduated from high school the previous year and was waiting to go into the military. He had a girlfriend who was a blonde outgoing cheerleader. She was a nice girl with many friends.

"He and his girlfriend would bring his sister over to my house to pick me up. My mother was elated about them stopping by the house. She always was wanting me to have friends. She kept emphasizing how glad she was to see my friends come over to the house."

Jim's friend had the latest popular records, and the two of them would practice the latest dances at her house. "In a lot of ways, we were like two girls, except she didn't realize it at the time. I guess she kind of wanted me as a boyfriend or something. Her girlfriends thought I was strange, but she'd reply, 'No he's cool like James Dean.' She thought that because I didn't put any pressure on her to make out."

After school a lot of the kids in Hailey would go to the Star Cafe in the late afternoon to visit and drink soda pop and eat ice cream. Sometimes after school Jim would go there too for a soda pop. Since he had turned 16 years old a month or two earlier, he was old enough to drive there from school like a lot of other kids did—but he had neither a driver's license nor access to a car, so he walked everywhere.

One day Jim went home from school and passed by his sister's room next to his. She and Fannie were gone. "Suddenly I got this crazy idea to dress up like a girl. This would be the first time I tried this on my own. Previously in LA, Bunny and her friends had taught me what I needed to know about dressing up as a female."

So, Jim dressed himself in his older sister's clothes, which were stored in a closet waiting to be handed down to his younger sister when she grew into them. Both the skirt and blouse Jim picked out to wear ended up fitting him tight. For his breasts Jim stuffed socks inside a bra. Since Jim's hair was short, he put on a scarf. He wore red lipstick and hoop earrings. He slipped on high heels and stockings and even added a purse. Now no one would ever know.

"My idea of looking like a fine woman was borrowed from the Marilyn Monroe kind of sexiness. I thought I made a pretty good female. In my reflection in the mirror I saw a very sexy woman looking back. I didn't realize that I was over-exaggerated. In reality I looked more like an odd combination of Marilyn Monroe, Jane Russell and slut."

Jim decided to go out and pretend to be a female. He walked downtown swinging his hips and entered the Star Cafe. Teenagers were having fun inside. The girls were dressed in typical fashion that young women at that time wore—full skirts, bobby socks and ponytails.

"As I think about it now, I probably looked like a young whore from some red light district compared to the other girls there."

Jim passed by the booths on his way to the jukebox. "I was in clear view of everybody as I bent over the jukebox picking out songs and showing off my twitching rear end."

Inside the Star Cafe, good girls were talking to friends. "They hadn't yet developed a sensuality to themselves. I'd hear the high school guys call them prick teasers. It was a small town, and good girls were careful. If they dated too much, guys would spread the word among themselves that the girl was easy, and the attitude among guys would be, 'Well, you gave it to him, why don't you give it to me?'"

Girls had their reputations to lose, not to mention the chance of getting pregnant, since birth control pills had not yet hit the market at that time. Other birth control practices often ended up used in a haphazard manner and often incorrectly. "The reputation of a good girl could be ruined, so they guarded their vaginas and usually waited until they got married. That was the basic belief most young women had at the time."

As Jim passed the booths to leave, a couple of guys in one booth asked him to sit down. They were not naive. Jim's skin-tight butt was sticking out, and he looked ready for adventure. He sat down with them and changed his voice telling them a story about how he was just in town for the weekend. He claimed he did not know a soul in town. The guys were excited to be sitting with the sexiest gal in the place. The guy sitting next to Jim hinted about driving his pickup out to the boonies where they could neck.

"One guy put his arm around me, but I moved it off. I couldn't let some guy put his hands on my blouse and discover that my breasts weren't real or put his hands on my skirt and feel things between my legs that weren't supposed to be there. Everything seemed to be happening too fast, and I was feeling uncomfortable."

"My sisters would talk about how dumb men were, 'When a man gets horny, they just don't care. They'll screw anything.' My older sister Ruth was very knowledgeable. She knew I was gay and told me, 'Remember that a dick has no conscience once it gets hard.' I guess that might be convenient for some people at sometimes, but this Star Cafe scene was getting too complicated."

"Then in walked a guy who was a real creep—an overweight ugly bully. He had no class and said dumb things. Most people found him irritating. He didn't have a girlfriend, and he'd always make obnoxious comments about other guys' girlfriends. He was the type to always walk up to a booth with the most popular people in school and barge in. I could hear him stopping and talking to people. He was loud and always wanted the world to know he was there. I thought, *'Oh, no. Don't come over here.'*"

He made his way to Jim's booth and flopped down right across from Jim. While he talked with the two guys in the booth, he kept glancing at Jim. "All I wanted was for this creep to get out of there. I kept thinking, *'Hurry up and leave.'* Then he started talking to me. I said I was from Twin Falls. Well, that was the wrong thing to bring up. He asked if I went to such and such high school."

Jim could tell that the guy somewhat recognized him but was still trying to figure out where he had seen Jim. Although Jim seemed familiar to the guy, Jim was not about to give him any help. "I kept trying to change the subject to ignore him, like any woman who had a crude guy pestering her."

"He began peering at me—really intensely. I thought that something had slipped. Maybe one of my breasts was falling down or my makeup was coming off or maybe my scarf was crooked."

Jim excused himself to freshen up and went into the women's restroom. He was alone checking himself out and was relieved to find everything all right. But he was feeling leery of the situation. "There was a window in the bathroom that opened up. It was sort of common knowledge that certain women who got into predicaments they didn't like would go to the bathroom and escape by disappearing out of the window. My instinct told me, *'This is not going to end well. This bully's going to be trouble.'* But I always had a theatrical side to my nature. I figured I could outsmart this dummy. I'm too smart for them. After all, they're just hicks stuck in this small town. I've been to California, and I'm more sophisticated than them."

Jim returned from the restroom and sat down again. Within a couple of minutes Jim told them he had to leave. The guy next to Jim coaxed him to stay, but Jim insisted that he was sorry and must be going. It was getting late.

All of a sudden the bully reached over and grabbed Jim's scarf and pulled it off, then yelled out, "Goddamn! It's that homo, Foshee!" The other two guys in the booth looked dumbfounded."

"Without my scarf, I'd been exposed with female accoutrements on my male body. I got up and decided I'd have to make my exit, graceful or not. My number one priority was getting the hell out of there fast. But it felt like I was in a slow-motion movie. I couldn't seem to move fast enough. I heard the bully's voice yelling, 'Shit, he's dressed like a woman!' The other people in the booths and along the counter were turning around staring at me in disbelief—absolute contempt. The girls looked horrified."

Jim flew out the door and ran down the street. The guys raced to their pickups and old cars to track him down. The guys had girls in tow with them, and the young ladies were screaming as much as the guys. "It was like they all were trying to catch an animal with rabies."

Jim had no choice but to pass all of the stores where his folks knew the proprietors and clerks. Jim braved it, hoping they wouldn't notice him. Behind Jim was the mob in a caravan racing to catch up with him. People had gotten themselves worked up into a frenzy. They had decided they were going to track down the homo. "I was afraid they might actually kill me, because they were screaming, 'Kill the queer! Get him!'"

Jim only had another three or four blocks to go, running down the street in high heels, a garter belt and a girdle trying to dodge bushes and climb fences. He fell down causing a couple of runs in his nylons. "I discovered why women don't wear those kinds of garments anymore and why most young women now prefer slacks or shorts. At that moment I realized the clothes I was wearing seemed designed to keep women subservient to men. If you're wearing all of that, you really can't defend yourself or run very fast."

Since the tight clothes and high heels impeded Jim's escape, he ditched the heels, got back up and ran down an alley. All the while the caravan of ten or twelve cars and trucks with shotgun racks was on the hunt. "They really hadn't known any gay people. I had experience in a gay community, but this crowd wasn't familiar with any of that."

Jim ran into a garage through a partially opened door and hid. His pursuers cruised up and down the streets looking for him, hollering and honking their horns. "I was absolutely terrified. They'd all chase off in another direction, and I'd sneak a little closer to home, and when they would get near again, I would hide behind big trash cans or fences or whatever safety I could find."

It began getting dark, and the mob gave up. Jim had managed to escape and arrived home. He ran into the house and up the stairs, avoiding everyone in the family. He removed all of the female clothes and put them back where they belonged. He washed off all of his makeup and went downstairs where his mother told him supper was almost ready.

Jim gave a huge sigh of relief that it was all over—except it was not. He had not considered that everybody in town would talk about it.

"This absolutely ruined me in Hailey. Things got worse, and I knew it wouldn't be long until my folks found out. I went to school the next day. My friend informed me that everybody was talking about it. They all acted like I'd committed a heinous crime. Certainly I'd done less than others—like the two guys who'd been caught stealing stuff from a couple of local stores. They were accepted back in school by the teachers and students as if nothing really important had happened. Nobody at the school made any kind of united stand against them as they all did with me."

"There was not one sympathetic person—including my only friend. Before the incident, she had been trying to date me as her boyfriend. She saw that I would never touch her, and she simply thought I was cool and laid back. But now she really didn't want anything more to do with me. I wasn't boyfriend material anymore."

That afternoon after school, instead of the kids going to the Star Café, they drove around Jim's house on the corner and hollered, tooted their horns and yelled out loud, "Queer! Get the Queer!"

"I was getting harassed so much I couldn't go to school. It was impossible. After the second day, I just gave up. I stopped going to school. Essentially I just dropped out and became a virtual prisoner inside my mother's house."

Fannie wanted to know what was happening, and Jim finally explained it to her. She had no sympathy, telling Jim that his silliness would teach him. "Since my mother was very religious, we never discussed anything about me being homosexual or what everything meant beyond the situation at hand."

The only time he walked downtown was with his mother. "All the sales people would look at me. They all had someone as the enemy, someone to take out all their hostilities on. Their ideas of morality certainly were different from mine."

Jim's parents figured the ruckus of yells and vehicles consistently passing by their house would cool down, but it never did. Every night the same disrupting scenario played out over and over. The disturbance of the peace for a couple of hours every night frayed Fred's and Fannie's nerves. "To me it all seemed like mass hysteria. I didn't think anybody had to accept me or my situation, but I didn't think it was right to be so harassed."

Fred and Fannie started calling the police. The cops would arrive, and the kids would leave. But the cops could not be present every night. Their attitude was that the disturbances would die down and the tormentors would get tired of it soon. However, it did not die down, so Jim's parents repeatedly called the police. The cops said they would talk to the mischief-makers, but the trouble continued. "I was miserable. If only my older sister Ruth had been there, she would have had the knowledge and boldness to fight it. I was weak and too passive."

"One night my folks called the police again for the umpteenth time. I was told to go upstairs, and they all had a long talk. The police told my parents that there was nothing they could do. The tormentors were the nice kids in town and came from decent families. The police said that since I was at fault, the best way to deal with it all would be for me to leave town. My mother decided that it would be best for me to return to the mental hospital. I packed that night, and the next morning my mother and Fred drove me back to the mental institution."

Not long after that, Jim's family moved from Hailey back to Ketchum, so Jim never was required to go back to Hailey again. "This incident was extremely embarrassing for my mother. She was a good religious woman. I felt sorry and sad for her and Fred. They were good preachers, and I was the black sheep who was supposed to have set a good example to everyone."

"When something like this would happen to me, I had the ability to sort of brush it out of my mind. I always had delayed reactions to things. I hated that little provincial town with those people. I thought what all of them had done to me was wrong. People told me that homosexuals were evil; but no matter what they said, I believed they were wrong and were not talking about gay people I knew."

Chapter 11

Gay at the Hospital

There were times when California authorities came into contact with Jim and sent him back to Idaho. Hospital records tell the story:

"On two occasions he has been deported from said California institutions to State Hospital South. He has eloped from this institution and from many others on numerable occasions. He admits frequently on interviews his homosexual tendencies and activities and feels that society is rather naïve for not accepting this as being normal. His trips to California were described as attempts to find a place where homosexual activity was liked and accepted as a rule rather than the exception."[20]

"As far as I was concerned, the hospital was way better than living with my mother and her husband."

Each time Jim returned to the Idaho mental hospital he brought back copies of *ONE* magazine—one monthly edition for each month he spent in California. He gave copies to hospital staff members. "I knew they had passed along their copies to others, because a social worker mentioned to me that Hospital Superintendent Mr. Cromwell had discussed something with her that he'd read in *ONE*."

During the time Jim was in the mental hospital, it was a fairly progressive institution. In 1956 Dr. John L. Butler, temporary chief of Idaho's Department of Mental Health, told government officials and politicians in the state capitol of Boise that he opposed sentencing homosexual adults to prison terms. He stated, "We have to build up community supports for them ... let them form their own society and be left alone.[21]"

"I had accepted my homosexuality and decided to be gay and live my life truly how I wanted—no hiding behind lies. I told one of my psychologists in an individual psychotherapy session about my homosexuality, and she explained why she saw nothing wrong with it. As the years at the hospital passed, more social workers and psychologists concluded that my homosexuality didn't automatically make me mentally ill."

$$\nabla$$

Most of the hospital buildings had been constructed a long time before Jim arrived. Each wintertime the hospital would encounter deep snowfalls making it hard to traipse around the snowy grounds. About 40 years before Jim began living there, the hospital had built a vast network of tunnels that interconnected the entire hospital complex so everyone could walk conveniently from building to building—all underground. The tunnels were used by orderlies to escort patients in wheelchairs and to transport severely disturbed patients between locked facilities.

"It took me a while, but I discovered there were certain hidden side tunnels and vacant rooms down there that nobody seemed to use anymore. Eventually during my mid-teenage years at the hospital, I began getting together with a guy, and we would play around sexually with each other. Ronnie was a year older than me and was committed to the hospital for his sexual deviation among other things. He was quiet but good-looking. He would have me meet him in one of our secret places in an unused portion of the tunnel system that no one ever seemed to think about."

"I was just beginning to figure out how to cruise guys who were interested in me. I was a stereotypical little teenage queen. One patient really liked hanging around with me, so after a while I made a pass at him, but it scared the poor guy to death, and he ran off. He obviously wasn't interested."

The staff found out and disciplined Jim for it—placing him in the "psycho" ward, assigning him to work there for two solid weeks. The ward constantly was on lock-down because patients there were so severely retarded. All patients there had major problems—talking to themselves, mumbling, drooling, moving spastically, banging their heads, picking at imaginary bugs and staring into space for hours.

"Some of them went to the bathroom whenever the urge hit—in the hallway, in their beds, wherever. It was the most awful thing. My punishment was that I had to scrape up all that shit they left behind on the floors and sheets. Then I had to carry everything to and from the laundry wash room. It was terrible."

While the hospital staff believed that Jim's homosexuality was not a mental illness, they were not about to allow him to induce other patients into homosexual hanky-panky. They emphasized that he was working on the psycho ward to learn a lesson about the proprieties of public decency.

"It didn't take me long to figure out that it was a bad idea to come on blatantly to just any guy. I was learning."

Chapter 12

Idaho Cornfield

It was late summer when Jim returned one year from California to Ketchum. Within a week or two he received a letter from friends who had moved to Boise telling him they were having a party there. That meant that older teenagers would gather at someone's house.

"We would all dress up in drag, act silly and drink—and hope that a 'real' man would show up—which hardly ever happened. I had packed my suitcase with an extra skirt, blouse, sweater and scarf. For some reason it took a long time to hitchhike, even though Boise was only 150 miles west of Ketchum. I didn't end up in Boise until early evening. We ended up having a fun weekend. As always, we had to keep fairly quiet, because the police would haul us off to jail if they caught us."

Jim woke up Monday morning, and the festivities were over. Time to return home. So, Jim walked to the edge of town to hitchhike back home. By then it was afternoon, and Jim could not seem to get a ride.

"I remember seeing a movie where this woman was hitchhiking. She sat on her suitcase with her legs crossed in a provocative pose, and she got a ride real fast. So, I crossed the street to a gasoline station and went into the restroom and dressed up in my female clothes. I thought I made a pretty good-looking woman, although most people probably assumed I was a trampy female hitchhiker."

Jim started hitchhiking again, and it was no time before a semi-trailer truck pulled up next to Jim and stopped. The truck driver was a respectable-looking guy. He asked Jim where he was going, and Jim told him he was heading home to Ketchum; so the driver told Jim to climb on in.

"It felt odd climbing into the truck with my skirt on having to make that giant step up into the cab, but I made it there."

The big semi was bumpy and noisy. Jim's voice was soft compared to all of the din surrounding him. The trucker said he was driving down to Salt Lake City. Jim's plan was to ride with him until they reached Jim's turnoff, another 90 miles ahead. He figured he would get off at that location and change into his male clothes and continue home.

As they drove east the trucker asked Jim why go home to Ketchum? Why didn't Jim just ride with him to Salt Lake? The driver was delivering a full trailer and picking up an empty one to take back to Portland.

"I replied that I didn't have any money, and the driver told me that was all right, that he'd take care of things. So, I thought, *'Gee, why not? It's another adventure!'* I was eager, and I was always doing compulsive things, so I agreed to go with him."

It was night when the driver pulled into a motel just north of the Salt Lake City warehouse destination. They both went into the lobby, and the trucker registered for a room with twin beds.

"In the room I got undressed. Luckily, I wore a scarf and had all the proper things underneath. I changed into my slip and got into one of the twin beds, figuring he would get into the other. Well, he didn't. He sat down on my bed and began a game of trying to caress me and putting his hands where they shouldn't be. I'd been taught by my older sister that if you want to put off a man, you just say that it was your time of the month. So, I told him, and that seemed to do the trick. He was nice and slept in the other bed."

Early the next morning the trucker and Jim traveled the last couple of miles to the Salt Lake City warehouse where the driver swapped trailers. Then the two stopped and ate breakfast at a big truck stop.

"I really looked good, but I was in my day-old clothes." The trucker was curious why Jim didn't have any new clothes to wear since he had his suitcase. Jim had prepared to spend only one day hitchhiking home, so the suitcase contained primarily his men's clothes. Jim told him his suitcase contained just ladies' stuff, and since he hadn't expected to spend the previous night away from home, he didn't bring along any extra clothes.

The guy offered to buy Jim an outfit more suitable for traveling. The two went into a large women's department store. "He suggested that I ought to get some ladies slacks, because it would make it easier to get around. I figured that was good—slacks and a blouse. I knew my waist was a thin 27 inches, so I sort of guessed at the sizes."

"I took the slacks and blouse into a woman's dressing room. I'm in there undressing, and in pops the lady sales clerk. I hadn't realized at that time and certainly never had experienced this in any men's dressing rooms, but women sales clerks came into dressing rooms to help ladies undress and try on new clothes. Of course, I realized it would never work if I undressed in front of her. I couldn't risk her catching on. So, I told her that I thought the outfit I was holding was just fine. The trucker paid for it, and I went back into the dressing room and put on the new clothes. They fit fine, so I lucked out."

Throughout the day the truck driver and Jim rode the highway heading back home. The trucker offered to take Jim to Portland, but long before they approached Jim's turnoff again, Jim decided it was time for him to head back home. He could not run off to Portland.

"Who knows what could have happened if I traveled to Portland with him. Here was this guy who was really sweet to me—feeding me, buying me wonderful clothes, treating me just like a princess. Yet I wouldn't give him any. I felt terrible about it, but he saw things differently and seemed to respect me for not giving it up. After the time we spent together, he obviously liked me and asked for my phone number. He thanked me for the wonderful company, and he drove off. The name and phone number I gave him were both fake. I really hated that I lied to the guy, but it was in my best interests—and his—to keep this situation from progressing any further."

$$\nabla$$

It was night and Jim had 90 more miles to hitchhike north to get to his mother's home in Ketchum. Jim considered taking his men's clothes from his suitcase and putting them back on. However, the women's clothes had worked pretty well so far, so he decided he could hitch another ride in no time if he stayed in the women's clothes he was wearing.

"And what luck! A guy in his early twenties in a pickup truck pulled up and stopped. I got in the truck, and he tossed my suitcase into the bed of his truck. And away we went. The radio was playing Elvis Presley, which he thought was really cool. Before I realized it, he had his hand all the way over touching the side of my blouse. He was a young working-class guy who wanted some action. He was frank and wasn't wasting any time. After all, what the hell was a young woman doing out there hitchhiking at night? He figured I was ready and willing."

Jim sat on the passenger side next to the door trying to not lead the guy on or flirt with him. Suddenly the guy pulled off the main road beside a cornfield.

"He was really horny, so I used the same old excuse, that it was my time of the month. He was okay with that, but now he wanted a blowjob." Jim realized it was best not to provoke him into a fight, so he went down on him to get him over being horny. The guy enjoyed the release and then dozed off.

"Here we are next to the cornfield. Something told me I should get the hell out of there. I would have to get out of the door and fetch my suitcase from the back bed of the truck. I couldn't just leave my suitcase. I reached for the door, but I must have made too much noise, because he woke up and leaned over to me and started kissing me to have another go. His hand went up my skirt and—surprise!—there's male genitalia that shouldn't be there."

The shocked guy ripped off Jim's scarf and realized without a doubt that Jim was a guy. He jumped out of the pickup, marched around to Jim's side and jerked him out of the truck. "He started beating me. 'I'll teach you, you fucking homo.' I kept thinking, *'Save the face, save the face.'* He was so mad that he began ripping my clothes right there in the cold night while he was beating me."

The guy quickly had enough and stomped back to his pickup, got in and peeled off. Then after a few yards he stopped and backed up the pickup to where it had been parked, so Jim ran into the cornfield to escape. The young pickup driver got out, grabbed Jim's suitcase and hurled it at the cornfield so hard that when it hit the ground it busted open. He got back into his pickup and skidded his tires as he rammed the truck down the road.

Jim was uncertain whether the guy was gone for good or would return. After a while Jim ran into the opening, grabbed his men's clothes and ran back deep into the cornfield.

"I was in a lot of pain. My beat-up face ached. My ribs were sore where he'd kicked me. I didn't quite know what to do, but I knew I had to get dressed back into my men's clothes. Thankfully he hadn't ripped up those also, so I put them on. As the sun rose, I retrieved my suitcase and walked down the road adjacent to the cornfields until I came to a farmhouse."

Jim knocked on the farmhouse door around 6:00 a.m. or so. A nice farm lady came to the door. She glanced at the way Jim looked and was alarmed. "I hadn't prepared exactly what to do or say. I knew if I told the truth, nobody would help me; and in fact, they'd probably arrest me. So, I told her and her husband that I was hitchhiking and that this guy picked me up and robbed me. I'd never quite heard that twist, since the normal hitchhiking story had the hitchhiker doing the robbing. I just switched the story around. Well, it was the best I could come up with on the spur of the moment."

The farm lady offered Jim a cup of coffee. He was anxious to look in the bathroom mirror and check out his face. "I was a terrible mess. I had swollen eyes and puffed out face and bruises. I just stared in the mirror thinking, *'Honey, Max Factor's never going to cover this up.'*"

Jim had not planned on getting the authorities involved, but when Jim exited the bathroom the farmer said he already had called the sheriff's office. Jim originally thought he would get cleaned up and hitchhike back home, but two deputies showed up and wrote down Jim's deposition. They were helpful and sympathetic and gave Jim a ride to the hospital.

Jim ended up staying in a semi-private hospital room. The nurses and doctors were busy but caring.

"No one asked me if I had health insurance. They didn't ask any of those types of questions in those days in contrast to the questions they require you to answer nowadays. The staff gave me something to sleep, and since I was already worn out from being up all night, I fell asleep right away."

Jim was sleeping when the two deputies returned. They informed him they had investigated the crime scene and had a few questions.

This time they were not in a good mood. Their attitude had changed, and they became aggressive, wanting to know what really went on.

"I figured they had caught the guy. I worried that I'd be in some serious trouble if the guy told them what actually happened. So, I stuck to my story that I was hitchhiking, and this guy drove up and robbed me. But I made up a false description of the guy and told them he was going in the opposite direction."

"All I wanted to do was recover and get home. I promised myself I never ever again would go in drag. I got into too much trouble in drag."

The deputies wanted to know where the guy went, and Jim realized they had not found the young pickup driver after all. They started quizzing Jim, claiming they knew what happened. "My heart sank. I wondered how in the world they found out what happened."

One deputy asked, "Where's the woman?"

Jim was puzzled, "Woman?"

The other detective said, "You might as well cough up the truth. What did you and your buddy do with the body?"

The deputies had it all figured out and asserted, "You and your accomplice picked up the woman and raped her and then killed her, didn't you?"

"I'm in bed wondering what in the world they were talking about. How'd they come to this ridiculous conclusion?"

Then one deputy told Jim, "We found the woman's clothes and purse scattered at the cornfield."

"Uh, oh! Well, I know when to give up a fight. Suddenly I'm faced with them accusing me of murdering some woman? Being homosexual wasn't so bad after all. There were some things I would refuse to admit, but fuck it, to save my neck I'd admit to anything that really happened. They weren't going to pin no murder on me."

So, Jim told them the truth about hitchhiking dressed as a woman and getting picked up by the guy. At first, they looked at each other with baffled expressions. Jim's tale was too far out of reality to wrap their heads around what actually happened. They did not believe him. So, he told them to bring the clothes, and he would show them that they fit him. That was all the deputies needed to hear.

"I began recounting in detail what happened. When I got to the part that I had sex with him, their attitude suddenly changed, 'Well, we would have done the same thing he did.' By admitting what I'd done, everything that happened to me was suddenly my fault—and I deserved what I got. They assumed they had this big juicy murder case, but once I showed them that they were mistaken, they realized I was just some homo that got the beating he deserved."

After the deputies informed the medical staff of some details of the case, Jim began getting the cold shoulder from the medical workers. As he prepared to go for X-rays, the deputies came back in and intervened. They yanked Jim out of the hospital and placed him in the local jail.

"Here I was in jail again—another bad situation I got myself into. To say the least, I wasn't at my peak."

Jim figured he would wait this one out, and hopefully he might end up without a long jail sentence. Jim stayed in that jail for two or three days. "I was pretty miserable. The jailers kept making comments. They'd come around to see the homo, as though they hadn't seen a real one before. No matter what, I tried to maintain my dignity."

"After a couple of days, they transferred me—to of all places—the state mental hospital. I was back home! The last thing the deputies told me as they handed me over to the hospital staff was, 'Don't ever come back.'"

Chapter 13

In the Hospital with Cassie

The mental hospital required patients to attend group therapy sessions. Patients sat around in a semicircle with a therapist guiding conversations.

"I told the groups about my trips to California, how gay life there increased my chances for happiness. For the most part, the others in the therapy groups thought it was just terrible, horrible. Usually what would happen in group therapy is they'd all ignore me, because I would dominate the conversation. I've always loved to talk. Later, when I would begin a story about one of my adventures, the other patients would remind me, 'Oh, we've heard that one before.'"

As time wore on, Jim could tell that he had gotten some help and insight from the therapy groups.

"That's where I met my dear friend Cassie[22] who was a little older than I was—a fascinating character who came from an Idaho rural community. In group therapy sessions Cassie was kind and understanding of everyone. Cassie was intuitive and one of the most intelligent people I've ever known."

It is unknown for certain if Cassie was an intersex individual or only had male genitalia. "Cassie was 'born' a male, but the boy had 'died' a long time ago when Cassie was young. Only Cassie, the female, remained. She never played any con jobs to cheat anyone out of anything. Cassie just preferred living life as a woman. She always had been effeminate and preferred to dress as a female."

"Cassie had a high voice and actually was closer to being a real woman in most every way except for one—her dick and balls."

She stood about 5'7" with sandy blonde hair that she curled and fixed up in cute styles. She didn't wear a wig, yet she looked just like a woman. Her body structure was very feminine—somewhat undeveloped and very thin—so in female attire Cassie easily passed as a natural woman.

For years Cassie had lived life as a woman. In the year previous to her being committed to the hospital, Cassie was running off and shacking up with men. Her parents were confounded by all of the baffling stuff going on and had no idea how to handle the situation. They thought it was obvious that Cassie was mentally ill. In those years, they never had heard of such mixed-up behavior and had no idea what to do with Cassie. So, they sent Cassie to the mental hospital thinking the institution might be able to do something to straighten out whatever was wrong.

The mental hospital discovered that Cassie had more female hormones than male. That gave Cassie bragging rights, and she assumed that she had the green light to live her life as she wanted. "It was as if they issued her a card or something that stated she was the way she was because of her hormones."

Cassie would tell Jim, "Well, Honey, if your chromosomes were like mine, you would understand. I'm not really gay. I've just got these chromosomes."

During warm late spring days Cassie and Jim would recline in hospital patio chairs and indulge in their mutual love of reading books. Some days were lazy and others hectic. Patients would walk nearby—some of them in a daze. One patient saw imaginary bugs on the sidewalks. Another patient whom everybody called Cookie would walk around carrying her pillow, which she believed was her baby.

On one particular laundry day, a new hospital attendant was gathering laundry. He passed by Cookie and snatched her pillow announcing, "Wash day!" Cookie began screaming and reaching out for her pillow. "My baby!" She started sobbing uncontrollably and stomping her feet. "No! My baby! Give me my baby!"

It was quite a commotion. Cassie was irritated with the disturbance, so she and Jim walked out to big bushes and sat on a secluded bench by themselves in peace, as they had done so many other times. The two would daydream together and fantasize about where they intended to go someday. Cassie fancied running off with

Jim to Los Angeles. She never had been there and was intrigued by Jim's stories of his adventures in California.

"I thought it would be fun taking a friend with me to LA. But I had to tell Cassie about my one major problem. I explained to her that if I ever got stopped by the cops, they could lock me up, and she probably would end up having to fend for herself on her own. I told her that I was officially banned from California. I explained my run-in with the law and told her that when the judge banned me he threatened me that if they ever found out I was back in California they'd lock me up."

"I remember Cassie chuckling, 'Oh Honey, they can't banish you from a state. That would never hold. They rejected those sorts of things back in the 1850s around the time Edward Everett Hale was writing about Philip Nolan.' It sounded convincing to me. I assumed she obviously knew what she was talking about—like usual."

Cassie yearned to get away from the hospital. She believed she never should have been placed in the state institution. She maintained that if her grandmother were still alive the old lady never would have allowed Cassie's father to commit her to the mental hospital. And Cassie intended to leave at the earliest date allowed.

Chapter 14

Home Visits & the Ski Resort

During Jim's home visits he stayed with his mother and the family. Most of the time they lived in Ketchum. Living a couple of miles from the Sun Valley ski resort was exciting. It was one of the first big ski resorts in the western USA—owned by Union Pacific Railroad, which promoted it quite extensively.

Fred and Fannie believed that if Jim had a solid job in the Ketchum area, he would not be so quick to take off for California. So, during that home visit in the late-1950s he went job hunting and got a position right away working in a Sun Valley ski resort restaurant as a bus boy.

"I felt so independent. Even though my folks lived in Ketchum, I stayed in swanky Sun Valley in sort of a cabin with a bunch of rooms where employees lived. I remember relaxing during my off-hours listening to the new Johnny Mathis album *Open Fire, Two Guitars*. He was still big at that time."

Jim set a lot of trends in Idaho that he brought back from California. People at Sun Valley were a lot more tolerant than those in Ketchum. "I was the first person in town to wear Bermuda shorts and the first to wear colored corduroy pants. I was the first in the area to come back from California and actually wear men's cologne."

Jim splurged one of his first paychecks on an expensive $50 sweater from a local boutique shop for the rich. "I wasn't being practical, but I always liked nice clothes, and money always did slip through my hands."

During the late-1930s, 1940s and 1950s, the rich and Hollywood types would vacation in Sun Valley, especially people into outdoor activities like Clark Gable and James Cagney. Most of the famous people who spent time there did so in wintertime for the skiing. A few would visit in the summer.

"I was riding a Sun Valley elevator from a basement to a first floor where there was a night club, and Gary Cooper got on. I noticed he had a fairly young face but a shriveled neck. This was right after he made the film *Love in the Afternoon.*"

"I saw Lucille Ball. She blended in with everybody else and looked like any other person—not fancy at all. She was still married to Desi Arnez, but the *I Love Lucy* TV show already had ended its broadcast run."

"Every year it seemed as though the vacation area was becoming more dynamic."

Local residents would see all of the famous people among the crowds of business owners, doctors and lawyers. Visitors would also shop in Ketchum, which had all of the gift stores, but the rich and famous lodged in Sun Valley. Local townspeople were taught and learned very fast that if they saw a celebrity, they were not to run after them or ask them for autographs. These people did not look their best without the makeup that made their fabulous faces—and locals were not to pay them any undue attention.

"One day Marilyn Monroe came to town. The newspapers were full of stories about Marilyn acting in a new movie filmed in the Ketchum area called *Bus Stop*. In reality they were filming only a very small part of the movie there. Of course, everybody got really excited. I was a real fan of Marilyn."

The locals learned the movie crew was filming about six miles outside of town at a gas station with a gift shop attached to it. The movie people transformed the station into the motion picture's bus stop.

"A lot of us gathered out there to see Marilyn, but she didn't appear very often. You could see her as long as you stood back behind the lines. The movie crew would tell everyone to keep quiet during filming, but later I learned that most movies that are filmed outside are later dubbed over because of the small natural sounds surrounding the actors, maybe even an airplane going overhead."

The crowds would watch as crews filmed a scene of Marilyn Monroe entering the bus stop with the rest of the bus passengers. They also watched a scene being filmed with Don Murray. "Crews were filming scenes that looked very artificial, but on film it worked. Watching the scenes being filmed over and over and over became real boring real fast. Most of us got tired of the movie set. It wasn't like we could go up and meet Marilyn. We couldn't even get her autograph."

$$\nabla$$

"Fred was a good decent stepfather. Looking back on him, I would say that in some ways he was sort of a friend to me. He always was trying to make a man out of me. If I'd been a masculine kid, he would have been a model stepfather."

Figure 26: Fred Hoffer and Jim in Ketchum, Idaho.

Fred always had been a hard worker and was always looking for a way to make an extra handful of money. He worked side jobs to supplement the money he and Fannie made. A few rich people living in Ketchum would hire him to do jobs like trimming trees, painting homes or repairing fences.

When Jim had returned from one trip to California, Fred told him that he had just painted Ernest Hemingway's house in Ketchum. "I'd seen the movie versions of his books like *The Old Man and the Sea* and *For Whom the Bell Tolls*. But up until that time I'd never read him at all. His books were about pursuits in the wilderness and adventures involving soldiers of fortune fighting wars. Those were not the types of books I previously chose to read. I began reading about him. He'd been featured in *Life* magazine, which included a photo of him with his white beard. He was called Papa, and he had been awarded the Nobel Prize for Literature and the Pulitzer Prize for Fiction. I was impressed that Fred actually knew Hemingway."

As Jim grew into his late-teens Fred included him in a couple of his money-making pursuits. One time when Fred was unable to find fence posts to purchase, he got the idea to go up into the higher mountains and make fence posts to sell. He cut down trees, skinned off the bark, cut the wood into lumber posts and treated the poles with wood preservatives. He not only sold fence posts to individuals and businesses, he also was able to sell some gigantic-sized posts to the phone company to use as telephone poles.

Fred told Jim that he could make good money that summer. Fred thought it would be good physical work for Jim and would keep him in Idaho instead of running off to California. Jim went up to the worksite and stayed in a camp space that contained a trailer the two guys lived in.

"Most of the time Fred and I were supposed to just bach it up there and work together by ourselves. Actually, I never really liked camping. It was very uncomfortable in the cold night air. There were no bathroom facilities but plenty of mosquitoes during the day. I wasn't a real happy camper."

Fannie would drive up with Anita to the campsite every three or four days. Fred and Jim took turns going back with her to Ketchum for a few hours to take a shower, get a decent home-cooked meal and haul supplies back up to the work site.

"Fred ended up making a whole lot of money that year. At the end of the summer I had more money than I'd ever had. Plus, my muscles grew pretty big from that work."

Chapter 15

New York, New York

Hollywood was a bust, but Jim was not about to give up on his starry-eyed dream of becoming an actor. He was an older teenager and had bounced in and out of the mental institution, survived the streets of LA and hustled himself in exchange for a dinner or a warm bed. He hitchhiked his way to his next intended destination and had found himself in the company of kind-hearted strangers, kindred souls and drag queens as well as con artists, liars, wannabe Hollywood types and ruthless cops.

Whenever Jim returned to Idaho after spending months in LA, he usually became bored. During one summer in LA, Jim worked as a restaurant busboy. He lasted there the entire four summer months before deciding it was time to return to Idaho. He had saved almost two hundred dollars from that job and headed back to Idaho, but there was nothing worthwhile to spend his money on back home and nothing worth doing in Idaho.

Jim recalled that in the Los Angeles libraries he had learned a lot by reading *Variety* and other film industry trade publications. Actors in Hollywood did not necessarily live in Hollywood. He read about actors heading to Broadway in New York to learn acting. "A lot of them would work in summer stock. Budding actors would be in one little play, then another play, and then perhaps if they got good at their trade, they might get into Broadway shows. At a certain time in their career, the film industry would send for them, or they would go to Hollywood hoping their time had arrived."

"In Idaho there was no way to develop my acting career. One day this great idea came to me. I would go to New York where I could kick-start my career on Broadway. I already had some experience singing and dancing on stage in the Idaho mental hospital. I just knew that when I arrived all kinds of people would be falling over themselves for my talent. I was like a lot of young dreamers."

"My dear, I was going to Broadway!"

Jim's cross country bus fare cost less than $40, so that gave him plenty of money to spare. He thought he was rich. He started on his cross-country trip and lived on the bus for almost four days.

Each mile the bus traveled became the furthest point east that Jim ever had ventured. No palm trees, no starlets and no wannabe stars on the boulevard. The cities he was traveling through seemed cold and hard. "Chicago wasn't that bad, but I didn't particularly like its midwestern metropolitan atmosphere. In downtown Detroit, people were moving out of the city, and the inner-city stores were beginning to close and board up. It looked and felt like a city on the verge of a downward spiral."

Each time the bus stopped, Jim became more excited about getting closer to his destination—The Big Apple. "When I finally saw the morning New York skyline from across the Hudson River, it was beautiful, just like in the movies." The bus drove through the Lincoln Tunnel underneath the river and emerged in midtown Manhattan, a mere couple of blocks from the Port Authority Bus Terminal.

Jim wandered around the terminal, gathered some brochures about the city and studied maps in preparation for his first few days in the city. Times Square was only a half dozen blocks away. Central Park was less than a mile away. He had made it. This was New York, the city that never sleeps. Jim's dreams were within reach—as close as Broadway. Or so he believed during his real New York welcome his first day there.

While Jim was analyzing the city maps planning his first move, somebody stole his luggage. His billfold and money remained safe in his back pocket, so he transferred them to his front pocket for extra protection to ensure no one would pickpocket him.

Walking down the frenzied streets, Jim saw the city up close. "It was dirtier and more run-down that I'd expected it to be. People seemed to be irritated and easy to anger."

Jim ended up staying at the huge Sloane House YMCA in a room up on the eleventh or twelfth floor. He went to Broadway productions to get an idea how the whole scene operated, and after the shows he hit the nightclubs hoping to make solid connections.

"I wasn't about to go around trying to find a job working in some ordinary place. I was in New York for a career." Jim read the Broadway trade papers, which listed the casting calls. He found a perfect open audition for a show and went to try out.

"Inside the theater I stood in a long line. Finally after a couple of hours I got up to the microphone. I'm on stage by myself and the audience area is dark. I couldn't see anybody with the bright lights in my eyes. I heard a voice from nowhere say, 'Okay, what can you do? What experience have you had?'"

Jim answered, "Well, I don't have any real experience here in New York, but I've done a few things in Idaho. I thought I'd come here and have you audition me and give you a chance to sign me up."

The voice replied, "Come back again when you've got more experience."

Jim explained, "But I can sing and dance. I can be an actor. I love to stay up all night. I've been in Hollywood for three or four years in the industry trying to become a movie star. That hasn't worked out so far, so I'm here to give my career a boost."

The voice said, "That's all. You're not ready for a Broadway show. Get some experience and then come back. Try out for an off-Broadway show. Start there."

It was disheartening for Jim, but while he was at the theater, he got to talk with some of the other young people and found out where they gathered and visited. For a while Jim went to the cafes and places where they met up, and he hung out with them. The people he sat with would ask him what show he was in. Some of the young people were working, but a lot were just hoping. Jim learned to tell people that he had been on the road in a show that folded before it got to Broadway. Or he would tell them he was between engagements. Jim pretended to be a dancer, and the others accepted that as true since he was both svelte and gay.

"My attempts hadn't accomplished much. Again, I'd made a serious miscalculation. It was taking longer to make my big splash on Broadway than what I first had assumed. I never was able to plan ahead very well."

Jim finally had to find a regular job to survive since he was running out of money. He landed a job in the mailroom of a big Manhattan high-rise. The company required Jim to wear a white shirt and tie and black pants. He bustled through the various floors delivering mail.

By the time Jim started working he was down to almost no money. He couldn't pay his rent at the YMCA. He told the YMCA clerks that he had a job but would have to wait three weeks before he received his first paycheck. They told him they were sorry, but they were not allowed to give people advances. He would have to leave.

"Here I had a job but no place to sleep, so I left the Sloane House and slept a couple of nights in the tunnels between Grand Central Station and what was then Pennsylvania Station. In the morning I put on my work clothes and went to my job. During my second night in the tunnels the weather turned cold. Wintertime was hitting, and the bottom of the man-made canyons between the tall buildings was bitter cold."

The next afternoon after work Jim scouted around and checked out Grand Central Station. He followed a stairway up above the crowds and discovered a storage room filled with rolls of wallpaper. He crawled between the big rolls and began sleeping there. In the mornings he would get up and go down to the restroom to change into his work clothes.

"I was too proud to admit to people at work about my problems. It was a disgrace to be in this kind of predicament. I just was glad I had this job. I was trying to hang on until I got my money. The wallpaper room was going to have to be my home for a few nights."

"The hardest part was finding food. I'd go two or three days without eating. One time they had doughnuts at the office, and I ate four or five. The worse thing was that there seemed to always be someone at the office who would want me to eat lunch with them. Of course, that meant I was supposed to bring my lunch. They would wonder why I didn't bring anything, and I'd tell them that I'd already eaten."

Jim was unable to wait things out before he received his paycheck. "The situation was getting too unbearable. I went to the boss and quit. I don't know why I just didn't admit my problems to him."

At least Jim had the wallpaper room to sleep in while he waited another half week for his paycheck. But in the middle of one night,

Jim woke up with flashlights in his eyes and security guards ordering him to get up. Maybe the guards who patrolled the premises had followed him, or perhaps somebody had seen him too often on the stairways or using the restrooms too much. The guards were surprised that a teenager had been living in the wallpaper room.

"At that time being homeless was unheard of, especially if you were young. The only people on the streets were a bunch of tired-looking old winos who panhandled. And you didn't even see them around unless you went into the seedier sections of a city."

The guards escorted Jim down to the main floor and handed him over to New York cops who took him to the police station.

"I only had one shirt, and it was getting pretty grubby and smelly by that time. I was so tired, and the police were so nice to me. I just broke down in tears. No one had been kind to me in New York up until that time. I told them my story of how I ended up living among rolls of wallpaper. These policemen were the nicest people. They ended up taking up a collection and sent me home all the way back to Idaho."

"My parents never sent money whenever I was stranded. I got myself into these situations, and therefore I was expected to find my own way out."

Jim returned to Ketchum during Idaho's busy winter season and promptly headed to the warmth of Southern California. He swore to never return to New York.

Chapter 16

Mistaken Identities

"In California, people would mistake me as the son of famous people. I guess that was because of the upscale way I always dressed."

One day Jim splurged on ice cream on the Sunset Strip at Wil Wright's fancy old-style ice cream parlor. The interior looked like the early 1900s. The parlor sold ice cream that was decadently rich in flavor, very expensive and very popular. As he ate his dessert in front of the parlor at a bus stop, an antique store next door beckoned him.

"Well, I never could resist window-shopping. Everything inside the store was elegant and expensive. The lady owner came up to me and told me how glad she was that I was back. She inquired how my father and mother were doing. I said very well and played along. After a couple of minutes, I figured out she was talking about actor James Mason who starred in *20,000 Leagues Under the Sea* and *The Desert Fox*. After a minute I remembered his actress wife's name was Pamela Mason, so I was able to drop her name. I didn't know if the Masons even had a son or not, but I faked everything the best I could."

The store owner and Jim discussed antiques, including a couple of old pieces he especially liked. The antiques were authenticated. Some of her oldest treasures included Louis 14th furniture. When it was time for Jim to catch the bus, the owner told Jim to tell his parents hello and to tell them about the antiques that Jim liked, claiming the pieces would be excellent investments.

∇

One winter day when Jim was about 19 years old, he packed his suitcase and took a bus from LA to try living in Palm Springs. He never had been there, but he knew it was nearby, sunny and warm. He might be able to make a lot of money from all of the rich people there. On his first full day in town he got a job as a waiter in an Italian restaurant. "A little old Italian woman owned the place and was the cook. The scene in there was just like you'd see in some movie. She was always hollering in Italian and cussing out everybody. Over the restaurant's speakers she played music by Italian-American singers like Frank Sinatra and Dean Martin and Vic Damone."

Jim discovered that Palm Springs had a shortage of affordable housing for laborers. The available rentals were all expensive and primarily for the tourists. Workers lived in trailer parks and old shabby buildings behind the city's tony mid-Century facade. Jim stayed at an old run-down hotel but was happy to have a job where he earned good tips, enough to get by very well.

The restaurant was closed on Mondays. Instead of sitting in his room, he always put on stylish attractive clothes and walked around to explore the area or watch a movie. Jim window-shopped along Palm Canyon Drive, a classy strip where many of the expensive stores were located. It was Christmas season, and palm trees that lined the street were lit up at night.

In front of one of the stores an older guy wearing a 1930s-style tie stopped next to Jim. Jim looked familiar to him, and he asked about Jim's family. "I didn't have anything better to do, so I played along. He said he had known Mr. Weyerhaeuser for a long time and wanted to know how my dad was doing." The Weyerhaeuser family harvested trees and sold a popular brand of lumber and wood products across the USA. The gentleman chatted about the timber and lumber business. He told Jim he was a developer at the Salton Sea just southwest of Palm Springs and was selling his shares of that subdivision project.

The gentleman said he was getting ready to go to Las Vegas. All of a sudden, he had a great idea—his son was visiting him from Connecticut for the week, and he was about to take his son with him to Vegas. Since his son and Jim were the same age, he invited Jim to go along with them. Jim told the gentleman he would have to wait until the following week when he would receive his paycheck. Jim didn't know whether to believe the guy, but the gentleman turned out to be true to his word. He said everything was fine, come along—he would treat Jim. The older guy thought Jim would be a good traveling companion for his son during the next couple of days. They would all stay at the new Tropicana Hotel, and the next day while he attended a couple of business meetings, the two boys could explore and have fun.

"Well, I wasn't about to refuse a free trip to Vegas just because I was supposed to work. Fuck that job right out the window. I could always get another job. Besides, I was sick and tired of that little old woman screaming her head off all the time at everybody."

While the gentleman called home to tell his son to take a taxi to the airport, Jim pretended to call home to tell his family he was going to Las Vegas and would be back home in a couple of days. The gentleman drove Jim to the airport, and the three of them boarded the guy's private plane and flew to Las Vegas. The gentleman sat in the front of the plane with the pilot, and his son and Jim sat in back having a good time getting acquainted. "I answered questions about the lumber business by saying, 'Oh, it's so boring. That's all we talk about at home. We're on vacation. Let's have a good time!'"

The next morning at the Tropicana, the older gentleman gave his son and Jim a hundred dollars apiece. "I couldn't believe they thought I was this Weyerhaeuser kid." The son and Jim were too young to gamble, and there were few things in Vegas for young people under 21 to do. The two window-shopped, ate and amused themselves amid the bizarre bazaar of barkers offering cash deals to separate the boys from their money. "His son was a nice guy, sort of Ivy League. He was going to Yale, so of course I had to tell him I was going to Harvard. And then I thought, *'Why did I have to pick Harvard?'* I didn't know a thing about Harvard."

In the late afternoon the two boys met up with the father. "I saw a roll of bills he had that would choke a horse. He spent money to show us a good time, and he bought a couple pieces of beautiful jewelry for Christmas gifts."

The following morning after breakfast the three took a cab back to the airport and flew back to Palm Springs. The older gentleman offered to drop Jim off at home, but Jim told him that he was supposed to meet his girlfriend. Jim had been trying to save as much as he could of the hundred dollars the older gentleman gave him. "I was afraid the guy was going to ask for the change back, but he never mentioned it. He dropped me off in the same area where we had met, and we said goodbye. He said he hoped his son and I would become friends. I told him that sounded good; however, I just didn't have the energy to contact them again and play along anymore."

Chapter 17

Called Up

The U.S. military had a long history as far back as the Revolutionary War of kicking service members out of its ranks if they were caught engaging in homosexual behavior. Excluding homosexuals continued throughout the 1900s, and Jim understood that to successfully enlist, gay people had to conceal their sexuality from their draft boards and the military.[23]

When Jim was 18 years old, he signed up for the draft as required and carried a draft card for years. According to Selective Service rules, whenever a draft-age man moved he was supposed to notify the draft board. "I figured there was no way they'd let me join, so after I signed up I honestly never gave it a second thought. After all, the country wasn't officially at war. The Korean War had ended in a cease fire, and the United States hadn't yet committed itself to what would become the tragedy of Vietnam."

During one of Jim's infrequent phone calls to his mother back in Idaho, she told him the FBI had called looking for him.

"I went down to the FBI main branch in Los Angeles to see what in the world the FBI wanted to talk to me about. An agent told me I was supposed to report for the military draft. I'd always been disappointed because I knew they wouldn't let me join the Navy. I was pretty effeminate, and all these trips to California hadn't butched me up. I asked the agent why I should report when they wouldn't take me since I was homosexual."

The agent said okay, and Jim provided the address where he was living. The agent said everything was settled as far as the FBI was concerned, and Jim could go.

"From the time I was a little kid I had this desire to go in the Navy. When I was a younger teenager a sailor gave me a Navy hat. I took it back to the mental hospital and showed it off. I read books about ships. I loved the cute sailors. It was fabulous walking down the streets in San Diego and Santa Monica and Long Beach—seeing the sexy sailors wearing tailor-made pants that buttoned around in front with no pockets."

"During and after World War II, sailors took advantage of victory girls. These women would go around giving it away free to all the guys in uniform in appreciation to these guys for their service to our country (or so these easy girls claimed). When I dated sailors as a teenager, I used to daydream about myself as sort of a victory girl of the 1950s."

Three weeks after Jim's FBI interview he received a letter notifying him to report to the Selective Service Center in LA. He was going to be drafted. "I told friends, 'Can you believe this? They're thinking about drafting me.' Friends told me, 'Oh girl, they get one glimpse of you, and they'll never take you.'"

Jim's friends warned him not to try to get into the Navy—be honest about being gay, because if the Navy discovered the truth after he joined, things could get bad. He could get locked up in the brig and kicked out. Who needed a court-marshal and a dishonorable discharge?

So, he went to the Selective Service office. It was full of civilian men sitting around on benches waiting their turns. "I was pissed because I was wasting my time waiting so long during this useless effort they made me go through."

Finally, it was Jim's turn to see a doctor. Jim let him know that he was irritated having to wait so long for such nonsense since they never were going to take him because he was homosexual. The doctor halted any further interactions with Jim and sent him to another doctor—and another long wait.

"I finally saw a psychiatrist and told him I was gay. He replied that they had lots of guys pretending they were gay so they wouldn't be drafted. On the other hand they didn't want a breakdown of morale because homosexuals were having sex with other servicemen. I explained that I wasn't the type to have sex with a bunch of other servicemen, that I'd prefer to find one guy in the service and settle

down with him. The psychiatrist replied that I would be getting my
A-1 classification changed, and I would not be allowed to enter
military service. He would write a note and send it to my draft board
in Idaho."

Chapter 18

Ruth & the Beats of San Francisco

In the late 1950s Jim's older sister Ruth divorced her first husband and moved to San Francisco. Jim decided to go to San Francisco to visit her for a while. It was heartwarming for Jim and Ruth to spend time together again.

Figure 27: Mexican Federale policeman & Ruth.
Ruth had fun riding on the back of his big Harley hog.

"I basically liked Los Angeles more than San Francisco. There seemed to be two types of California guys. First there were the southern California types. We'd go to the gay beach area in the summers to swim and show off our bodies. I was the young type that the LA crowd wanted. I really didn't like to drink, and gay guys in LA didn't have to go to bars to have fun, because a lot of things happened outdoors. I used to try to sneak into bars before I was 21, but after I turned 21 it didn't take me long to get tired of that drinking scene."

"Then there were the San Francisco types. San Francisco was too cold for me. I didn't feel like I quite fit in there. People weren't as outdoorsy as they were in LA. It seemed to me like the main activity in San Francisco was drinking. I guess that's because the weather's so chilly."

Jim's visit with his sister was his first trip to the city. Ruth lived a couple of blocks east of Golden Gate Park. She made excellent money, yet she only worked half-time. She woke up before dawn and drove across the San Francisco-Oakland Bay Bridge to her job at Golden Gate Fields horse racing track in Berkeley. She observed the horses during morning workouts, studied their backgrounds and reviewed their ratings from the previous few races. Then she handicapped them and picked the horses to bet on that day and night. She returned home mid-morning and relayed her predictions to the betting company, which in turn advised clients on which horses to place bets.

"I had a lot of freedom at Ruth's place. Long before I ever went to San Francisco I learned that North Beach was the gay area in the city. I started walking all the way back and forth between Ruth's home and San Francisco's North Beach area. When Ruth would give me extra money, I'd treat myself to a cable car ride midway. I found it difficult to hitchhike around San Francisco—there were so many twists and turns that it was hard to navigate around, let alone hitchhike. All the vehicles seemed to be going all around in mixed-up directions."

In the late 1950s the North Beach area was known for its concentration of bohemians, beats, radicals and longshoremen. There was an abundance of artists, musicians, poets, sex and dope. Gay people who lived in North Beach melded into the trendy beat scene. Popular gay and lesbian bars served the gay crowd in the area.

Three years before Jim's arrival in North Beach, gay beat poet Allen Ginsberg's groundbreaking poem "Howl" was published. The abstract poetry contained spontaneous reflections of the madness and mental illnesses that Allen had witnessed among his friends and relatives:

I saw the best minds of my generation destroyed by madness,
starving hysterical naked[24]

Figure 28: Legendary beat writers (left to right) Bob Donlon (Rob Donnelly), Neal Cassady, Allen Ginsberg, Robert LaVigne and Lawrence Ferlinghetti stand outside Ferlinghetti's City Lights Bookstore in San Francisco, California, Spring 1956.
[Photo by © Allen Ginsberg/CORBIS/Corbis Premium via Getty Images]

San Francisco's City Lights Bookstore co-founder Lawrence Ferlinghetti published "Howl" in the booklet *Howl and Other Poems* as part of a series of booklets of poems released by his publishing company, City Lights Books. Allen Ginsberg's booklet of poems became an immediate success.

It was the tipping point for a literary and artistic movement influencing North Beach and the gay civil rights movement over the next decade.

In North Beach, the Six Gallery featured poem and literary public readings, and Allen read aloud while his friends Neal Cassady and Jack Kerouac lent him support from the audience.

Literary critics reviewed "Howl" as an epic poem that helped kick start the beat movement and ultimately raised the high banner of free speech and artistic freedom. National publications printed positive features about the poem and about the top poets who occupied San Francisco's new exuberant poetry and writers' movement.

In contrast, many moralistic readers considered "Howl" to be a scandalous display of pornography and homosexuality, shocking many readers with its graphic, sexual language:

> *...who let themselves be fucked in the ass by saintly motorcyclists, and*
> *screamed with joy,*

Further troubling, the poem condemned the conformist society that the post-World War II establishment had promoted through public schools, mass media and entertainment.

U.S. Customs Office confiscated copies of "Howl." San Francisco police busted City Lights and arrested a clerk and prosecuted owner Lawrence Ferlinghetti for printing and selling what prosecutors called the indecent and obscene *Howl and Other Poems*. At the end of a significant trial, the presiding judge ruled that "Howl" was not obscene because of its redeeming social importance and its protection under the First and Fourteenth Amendments to the U.S. Constitution guaranteeing freedom of speech and freedom of the press.

North Beach in San Francisco had become a Mecca for the beats and was known for being hospitable for those choosing to live by their own standards instead of the establishment's standards—including artists of various disciplines, hipster musicians and young people who gathered in coffee shops for poetry readings and jazz music.

It was against this backdrop that Jim had landed in San Francisco's North Beach at the height of the beat movement. He had little interest in the beat lifestyle or its literature. He headed to North Beach for fun.

Storefront Italian cafes lined the streets selling slices of pizza. "Sometimes I'd buy an Italian sandwich when I could afford one."

Jim was eating in one small busy joint, and a beat asked Jim if he minded him sitting on the stool next to him; and they started talking. Jack was a gay beat musician who was a half dozen years older than Jim. He lived in Seattle, and he wrote some beat songs among other songs he performed. "I remember him singing *Daddy-O Has Got the Bongo Beat*. I'll never forget that name."

The beats that Jack and Jim associated with were friendly toward gay people, although there were plenty of other beats whom Jim never encountered who were less than supportive.

A lot of people in North Beach were rebelling against the traditional attitudes in the USA that had prevailed after World War II. "We had to watch out, because the police were out to raid gay bars and bust gay people. They were also targeting the beats. It seemed like the fuzz were intent on suppressing the whole subversive bohemian counterculture."

Jim and Jack ended up spending a couple of weeks together. "I thought Jack was a sexy beat who was hip and exciting and had a fun attitude about life. I'd learned enough from the press and TV about beatniks that I had a good idea where his mind was coming from."

Jack was the first guy Jim ever dated who had facial hair. Jack preferred not making the scene back in Seattle because he thought it was dullsville compared to the beat generation lifestyle in San Francisco, which was a lot more vibrant than back home.

Jack took Jim to coffeehouses where cool musicians and beat poets congregated—places that were a lot more laid back than bars. "We went to a couple of poetry readings. We watched beat musicians singing with harmonicas and bongos inside establishments where the atmosphere always was mellow and the edison was always turned down to keep the places dark. Instead of clapping for the performers, all of those cool cats would snap their fingers in applause. The whole atmosphere in the coffeehouses seemed far out, but being with Jack made it a gas and a real wild thrill."

Jim did things with Jack that he never had experienced before, such as going to a nude beach and turning on to marijuana. "As we smoked a joint, Jack asked me, 'Like, you dig this fine grass?' I was thinking, *'I'm kind of dizzy. I'd rather be straight.'* I told him, 'Yeah man, this is good stuff.' I hoped he would see me as cool and hip instead of square."

Jack was staying in North Beach with other beat friends who were packing their belongings to move over to the Haight area of the city. Jack moved with them and stayed a couple of days longer in their pad in the Haight before he returned to Seattle. The Haight was not far from where Ruth lived; nonetheless, after Jack left, Jim had no more reason to go there. "The Haight didn't interest me in those days. North Beach was the place to make the scene."

Jim spent a good portion of his time with his sister. Ruth and Jim took late-afternoon walks in Golden Gate Park, wandered around Fisherman's Wharf and explored Chinatown. After a couple of joyful months with Ruth, Jim went back to Idaho. From that time forward, he would return to San Francisco again and again.

Chapter 19

Off to California with Cassie

In March 1959 Jim turned 20 years old. "I'd been homosexual as far back as I could remember. Although my mother knew it, she conveniently never had to acknowledge it. She dismissed everything as silly stunts."

Finally, Jim decided he needed to spell out the truth to Fannie. He said the words, "I'm a homosexual." He told her he had experienced homosexual relations and intended to continue to find the man of his dreams. Her response was one of horror. She took the attitude that Jim was a menace to society. "Although my mother's response didn't surprise me, it still hurt. I resented her. I just never seemed to have bonded with her—going as far back as when she moved Ruth and me from the orphanage into her home, and I began getting acquainted with her."

"Now in essence I was fully rebelling. I refused to conform to her determination of how I should live my life." Jim announced he was leaving Fannie's home and moving back with the gay people in LA. Within a day Fannie signed a petition for a judicial order to send Jim back to the state mental institution again (for the eighth time).

"I arrived into the safety of the mental hospital and announced, 'Here I am.' And they were sick and tired of it."

Long ago the hospital staff had determined there was nothing mentally wrong with Jim. They became increasingly concerned that Jim was becoming institutionalized there. They wanted him to leave, but they decided that Jim should not be released to his mother again, labeling his parental relationship as disturbed and atrocious.[25]

"They laid down the law to me. 'You absolutely have got to go.' It was terrible. I wasn't welcomed at my mother's house, and now I didn't have my home at the hospital. I didn't have anything out there in the world. I felt so lonely and abandoned. Being kicked out of a mental hospital—how low could I go?"

Jim and the Idaho State Mental Hospital parted ways for good.

Jim seemed lost. So the day after he left the hospital, he went to see Cassie who was living in a house trailer in Twin Falls. She invited him to move in with her.

Over the years Cassie had developed the knack of naturally fitting into life as a female without arousing anyone's suspicions. Cassie's main boyfriend was a 19-year-old who originally had approached Cassie in front of a theater. "He spent a lot of time at Cassie's place, and they were sleeping together all the time."

Since Cassie was so effeminate and not that well known in Twin Falls, nobody had an inkling about her male genitalia. Nonetheless, Cassie concluded that Twin Falls was too small for her and Jim to live comfortably.

"I thought we should move to Boise. I had a couple of friends who used to live there, and I had attended a couple of their parties. Cassie was firmly against living in Boise. She claimed the city was a queer trap for homosexuals—that it conducted witch hunts for homosexuals whom the authorities arrested and actively prosecuted."

Cassie feared Boise. She knew a former patient whom a half dozen years earlier had been committed to the state mental hospital in Blackfoot. When he got out of the hospital he was supposed to be rehabilitated, however he reverted to acting on his homosexual orientation and urges, and he got rounded up in one of Boise's hunts for homosexuals. At the trial the judge noted that the former patient had not lived with his wife after getting released from the insane asylum—a clear sign that he was not rehabilitated—so the judge sentenced him to a decade and a half in the Idaho penitentiary. The judge stated that this was a warning to homosexuals that if they refused to rehabilitate themselves, they had best stay away from Idaho.

"So, we took off and never returned together to Idaho again. We got on a bus and headed to Los Angeles, and I'll never forget that ride. We drenched ourselves in My Sin perfume and threw our coats over our shoulders and swished on the bus. We just gabbed and carried on all the way to LA. The other guys on the bus were attracted to Cassie's womanly charms, but they didn't know what to make of me as her obviously queer companion."

"It was night when we arrived in LA. We ended up renting a room at a small cheap motel in a tacky section of the city. Cassie went down the hall to take a bath. She came running back and knocked on our door. It turned out we were in some kind of sleazy dope house—a real trashy place."

The next morning the two made their way to Hollywood where Cassie was determined to rent a place. Instead of renting an apartment or room, Cassie ended up renting a small house for her and Jim. "I didn't know how she accomplished it all. She had an excellent understanding about money, but then she was successful at everything she did."

Each of the two tiny bedrooms were only big enough for a bed and nightstand. In the small living room, they moved in a chair, couch and table. After a couple of days, Cassie went out and found a job. Life was wonderful. Cassie planted flowers around the palm trees to accent the yard, and within a couple of months the whole place looked beautiful both inside and outside.

"Cassie didn't waste any time hitting the bar scene. She never went to gay bars. She wasn't sexually attracted to gay men and wasn't particularly interested in being around them. She was interested only in straight men. Cassie's idea of fun was going to honky-tonk bars and straight beer joints as a woman."

Cassie was extremely popular. All of the guys were interested in her. "She went with men who I'd call lower working-class guys. She had a fetish for tough guys and for bikers who rebuilt and modified and chopped their own motorcycles."

Most of the guys were in their late twenties and thirties. Cassie knew how to relate to those ordinary blue-collar guys. They were interested in having a good time. Cassie gave it up when other women would not. Sometimes she would have two or three different guys revolving through the home during the same week. Within a couple of months, she had attained the reputation as one of the hottest numbers in town.

"Cassie made it clear to her boyfriends that she was just a good-time girl who was not about to get married and settle down with only one guy. She set the rules. They could either dig it or drift on."

It was the fun-loving young guys who ended up coming around the house all of the time. Cassie always had plenty of beer and whiskey for them. She made it seem as though she was drinking large quantities of alcohol. She would look drunk—but the only ones who ended up getting drunk were the guys around her.

She entertained the young bikers in the backyard. They would kick back near the barbecue, drink and smoke cigars while Jim listened to them swap stories about their wild escapades.

Cassie seemed like a total woman, except for the penis and testicles. "I'd see Cassie dressed in skin tight skirts, and her private parts never showed. She had sex with the guys in her bedroom, and I could hear them moaning and groaning. And these were guys who had sexual experience. How she hid it and got away with it I'll never know. But we have to remember—this was a naïve time. Everyone just naturally assumed a woman was always a woman. Nowadays in our know-all society most everything would be truthfully out in the open to everyone close to us."

Cassie's boyfriends never saw her completely nude. She never entirely undressed. Even when she was on the sofa or in bed with a guy, she continued to wear her Chenille bathrobe.

"It was a strange thing. I never completely understood Cassie's fetish for these rugged tough guys she'd drag home. She didn't have sex with every one of them, but she certainly had her share. After having wild fun at our home, these macho hunks invariably showed up again for more good times."

One of Cassie's boyfriends commented to Cassie about how effeminate Jim was and asked if he was a homo. Cassie told him the truth about Jim, and from then forward she would introduce Jim to all of the guys as her queer cousin. "I was just being myself, whatever that was. Her friends would talk about her queer cousin, and she'd agree with them in a patronizing way. Inside myself I'd get upset at her for it. After all, I felt that she was just as queer as I was."

All of Cassie's friends treated Jim in a kind manner. The guys were all friendly to him and treated him like a little brother (or sister). Jim understood that since he was young, he could get away with a lot of things with them. They developed a rapport with Jim on a superficial level. "If they were traveling to a store or somewhere, they would take me along on the back of their motorcycles. The guys were too masculine and tough to give a shit what anybody thought of them associating with a homo."

Many of Cassie's biker friends were outlaws, not in the sense that they were evil, but outlaws in the sense that they were total rebels. They viewed Jim as a rebel also. Jim was what he was and made no bones about it.

"We all understood that the norms of the day dictated that Cassie's biker friends weren't supposed to like homos; but rules existed to be broken by these rule-breakers, so these rebels all liked me—to hell with fucking rules. Their attitude was: What a guy does with his life should be his own damn business."

One day some bikers treated Cassie to the amusement park and Jim tagged along. They took Jim on the rides, and he screeched and screamed and acted like a young girl—and the guys liked it. Jim was different, and he was fun to be with. "I guess I was fulfilling their idea of some little faggot, and they got a kick out of it. I was like a teenage girl to them."

As for Jim, there was nothing romantically going on for him. After all, these guys came over to the house to see Cassie, not her homo cousin. Jim began getting bored watching Cassie get all the men while he got nothing. "I felt isolated watching her and the guys. They were really interesting guys, but they weren't attracted to me. I would have loved to do something with a couple of them, but I knew I couldn't. So, it all felt very frustrating."

Jim and Cassie ended up living together for a few weeks. Eventually Cassie decided that LA was too large and impersonal for her comfort and wanted to move up to the Pacific Northwest. So, Jim and Cassie went their separate ways. Cassie moved up north, and Jim remained in California.

$$\nabla$$

In late autumn Jim went on a two-week vacation. First, he stopped in Las Vegas to see Ruth for a couple of days. She had been a showgirl and a go-go dancer. Now she was a golden mermaid at the Silver

Slipper Casino where she swam around inside a giant fish tank circling around a big submerged globe. Jim explored the tourist spots on the Las Vegas Strip, but he was not old enough to go into any casinos and gamble. He saved his money and bought nothing from the hawkers whose purpose was to separate tourists from their hard-earned cash.

After a couple of days with Ruth, Jim headed up to Idaho. On Jim's journey to his mother's home he stopped in Blackfoot at the Idaho State Hospital South. "I wasn't a patient there anymore, but I wanted to see my friends. After all, I'd lived there for years. Friends and staff members were all happy to see me and loved hearing the good news about my life. I told them how well I was managing—and all of a sudden I started feeling a lot of pride about myself. It was a really good feeling."

Then Jim stopped by Ketchum to see his mother, Fred and Anita. He told them all about how good he was doing in LA. This was the first time seeing them since Jim had come out to Fannie. "The environment at my mother's place seemed a little hostile, so I only slept overnight and left the following day. I never again lived or stayed inside my mother's home with her."

Next, Jim headed from Ketchum to the Portland area to visit Cassie for a week. Cassie met Jim at the Portland bus station. "We climbed into her great big 1956 Packard Patrician that she had just bought. She drove me to her home in a suburb of Portland located just across the Columbia River—the small town of Vancouver, Washington. It certainly wasn't the center of gay activities, but Cassie was very content there. She had settled down there with a guy who was a couple of years older than she was. She had given up all other men."

Cassie and her boyfriend treated Jim to dinner at a couple of fine Portland restaurants. They also took Jim sightseeing up and down the Columbia River. They would climb into Cassie's Packard with Jim in the back seat wearing jeans and a jacket. It had turned cold, so everybody there was wearing large car coats.

"During my short stay with Cassie I talked a lot with her boyfriend. He was a rough gravely-voiced guy. It was obvious that he knew the history between Cassie and me, because he alluded to the hospital in Blackfoot. Also, he knew the whole truth about Cassie. He told me, 'I got the best of both worlds—Cassie's got the bitchin' body of a hot sexy woman and the sexual drive of a man. For me there's nothing as boring as women who don't totally enjoy sex.' He believed that his and Cassie's energies intensified each other's passions."

"Those previous months in LA when Cassie and I lived together certainly were exciting to say the least. Now I felt good knowing that Cassie was settled and happy and satisfied. I don't know if she ever got a sex-change operation—it was a very complicated procedure back then."

After a week in the Portland area, Jim headed back to southern California. He was ready for warmer temperatures and another new job.

Chapter 20

Dallas

Jim loved the West Coast, but his spirit continued to move him to explore new places. In summer 1962 he decided to travel to the southeast Gulf states of Louisiana and Texas.

Jim visited Louisiana first and found New Orleans to be a lot more fun than most other places he had visited. "New Orleans was a pretty wild place, very nice. I'd heard a lot about it. It had a large gay community. I didn't go during Mardi Gras, which I wanted to. I chose an off season and went there and looked around for myself."

Jim found New Orleans rich in culture. He spent most of his time in the French Quarter with its unique architectural style that made Jim feel almost as though the area was a foreign country and not part of the USA.

Jim checked out the riverfront parks and walkways along the Mississippi River and watched large steamboats paddle the river and barges haul oil and tons of cargo to and from the Port of New Orleans.

"I also spent time in the Garden District and rode a streetcar named St. Charles."

"There were a lot of fun-loving gay people in New Orleans. It's a real paradise for people who like to drink. The bars never close. But for me, I didn't drink that much. Nonetheless, there were a lot of gay bars. One of the bars was Café Lafitte in Exile. It claimed itself to be the oldest gay bar in the USA. It was a real famous place, one of the premier gay bars at that time. It was named after the pirate Jean Lafitte."

Jim wasn't in New Orleans very long. He left there and decided to stop in Dallas for a visit.

Jim checked into the YMCA to spend a few days. "YMCAs were all over the country in whole lot of cities. It wasn't that they advertised themselves, but everybody knew about them. When I'd go to all of these cities, that's where I'd often stay. I could usually afford the YMCA."

"I met many butch guys and military types there. I guess World War II might have had something to do with it, maybe before. But certainly many military men stayed at them because they were cheap. The only thing was that the guys couldn't have women in there with them."

"I'd been registered at the YMCA for about a week or ten days. I had spent all of my money and owed one day's rent, which I didn't know how I was going to pay."

It was the middle of the night during early morning hours. "I walked down the hall and saw a door open. The door was open three or four inches and a shoe was prying it open. The night chain was on. I reached in and got a man's billfold. This billfold was on the table. I put the billfold in my pocket."

The billfold contained no money.

Jim went out on the building's fire escape and entered through a window into another room rented by a sailor and stole both the guy's billfold containing $101 and personal papers. Jim tossed the billfold and kept the money. He checked out of the YMCA paying his bill with part of the stolen money.

He then took a taxicab to a nearby hotel.

One of the guys whose billfold was stolen summoned the police and made a formal complaint.

Every law breaker sooner or later screws up. Police contacted the taxicab company, learned the cab number, identified the name of the cab driver and tracked the cab's route to the location where Jim had been dropped off.

Police busted Jim in his hotel room, recovering the stolen billfold, money, papers and his suitcase and umbrella.[26]

Police also discovered that Jim had cashed a forged money order while in Dallas that had been stolen in New Orleans.

Obviously, Jim's life had degenerated into stealing money to get by. Now as a young 23-year-old man, he was busted. This was one of the biggest mistakes of Jim's life.

The police slapped handcuffs on Jim and transported him to the Dallas city jail where they interrogated him. They already had sufficient proof of his crime and let him know that.

He could fight it in court, but there was little chance that he or a lawyer would be able to sway a jury. Jim would now have to face consequences.

The police fingerprinted, photographed and booked Jim. They had him change into jail garb, then gave him a mattress, blanket and bedding all rolled up together and placed him in a hot, muggy jail cell.

"I looked at it as another experience I'd have to go through. I had previous experience being locked up—I'd spent time locked away in LA when I was 15 when the courts had me testify during the trial of Bunny's boyfriend Dutch. And I survived that."

Jim waited in the cell until he went to his arraignment where he was supposed to plead. He stood in a long line of people. Finally, the clerk read the charges. The judge asked Jim to enter a plea, and Jim pleaded not guilty—in his mind it was worth a shot. The judge set his bail amount and told Jim he would be coming back to court to schedule a date for trial. A lot of the people paid bail and were released. Jim was from out of town and had no money for bail or for a lawyer, so they kept him in jail and assigned him a court-appointed public defender.

"I absolutely had no one to come to bat for me, so I resigned myself to remaining in jail for a while. After all, staying there didn't cost me money—it was all free. Besides, I couldn't accomplish much on the outside. I figured there was no use calling people. I certainly wouldn't call my mother. As usual, she wouldn't have done a thing to help me."

Jim had no cigarettes and was suffering through the cravings he had for a smoke. Although he had not eaten in a day, his stomach was too wound up to be hungry.

Jim met his court-appointed attorney during his arraignment. The two also talked another couple of times in an interview room at the jail for a few minutes each time.

During Jim's first legal consultation, the attorney explained that under Texas law his crime was considered a felony.

The court-appointed attorney recommended that Jim plead guilty to save the costs of a trial. He explained to Jim that he would try to get him probation. After all it was Jim's first major charge in Texas, and Dallas police had found no previous criminal records of Jim going as far back as Idaho. The attorney thought here was no reason why Jim should be denied probation.

"I kept getting the distinct impression what he wasn't particularly interested in my situation. Although the attorney was appointed by the court to handle my case, it was obvious he had too many more important things on his mind. This case potentially could burn up too much of his time. I told him that I was not ready to plead guilty."

"Back in the tank, the other guys didn't think I should go through with a big trial. All the men in there were straight. Two or three guys were locked up for petty crimes, but there were others locked up for armed robbery and other big-time crimes."

"At first, I was scared, but all the men there ended up being decent to me. One guy who'd been in the tank for months took an interest in me, telling me, 'Why don't you come over here and smoke this cigarette with me.' I jumped at the offer. In that jail the sex I had wasn't with no queens, I can tell you that. Even if I'd wanted to fight off those men, I wouldn't have succeeded. Nevertheless, these men didn't exactly have to force me into sex. I gladly gave them what they took."

"Most of the guys thought a trial wouldn't help, because if the authorities wanted you, it would always be your word against theirs, and few people would believe a defendant's testimony over that of the police."

During Jim's second legal consultation his court-appointed attorney explained the process of maneuvering through the court system. The attorney told Jim not to worry about the burglary charge and again suggested that Jim would be better off pleading guilty. The attorney said the State of Texas would appreciate it, and the judge would be more lenient—those deals happened all of the time. Jim was not so sure.

"My attorney said I wouldn't have to endure the hassle of a full-blown trial. 'Think of the expense the state would have to go through with an exhaustive trial.' Instead of me saying, 'What do I care about the expense,' I decided I'd better follow the professional legal advice instead of winging it on my own. What did I know? Obviously, I was guilty in their eyes. Even though I initially refused to plead guilty at our first consultation, I finally agreed to save the state its money by pleading guilty. After all, the lawyer was confident that I'd get probation. Then I could get the hell out of Texas—the sooner the better."

After agreeing with his lawyer to plead guilty, Jim was called before the judge. Now he had eliminated most of the expensive trial costs of lawyers, jurors and judge. There would be no trial. The cops who arrested Jim were there in court in case they were needed to tell their story. The court clerk read the charges, and the judge asked Jim if he pleaded guilty or not guilty. Jim pleaded guilty. The judge said fine and set a date for Jim to come back for sentencing. The proceedings were over fairly fast.

Back in Jim's cellblock the other men guessed that Jim likely would be sentenced to 60 days in jail and then would be given probation—and Jim already had served about half of that as jail time in Dallas. For the most part the men in the jail were savvy about legal matters. This was not the first time that many of them had been in jail or prison, so they understood the system.

A couple of weeks later Jim returned to court. The courtroom was crowded. Eventually court officials called Jim's case number. Jim's attorney said, "Your Honor, I suggest that my client get probation." The judge denied it. Jim sat at the defense table with his court-appointed attorney. The judge looked at Jim and had him rise.

The judge then sentenced Jim to five years of hard labor in the Texas State Penitentiary.[27] "I almost died. Five years in prison—that's not what I was led to expect. But that was the way fucking justice worked in the State of Texas, and that probably was the way it always had worked across the country."

Jim was young with no roots. He was used to going wherever he wanted. "I was 23 years old. The next five years of my life were being taken away. I was going away for what seemed like a very long time. I started crying. The judge looked at me and asked if I had anything to say. I told him, 'You've just killed me.'"

"Neither the judge nor my court-appointed attorney had anything to add. The attorney essentially had done nothing to help me. There was no caring concerned lawyer like you see in movies and on TV. The attorney really didn't want to have to talk to me after the sentencing. If I would have understood before what I then learned, I

138

would have fought every step of the way, maybe get a plea agreement or something as so many other defendants get."

All of the prisoners at the jail had been sure that Jim would get some sort of probation. They were surprised to find out that the judge had sentenced Jim to a nickel. Five years was more than they had expected.

Jailers informed Jim that he would be transported to prison within a couple of weeks.

"It was scary. After I got over the shock, I found that I could cry only so much. At that time, I was very adaptable. I might not like a situation, but I could adjust."

"I gave in to the fact that I was going to The Big House."

Jim talked to everybody in jail about what to expect. They told him about prison stabbings and shootings, how prisoners kill each other and how they intimidate each other. It sounded as though the inmates were too powerful.

The guys in jail told Jim that the one thing he should never do is rat on anyone. If a prisoner talked to officials and snitched on somebody, the other prisoners would never forgive, and they would put out a hunting license to kill the stool pigeon.

They warned Jim not to defy anyone—neither the guards nor the prisoners. He would not be able to beat the system. Once a guy was in prison, someone could arrange his death. The prison staff could lock up a disruptive prisoner in a dark solitary cell. The men in jail with Jim claimed that a prison administration could tell a family that a prisoner died of something and had to be buried or cremated before the family could get to them.

"I talked at length to one guy who'd been in prison systems before. He'd gotten to know me really well during my time there, and I trusted him. I asked him what I could expect, 'I want to hear the truth. Don't tell me stuff just to make me feel good.'"

He told Jim there were two things prisoners hate and despise above all else. The first thing is a child molester. The second thing is a straight guy who prisoners turn out. They find a young guy—and it did not have to be a young guy necessarily—and they work on him, make a deal with him, give him stuff and then end up getting their way one way or the other, and the situation might even conclude in a rape.

"I was getting more scared, 'I don't want that.' But the jail mate assured me that I wouldn't have to worry because I was a free-world queen since I was already a queen on the outside before I entered prison. He told me, 'They'll love you. If they put you out in the general population, grab hold of the biggest, strongest, meanest motherfucker there. You're young and pretty. He'll give you what you want because he'll be getting what the fuck he wants. And he'll take care of you like a rare diamond.' He told me, 'You'll be the closest thing to a lady most of those poor bastards have seen in a long time.' Another guy told me that prison worked that way because it keeps the prison population somewhat subdued."

"I was determined to survive. If I had to be a queen in prison, I'd be the best queen those guys ever saw. I decided I'd make it work for me. I would put on even more of an effeminate affectation than the way I normally acted. I'd be more like Marilyn Monroe than she herself was. That hopefully would save me. I had nothing to lose. What else could they do to me?"

"It couldn't be too bad. I told myself there'd be all these men—older horny men—who'd been locked up for years. Because I didn't find people my own age very attractive, I had this fantasy about all these older horny guys in the back of my mind. But then, I didn't realize that prisons are full of some of the ugliest people in the world who make a gay bar full of trolls look like beautiful people. That's not to say there aren't all sorts of fine-looking men in prison too. There are virile men for the most part stuck in prisons, and I figured that situation might be a real attraction."

Chapter 21

Entering the Belly of the Beast

The fateful day arrived when Texas authorities transported Jim to prison: October 9, 1962.[28]

Figure 29: James David Foshee prison mug shot. [Texas Department of Criminal Justice]

Jim was unsure what to expect, but he tried to prepare himself. That morning the guards gave him prison clothes to put on—jumpsuits that prisoners wore all chained together to keep them from escaping while being transported. The clothes had the name of the prison stenciled on the back. Officials wanted all people to know that these men were prisoners, especially in case they ran away.

"I was shown gratitude from one of the guys in jail early that morning when he gave me a pair of red nylon panties that he said had belonged to a girlfriend. How he ever got those smuggled into the jail I never asked. He told me to wear them on my way to prison, that they could make a big impression on someone. So that morning I slipped into the red nylon panties, then over those I put on the prison clothes."

Figure 30: Chain truck. [Texas Department of Criminal Justice]

Guards loaded the group of prisoners into a chain truck, connected them to long benches on each side with chains around their necks and transported them from Dallas to Huntsville where the main Texas prison was located. The trip took a half day.

Figure 31: Exterior Huntsville Unit ("The Walls") Northwest Picket.
[Texas Department of Criminal Justice]

Figure 32: Exterior Huntsville Unit ("The Walls"), Northwest Picket.
[Texas Department of Criminal Justice]

As they entered the small town of Huntsville, they approached the Texas main penitentiary, "The Huntsville Unit." It was nicknamed "The Walls Unit" or simply "The Walls."

"I looked out of the chain truck, and I saw the huge red brick walls and buildings looming in the distance. I watched the giant walls grow closer and larger. I had a real foreboding feeling in my stomach."

"The chain truck entered the prison grounds through a large gate. It pulled to a stop, and guards unchained us from our seats. We were told to get out by a guard with the bearing of a military drill instructor. It felt like some boot camp. He started shouting profanities at us the moment we arrived."

Figure 33: Inmate processing at the Huntsville Unit ("The Walls").
[Texas Department of Criminal Justice]

Guards separated the Black and Hispanic prisoners from the White prisoners who all had been transported together to the prison. Guards took the White prisoners into a room where they removed the chains that had secured the prisoners together. Then guards took them outside into a giant courtyard containing a handful of guards on duty. The afternoon sun was warm, and the surrounding buildings were beginning to cast their shadows from two and three stories high.

Figure 34: Texas State prison, Huntsville Unit ("The Walls"). [Texas Department of Criminal Justice]

Inmates inside the cellblocks looked down at the newly arrived fish. This was a common ritual every time a group of newcomers would arrive. The cons would watch all of the new prisoners to see if any of them were friends from the outside. It was an event that did not happen every day, so convicts always were curious to see who was arriving.

"First we were told to take off everything—completely undress. And this was all done out in the open. There were no women around, so I guess in their minds it was fine for us to be naked."

"The other fish started to undress, but I felt embarrassed, because I didn't like taking off my clothes in front of strangers. I was a prude in many respects. It was very uncomfortable. I was glancing around at all the men looking down from their cells. A guard began giving me this menacing stare, 'Get your goddamn ass out of them clothes!'"

"And all of a sudden it was like I was in a movie where somebody yelled, 'You're On!' So, I started slowly stripping. I didn't simply undress—I stripped like a sexy strip-tease artist. One sleeve over my shoulder here and the other sleeve daintily falling over my other shoulder there."

By the time Jim got down to his red nylon panties, convicts watching his act were hollering, "Whoo, wahoo! Baby doll!!" Their whoops and catcalls grew louder, "Whoa, hoo-ha! Baby, take it off!!" The loud pandemonium of wolf whistles and yells reverberated from all sides of the courtyard.

"I told myself, *'I will not be embarrassed. I'm a grand queen, and I'm performing for all of my appreciative fans.'* I was living out this fantasy. Here were all of these horny men, and here I was this sexy young stripper—and you could just feel the vibrations of lust sweeping over the whole place. I thought, *'Okay, they're going to keep me here a while, so Honey I'm taking advantage of it!'*"

Jim slipped out of the red panties and gingerly dropped them to the ground as his spectators cheered from the balconies.

Suddenly a guard grabbed him, and reality re-emerged. The guards wanted this mess cleaned up and Jim out of there—quick! The guard put him at the head of the line of White prisoners waiting to get their heads shaved.

As soon as Jim's head was shaved and before any of the other fish got their heads shaved, the guards moved Jim out of the courtyard. As soon as other prisoners joined him, the guards took the fish into a room and gave them a delousing, which they applied on all new prisoners. They used old-fashioned pump guns that people used to spray for bugs. They commanded the new prisoners to raise their arms and then sprayed their armpits, scalps and crotches. Then everybody had to bend over to get sprayed in the crack of their butts.

A few minutes later the prisoners took showers. The fish had a limited time to get their showers completed. "I'm showering with these guys and kept worrying that I'd get a hard-on, so I just looked at the ground and tried not to look at anybody. Plus, the whole thing was pretty traumatic."

Then prison workers issued the new inmates white prison clothes. The Texas prison system used bleached prison garb, similar to jumpsuits, which included white shirt, white britches and a white hat. Inmates made all of the prison clothes inside the prison system and grew their own cotton for the clothes.

The new clothes did not have prisoners' names on them—they would get those identifications later. At this point the clothes only had markings signifying them as property of the prison system.

The prisoners put on new black brogan shoes issued to them, and guards dispersed the group. They put Jim in a two-man cell. Jim met his cellmate who was a tall dark-haired inmate in his late twenties or early thirties.

"I already was pretty effeminate, but I laid it on even thicker becoming more lady-like than I actually was. In prison my approach always was to let these guys approach me. I was a lady. I didn't make the first move, but it was obvious to these guys that I'd be easy pickings. After all, I was a free-world queen, not some punk who they had to turn out through intimidation and violence. They wouldn't have to coerce me for favors. I liked it."

"My new cellmate and I talked. And of course, I was figuring out what would be happening between this man and me in a matter of a few hours when the lights finally dimmed for the night. What a treat he had in store for him! I didn't know how long he'd been in prison, but now I was there for his pleasure."

"I was in the cell for about an hour before the prison staff must have realized their mistake: 'Hey wait a minute, what happened to that young homo that came in here?'"

Guards arrived at Jim's cell and informed him they were moving him. They transferred him up into a cell by himself. It was over the Hispanic cells, which were on the bottom floor. "We called the Hispanic guys Mexicans. It didn't take long for them to find out there was a free-world queen upstairs. That generated lots of noise from down below. These guys were in their cells and couldn't see me, but I could hear them yelling up to me in thick Mexican accents, 'Baby! Baby!'"

Jim spent that first night alone lying on the bunk. As he wondered what would happen to him in the years ahead in prison he drifted off to sleep.

$$\nabla$$

The next morning the prisoners in the large cellblock stood outside their cells waiting to go to the chow hall for breakfast. A lot of them watched Jim locked inside his cell and began whistling. "So, I waved back and blew them kisses. They would grab their crotches and wink. Eventually this commotion was going on all the time, constantly! It was flattering, but the hoopla they made became just too much."

Jim was not allowed out of his cell to go eat with the other guys. He ate all of his meals in his cell. "In prison I decided I'd always try to look at the bright side of things. They'd bring me a food tray, so I rationalized that I was getting room service. How nice. The hoi polloi had to go to the chow hall, but I didn't. I was special. I would just dine by myself. After all, I liked my privacy. I didn't want to have 50 guys staring me up and down."

That first morning the prison staff began the process of checking him into the system, a process lasting a week or so. Jim thought it all had a very militaristic feel, almost like getting processed into boot camp. Guards took Jim to various locations—administrative offices for paperwork; tailor shop to get his name and number sewn onto his prison garb; and testing sites to check urine and blood to ensure Jim suffered no sicknesses such as tuberculosis, sexually transmitted diseases or any other communicable diseases.

"I took on the mindset of a queen, and thankfully I was a free-world queen who had some humor, because it helped me survive my years in prison. One or two guards escorted me to my tests and waited while I went through various processing procedures. They had this idea that they were keeping me separated from the bulls in prison. But we'd walk through the halls and across the courtyards, and of course the prisoners would recognize me twisting my little ass. I just viewed it as if I had two bodyguards who were protecting me from the common crowds of men. It was like I was this star stepping out to let her fans catch a glimpse of her."

The guards stoically remained silent and stone-faced while prisoners vied for Jim's attention with winks and wolf whistles. Jim returned their affections with delightful smiles and kisses he blew to them. "I wasn't the only queen they'd ever encountered in the big house, but I was the youngest and prettiest one at the time."

After tests, guards returned Jim to his cell where he stayed put. He was not allowed to attend movies or to go out on the floor to mingle with others. "I was allowed to do nothing. So, the more they acted that way, the more determined I was to revel in it."

Figure 35: Various prison cellblock wings holding incarcerated convicts inside the Huntsville Unit ("The Walls"). [Texas Department of Criminal Justice]

Prisoners were the ones who swept and mopped the tiers and delivered food trays. Runners wheeled carts to prisoners that contained commissary like soap, towels, cigarettes and newspapers. "I had one worker who would come by and always try to get me to suck him through the bars. 'Are you crazy? I don't do that.' I was too much of a lady to do such a thing. I wouldn't have minded something sensuous in a nice private setting, but certainly never through some bars of a jailhouse cell."

The main runner was a guy named Morse. Jim complimented him on his name saying he knew a guy on the outside whose last name was Morse. But no, this prisoner's name really was not Morse. That was only a handle he used. It stood for Morse code, because he passed around so many verbal and written messages between prisoners. "Lots of guys didn't use real names in prison—they didn't want anyone knowing too much about them."

Morse started passing small notes to Jim from other prisoners who would pay Morse to slip the little letters to him. "These guys all competed for my favors. They were promising me all kinds of things.

One guy sent me a pack of cigarettes with a note saying he'd give me all the cigarettes I wanted."

Morse told Jim that he was a valuable commodity and sweet-talked Jim, telling him that he had such soulful eyes, such beautiful long eyelashes. "He told me I looked just like Bambi. That was enough to sweep me off my feet. He left and turn back to look at me, 'Bye, Bambi.' Morse didn't realize at that moment that he'd just bestowed the nickname on me that stuck throughout my years in prison. In a couple of days all the sweepers and runners coming by my cell started calling me Bambi."

Jim's first few days had gone well, but he was still apprehensive. His physical tests all came back looking good. Staff workers told Jim they wanted to rehabilitate prisoners. Jim could benefit by learning things, and the prison system could benefit by filling job openings with free prisoner labor. The staff wanted to find out who had the needed prerequisite skills.

Jim continued through his testing procedures. The employment office analyzed the tests. The only abilities in demand in the prison at the time were typing and clerking skills. Jim could not type and had no office work experience.

Jim found out that the Texas prison system was divided into a lot of smaller prison units functioning as farms. All of the new prisoners in the system were processed and evaluated inside the Walls. Then most prisoners were sent to one of the prison farms.

"I realized the best place to do time was inside the Walls, not on a farm. One guy told me about working on a prison farm chopping cotton until you dropped and later picking the cotton until your hands got all cut up raw. What the prison system mainly wanted was fodder to work the fields. They believed in hard work. Thank goodness I was a queen. It was easy to figure out they wouldn't be sending a queen like me to do outside men's work."

After a couple of days, a psychiatrist talked to Jim to evaluate his mental health. He questioned Jim about how long he had been homosexual. Jim replied it was as long as he could remember. The psychiatrist wanted to know what role Jim took. Jim explained that he was passive. The psychiatrist's answer to everything Jim said was simply, "Oh, that's interesting."

"I explained that I didn't want to be involved in any trouble in prison. That I would stay out of the way and choose somebody who'd be my lover and stay with him—like a quiet married couple. In a way, up until this time I was keeping my eye out for a lover. All these guys were hollering out to me, and I was thinking, *'Hmmm, I wonder which one I should choose?'* After all, I had to make sure my choice was a good one."

The next day guards took Jim to the assistant warden who motioned for them to come into his office. He straightened up in his chair behind his desk and looked sternly at Jim. "He told me, 'So, you think you'll come to prison and have a good old time, don't you?' I was thinking, *'Yeah, you got that right!'* I cast down my eyes and answered, "No sir, not at all.'"

"The assistant warden told me, 'You think you'll find a husband and settle down while you're here, don't you?' Obviously, the psychiatrist told him what I'd said. I explained to the assistant warden that yes, that would be the right thing to do to stay away from trouble."

"He began roaring, 'No! Absolutely not! We segregate our convicts—especially your kind. We're not about to let you out in the general population. Why, you'd have these guys killing each other over you.' I hadn't realized I had that power. But I was cute and effeminate and acted like a young and well-mannered soft-spoken lady. I was both nice and naïve. Plus, I had experience in pleasing my man and loving him. That was the big difference between me and some punk."

As Jim turned to leave, the last remark from the assistant warden was, "Remember, we run this prison—not you convicts."

Chapter 22

Ramsey

One morning during Jim's second week in prison, a guard informed Jim that instead of remaining in the Walls, they were transferring him to one of the prison farms: Get Ready. So, Jim again dressed in chain clothes. Guards chained over a half dozen prisoners together inside the chain truck. Two guards locked the doors, sat in the front of the vehicle and off they drove. The prisoners in the back consisted of five or six White prisoners and a couple of Black prisoners.

After traveling over an hour the chain truck arrived at a farm. The guards unlocked the chains and removed the two Black prisoners riding in the back. The White prisoners remained chained together. Jim could see other Black prisoners there on what was called a colored farm. In the early 1960s prison system all inmates were segregated. Blacks and Whites were separated as were Hispanic prisoners.

"I was there in prison at this time when society insinuated that the melting pot theory was all wrong and that the races shouldn't mix. The thinking of the prison authorities at that time—and way back before that—was that if you put a Black man and a White man together in a cell, they hated each other so much that they'd kill each other. So, the Blacks were kept on separate prison farm units, and Hispanics also were at other farms. None of us White guys served any time on prison farms with Black prisoners."

The chain truck departed the colored farm and carried the White prisoners toward their next destination. "I was the only queen in the back, and they all had heard about me. They were horny and vying for my attention. I was the hit of the chain truck, but I was too scared and distracted worrying about my own unknown future."

Within another hour the truck arrived at another farm. Guards removed Jim and a couple of the other prisoners from the chain truck. "We received the normal cussing out by guards who informed us that we had it easy back at the Walls. The State of Texas had sent us to work our asses off, and that's what they intended for us to do."

The main guard told the newly arrived prisoners, "Welcome to Ramsey, boys. Y'all will be calling this home, and we expect you cons to treat it like one."

The exterior of the Ramsey Unit appeared as a typical farm with fences, but the interior of the farm's large building complex looked and felt just like a prison.

Figure 36: Ramsey Farm, 1960s. [Texas Department of Criminal Justice]

Inside the building was a large enclosed jail system divided into two companies, each within its own separate lockup tank.

Guards walked Jim down the big hallway, pulled a gate lever and took him into a massive room that held his company. Prisoners in the company were confined inside whenever they were not working outside or on chain gangs out in the fields. The room was encircled by two tiers of cells upstairs and downstairs arranged in a U shape. Essentially, it was a prison within a prison.

The new prisoners were assigned a cell and given white clothes to change into. Every prisoner had a roommate. "I'd learned by this time that you should treat your cell like your home. In fact, that's what I called it—my home. I refused to refer to it as my cell."

Jim fixed up his bed and wandered around. In the middle of the cells was a large common area for watching television and socializing. There was even a small barber shop area in a corner. Guards left individual cell doors open at certain times, and inmates were free to go in and out of the cells and move around the tank.

"We had about 40 or 50 people in our company. This company was notorious for containing the prison system's homosexuals. There were straight guys put in our company too. They weren't gay, but they'd been seduced or raped. Some tried fighting back but lost. Once they got fucked, their reputations were shot. We queens felt sorry for them. They were wonderful guys. In those days, when sexual assault victims complained, the authorities moved them into our tank so the prison could protect them. The administration did that for the benefit of the prison system itself, because that made it easier for the guards to maintain order."

"In the prisoners' minds they thought a real man couldn't be raped, that a real man would fight to the death. Once these guys were put in with the queens they were stamped as queer too."

"There were no Black queens in our company. I'm sure there had to be some somewhere in the prison system, but they must've been kept on one of the colored farms since everything was so segregated to keep us from intermingling."

To maintain law and order inside the buildings, the prison system utilized a prisoner-run discipline structure—each tank had a top prisoner called a building tender who prison managers selected. He would enforce order. These tenders were usually older lifers who were never likely to be paroled. Whenever prisoners were inside their individual tank, the tender had complete authority to impose discipline. "Our tender was a very kind and gentle white-haired man in his sixties who'd been in there for a very long time. We called him the Old Man. He said there were certain rules, and if I followed them, I'd get along fine. He advised me, 'Don't end up getting institutionalized here. A guy only has hisself to blame if he becomes another sorry old convict.'"

The Old Man would announce when it was time to go eat. The prisoners lined up, the picket guard pulled the lever on the tank's door, and everyone walked out into hallway and down to the chow hall.

"The system had some customs I'd never heard of, plus everybody used complete slang. They called a biscuit a 'cat head' and they called syrup 'dope.' But I refused to use those terms, because I told myself that I wasn't in there for some big crime, and I didn't intend to be in there forever. I was determined that when I got out, I was never ever coming back to prison. If I previously had any fantasy about an exciting life in prison, it certainly was gone now. This was not the life for me."

"The Old Man never mentioned to us anything about sex, but the guys in the company all realized that if they were going to have sex, they had to be discrete. The system threatened all of us in subtle unrelenting ways. For instance, we could lose good time. I found out that although I was sentenced to five years, I could get out in three years—two years early. But if I did anything wrong, I could lose not only my privileges but also a portion of my two years of good time. The guards threatened all prisoners with that, except for the convicts who never had any chances of ever getting out of prison. And I didn't want to lose any of my good time."

Jim witnessed one case of a couple of guys who lost some of their good time for stealing bread. Another guy ended up locked up for 30 years because he tried to escape and committed other peculiar hijinks that caused his sentence to keep increasing by years.

"There was this one guy younger than me, about 20. He had a boyish and charismatic quality. He was a sweet butch boy who'd been gang raped at another place in the prison system. This guy was very straight in appearance and attitude, but he was very aggressive with me. He kept pursuing me like crazy, coming over to me and grabbing me and hugging me and kissing on me, trying to get me. As the months went by, I'd be sitting there watching television, and he'd come over and do that, and it scared me to death—you can't do that out in the open without getting into trouble. One prison guard witnessed this, but all he did was chuckle to himself while he watched me getting flustered with this guy."

"In general, it was a miserable existence on the farm. We'd get up with the sun and would return to the tank when the sun went down. If you didn't do your job correctly out there, you'd be put on report. It was an effective way of creating dread among the masses of prisoners to keep them in line."

Jim's work crew set up watering systems, tended gardens, pruned bushes and took care of cleaning the prison farm grounds. It felt good for Jim to get outside in the autumn and mild winter weather. Some of the prisoners in the company worked at other full-time and part-time prison jobs. Guys who knew how to write, type and file worked in an office doing paperwork not only for Ramsey but also for other prison farms in the area. A former hair stylist served as the barber for both companies. One prisoner had worked in agriculture before being incarcerated, so the farm used him full-time to work with seeds, plan crop-planting schedules and manage technical controls.

Jim and other prisoners got a reprieve from the hard work on Sundays when everybody stayed inside the tank. They could watch TV and receive other special privileges like going to movies.

"I was careful to do everything the way I was told so I wouldn't lose any of my privileges. My bunk partner was a nice guy. I think he was in there for thievery or something, I can't remember."

"Many of the queens in there were nasty killer queens. There were a couple of pretty queens, but most were older ugly ones who resented me because I happened to be young and pretty and desirable to a lot of the bulls. They had insufferable personalities. Their attitude about themselves was, 'I ain't very pretty, but by God this is my area, and I'm the Queen Bee around here.' The majority of them wrangled among themselves for recognition as the number one queen."

Since Jim was new, he had not yet learned all of the unwritten rules. The queens told Jim to stop being polite to the guards. One of the guards was friendly and nice, so Jim in turn was nice to him. The two talked together for several days. "It was all harmless talk. One prisoner in the tank was depressed and wasn't doing very well. The guard told me he was worried about the prisoner. I was worried too. The guard wondered what was wrong with him. I explained that the guy was having love trouble. The guard was truly concerned and so was I, so we discussed the situation. This prisoner had some straight lover in another company that he couldn't get to, so they ended up only being able to write a couple of letters back and forth. They eventually were unable to keep in touch with each other, so apparently they ended up essentially having to break up."

The guard ended up passing my information up the Ramsey command structure. Then guards gave the love-sick prisoner the third degree: Who was he seeing, and how did he and his lover accomplish what they had done? The queens viewed Jim as transgressing the unbreakable law of ratting on someone. "I couldn't understand why they were so upset. I was only trying in my own way to help make things better, but I guess I screwed it up. I told the guy, I'm sorry, I was just trying to make it easier. That didn't matter to these queens. They began giving me the silent treatment."

"I'd never had to put up with such a group of devious queens before. They seemed to reinforce each other's ugly mindsets. I hated those bitchy queens, yet I couldn't escape them. I couldn't stand the downright long hard-working hours outside, yet I couldn't escape that either. It was all terrible. I'd never been so miserable."

$$\nabla$$

"Within three or four months, I realized I wanted the hell out of there. I couldn't remain there. I had to do something. The other prisoners would talk about the mental facility inside the Walls for people who couldn't make it anywhere else. This prison hospital had air conditioning, and nobody worked. That sounded great to me."

Ramsey's medical staff held sick call on the farm every day for prisoners with the usual physical problems. "The convicts constantly attempted to get out of work. But no matter what a guy at sick call complained about, he usually got two aspirins. That was their cure."

Jim had to figure out how to get himself sent back inside the Walls—not for some physical problem—but for a mental problem. He figured if he just could get sent to the Walls, he could play it one day at a time. A prisoner had to be very clever. Jim saw another inmate fake a mental problem, and it did not turn out well for him. It was easy for the medical staff to catch people who were pretending since they had identified fakers countless times before. "But I had a big advantage. I had experience. After all, I'd spent my teenage years in a mental hospital. I'd seen it all."

Jim realized there was no way he could confide in anyone that he was faking it. He began it all by talking to himself for a full day, but this itself would not accomplish anything other than laying the foundation of his plan. The next morning Jim added more mentally-ill behavior. As the company was going out the gate for work Jim stayed back in his cell, grabbed his pillow and hid under his bunk. He took off his clothes except for his underwear, and he refused to come out. Several guards and staff members tried to coax him out and then tried to nudge him.

Jim was staying put. "Come on, Bambi." They got a good hold on Jim and pulled him out. He jumped on top of his bunk with his pillow. They tried to take away the pillow as Jim clung to it, "My baby! No! Don't take my baby!" They were baffled and exchanged puzzled looks toward each other. Jim began talking to the pillow as though it was his baby. He rocked the pillow back and forth and attempted to breastfeed it.

"It was obvious to the staff that something was wrong with me, that I needed to see the doctors. At this point I'd gone beyond being embarrassed in front of my peers in the company, so there was no turning back. They paraded me out the gate and down the hallway in just my shorts with no shirt. Everybody was standing around making comments. By this time, I had built up some hysterics. It was ludicrous. I couldn't keep from laughing at the funny situation. Oddly enough, they viewed my laughter as more proof that I'd flipped out."

They took Jim to the sick ward on the farm. It was nice with beds and real sheets. Medical assistants gave Jim a shot to calm him down. He strategized what to do next and fell asleep.

If a prisoner had a serious condition, they might end up in the Walls infirmary for observation. However, it was hard to get admitted. Many prisoners wanted to get into there.

The following day Jim was transported in the chain truck to the Walls. It stopped at a couple of farms where guards unloaded and picked up prisoners. After arriving inside the Walls, guards took Jim and another prisoner to the infirmary. There were about a half dozen prisoners from throughout the prison system who were being treated and evaluated.

A psychiatrist called up prisoners to his table one by one. He would read through the prisoner's jacket, or personnel folder, and ask each guy why he was there. One guy had cut off a finger to keep from working. Once in a while, prisoners would hear the scuttlebutt about some desperate guy who had cut off some part of his body. The psychiatrist saw another prisoner at his table who had attempted to kill himself months earlier and was back for a checkup.

"The psychiatrist gave the same small lecture to each prisoner who came forward for evaluation. 'There's nothing wrong with you. You're here because you think you're going to get out of work. You think you're going to have it cushy and sit up here and just relax.' It was bullshit with a Texas Accent. 'You cons need to learn to stop making trouble—you can do this either the easy way or the hard way.' In other states some mental disorders might send a prisoner to a state hospital for the criminally insane. But in Texas, prisoners always did their time whether insane or not."

"I sat there waiting and talking to myself. I didn't speak with any of the other prisoners about my condition, because I figured they could've been planted there. You never knew if a prisoner would rat for a little extra point or whatever. I had no intention of ever seeing these guys again. I acted my craziness in front of the prisoners as much as I acted my part to the staff."

"Finally, it came my turn to be examined. The doc was reading my jacket and asked, 'Why are you here?' I told him, 'I don't know why. I like it back there. I never got in any trouble, and I've got friends back there. You're letting these other guys go back, and you should let me go back too. Why do I want to be in this stupid place?'"

"The psychiatrist asked me, 'What about this baby of yours?' The prison doctor hadn't heard of that problem with any prisoners before—but I had. I replied, 'They took my baby.' I played it sad and agitated but didn't say much. I figured everything the psychiatrist needed to know was already in my records jacket. So, he said, 'Fine.' And he called up the next person. That was easy."

After Jim's examination, a medical assistant told the prisoners they were going to various locations in the Walls for observation. A guard led Jim to a second-floor tier containing a whole row of individual cells. It was the queens' tank, where the prison system housed sexually nonconforming inmates when the system didn't quite know what else to do with them.

"Most of the prisoners in queens' row were normal guys, but others were strange. One guy had attempted to put light bulbs up his rectum and break them. Another guy was always on the make for sex from everybody around him. They beat him up and confined him, but as soon as they turned him loose again, he'd start chasing everyone all over again. The administration finally resorted to keeping the guy locked up inside a cell in the Walls all the time to prevent him from causing any more chaos."

Most of the guys under observation of the infirmary were kept inside the Walls because of serious physical ailments, but Jim was there under mental observation. There were few limited cells inside the Walls located far from the farms where thousands of prisoners were forced to toil away on the oppressive chain gangs. After a week in the Walls, medical assistants informed Jim they were sending him back to Ramsey since he had experienced no more hallucinations about his baby. "Before this I thought it all had been settled. One guy on the tier had advised me not to worry, that they always forgot about us once we were there, so I didn't maintain my act. What a mistake."

$$\nabla$$

Jim dreaded returning to Ramsey. This time instead of putting him back in his old company, the prison staff put him in the other company in the building, a place where he'd never been before.

Some men in Jim's new company may have been willing to engage in homosexual acts in prison at one time or another, but most of them only wanted women before and after their incarceration. The men in Jim's new company were individuals who either botched their incarceration or had fought back—the known troublemakers. They were butch and masculine. They prided themselves on being tough and looked down on the queens in the adjacent company. "I had to make all new friends, but I was glad. I didn't miss those killer queens in my old company."

"In my first company the Old Man was a kind and gentle building tender. The tender in my new company was notoriously dominating and evil—that's why everybody called him Evil. His age was late forties. When I was with my first company, I'd seen Evil in the chow hall. He was supposed to be a lifer, but his new legal case looked like it was turning in his favor, so there was a small chance he'd get released after all. This sadistic bastard always was beating up on some poor prisoner while the guards stood outside and watched in silence. If anything went wrong, the guards' hands remained clean. Discipline was his job. My guess would be that Evil would've made a good sadist."

"Evil had his own private boyfriend. After all, why should he do without. He might not let the other guys have any sex among themselves, but he sure as hell had his little blonde kid who was his old lady and had to service him."

Helping Evil was an assistant building tender. "He looked like a big wrestler. He decided he wanted me. So, Evil moved me into the cell where he held his private blonde concubine. It was located next to the tenders' cell so Evil and his assistant had easy access to us."

"I figured okay; I'd be protected. I'd heard that if you go to prison and there's somebody there who was really mean, become his friend and let him protect you. So, I was the property of the assistant tender. Sex with him was okay most of the time, although a lot of the time it was very rough. But it was my job."

One night Jim and his blonde cellmate got it on. It was nice for the two young guys not having to put up with the two old thugs and their crap. But the two young guys got caught. In attempt to spare the kid, Jim told Evil that he had been the instigator. The two waited for the beating they knew was coming, which Evil always inflicted on guys who screwed up. But Evil did nothing to Jim and his cellmate. After that Jim was no longer welcomed as the assistant building tender's girlfriend because Jim was guilty of infidelity.

For Jim the worst parts of life at Ramsey were the long hours of hard work the prisoners were forced to endure on the chain gangs. As spring passed into summer the real horror of the farm became apparent. "They made us work our asses off, just like all the other

Texas chain gangs that were made up of masculine men. Nobody ever physically abused me with fists or straps, but the work itself was physical abuse. Nobody wanted to work their asses off for the state under that hot stifling sun. That was backbreaking work we were forced to endure, and the human body at a point drenches itself in constant sweat to keep alive. The climates of the Idaho summers and the California beaches hardly ever caused any perspiration, but never in my life had I sweated as profusely as I did on that fucking Texas chain gang."

Figure 37: Hauling chain gang convicts to cotton fields. [Texas Department of Criminal Justice]

After breakfast, the sun came up and the prisoners loaded themselves onto a flatbed wagon. A tractor truck would pull the wagon to the day's work site. Jim and the other prisoners never knew where they would be going. It was not yet harvest time, so instead of picking crops, the men on the chain gangs were kept busy removing tree stumps, digging ditches, repairing dirt roads and installing culverts.

The prisoners wore unbleached cotton outfits with their names and numbers sewn on both the fronts and the backs. To keep the sun out of their faces, prisoners wore wide-brimmed hats made from the same material as their clothes. The prison system also issued bandanas to chain gang convicts to help sop up the sweat from their foreheads.

"My aching feet got blisters from those awful brogan shoes that never fit right. You could wear gloves if you could afford to buy them, but they didn't help much. I was ruining my hands. They were marked with blisters and callouses. My back hurt. You couldn't wear shorts, and the long pants caused you to sweat even more."

Jim complained to the other convicts, but they told him that he just had to put up with it. It was neither fun nor adventurous. The distress was more genuine than any movie Jim ever had seen. While the crops were growing, the chain gang would till the crop rows with hoes that everyone in the prison system called aggies. Prisoners worked in a line. The fastest worker was called the lead, and he would act as the pacesetter.

Figure 38: Texas chain gang. Convicts and dragline building a dam & flat bedding sides of gullies.
[Texas Department of Criminal Justice]

"We constantly worked. We couldn't stop. We couldn't say we were tired. It wasn't like the free world when you just stopped if you got too tired. We were forced to keep going. If you started to fall down you simply got back up."

Always watching over the prisoners was a uniformed field guard in khakis sitting on a horse in the hot sun, bored out of his mind—an overweight frustrated John Wayne type cowboy. All prisoners called him Boss. The chain gang was based on a military system. On his hip, Boss always kept a big riding crop and short whip used to stir horses (and men). Boss could be very formidable.

Whenever a prisoner needed a drink of water or had to go take a leak or whatever, he was required to turn around, stand at attention, take off his hat and ask for permission, "Getting a drink, Boss." Boss would tell the prisoner either okay or get back to work.

Always in the background behind every field boss was a uniformed high rider on a horse. He always carried a rifle and backed up boss. The high rider was a solid convict who had attained the level of trustee, because he had been in the prison system for a long time and had earned the trust of the powers that be. If a prisoner attacked a field boss or pulled him off of his horse, the high rider would shoot to kill. He also would shoot any inmate who attempted to run away. If a prisoner got within 10 feet of the high rider—the dead line—the high rider would kill him. Every once in a while, some prisoner had put up with as much as he could take, was tired of living his life and walked over the dead line toward the high rider to end it all. The high rider didn't say, "Stop! Put up your hands." It was simply known that prisoners did not cross the line.

"If a high rider shot a prisoner, it wasn't a field boss who killed the prisoner but rather another inmate, so the prison staff remained clean and uninvolved."

The high rider had a fairly decent job sitting on his horse all day. He didn't have to toil like the rest of the chain gang. He also got perks and special foods. The only individuality among inmates were the trustees, whose white pants were pressed as a symbol of their status.

"I witnessed firsthand just how the Texas Department of Corrections was notorious for being rough. The field bosses out there could be real bastards. They were always yelling. If field bosses thought convicts weren't working hard enough, they'd cuss at them. If field bosses wanted to, they could kill you; and stories circulated about some bosses in the past who had done just that. All they had to say was that the prisoner tried to run. Your life was in their hands. Prisoners back in those years had no rights. In contrast, the prisoners today can be spoiled. Back then nobody wore long hair. Nobody wore a different hairdo because it had some religious significance. Everybody wore short hair, and they all looked the same."

Around noon Boss would announce it was chow time. Prisoners had 15 minutes to eat. Field bosses also allowed prisoners a five-minute break every two or three hours. It was a chance for prisoners to drink water, and they got a chance to smoke a cigarette, unless the whole crew was being punished for some infraction.

During the first few days that Jim was out on the chain gang, Boss studied him. Jim was stooping down like a lady, holding his hat with one hand and effeminately working the ground. Boss would call over other field bosses who all thought Jim's work postures were comical.

Within Jim's first couple of days on the line, Boss decided it was time to call him forward. He called out Jim's name, "Foshee"—but Boss mispronounced Jim's last name as "FAW shee" instead of "Foe SHAY." Boss critiqued Jim's work methods, "You ain't doing any damn good with that shovel there. Strike the ground fast, then push hard with your foot."

Jim answered, "Yes, Boss." "Permission to speak, Boss." Boss said, 'Okay.' Jim explained to Boss, "My name is not pronounced 'FAW shee,' it's pronounced 'Foe SHAY.'" Behind Jim, a couple of the guys on the line chuckled. Boss peered down at Jim, "Well, excuse me, Miss 'Foe SHAY.' I shall remember that. Now, get back to work.'"

"For Boss and me, it became a regular routine. Boss would sit on his horse bored out of his mind. He'd call me forward and gripe about my work methods: Keep my aggie near the ground when I hoed, don't bend my legs when I scraped the irrigation ditch, keep my feet apart when I shoveled, and on and on. Boss concluded pretty quickly that he wasn't going to be successful making me into a masculine laborer."

After a few weeks on the chain gang, Jim was feeling relieved about Boss. Jim had convinced Boss that his effeminate nature was just how he naturally was. "He'd question me about why I was so effeminate. I'd put on my feminine charms and tell him that's how my mother raised me, 'I've never done a stitch of outside work before.' And in truth, I wasn't a natural at doing that hard manual labor."

A few days later, Jim was in the line building irrigation structures and berms. Jim was barely keeping up with the other guys when Boss again called out, "Miss Foshee." Jim turned around and removed his hat. Boss ordered him front and center. Jim trotted up to him and stood at attention, "Yes, Boss." Boss leaned forward in his saddle, "You're getting in their way again, Miss Foshee."

"When Boss would pull me out of the work line, I'd start telling him stories about my adventures being young in the free world—how I first showed up in California when I was 15, how I was banned from California, how I ended up living in Grand Central Station in New York. I'd describe the ironies of my peculiar stories, and Boss would be fascinated. He actually would laugh. It didn't take me any time at all to figure out that as long as I was entertaining Boss, I wasn't having to work at the hard labor taking place under that searing sun. I did my best to survive by my wits."

Jim got away with it. It was his way of fighting the system. Prison had to be played as a game for someone weak like Jim in order to survive. "I played my cards as a sweet young lady, and the guards were kinder to me than to the other men—they expected more out of them. I was naïve and thin and helpless. I was very polite and charming to the officers. I called them all Sir and held my tongue and never talked back no matter what they said."

"Some prisoners tried to strike back at the guards or spit on them, and they'd end up getting beaten and then thrown into solitary confinement."

"To be fair to the guards, I left prison never hating any of the guards, because they were caught in the system as much as any other soul who steps inside a prison."

The men working on the chain gang longed for Boss to declare the day was over. Boss would whistle and announce, "Time to go." The prisoners then put their implements in a row and counted them.

At sunset they returned to the compound. As they waited outside to go in and take showers, they would be dreading the guard calling out names and numbers of chain gang workers who had not toiled hard enough or broke some rule during the day. The guard would tell them to "catch the hall."

The prisoners had to stand in line before entering the crowded open shower room as the various chain gang squads usually showed up at the Ramsey compound around the same time. The first ones to shower were the bulls, the real men. Queens and turnouts waited their turns.

After showering, the prisoners put on clean clothes. Most walked down the long hallway to their tank. The ones who had to catch the hall were required to remain standing in place. Then a guard took the detainees to the Lieutenant's desk and told him what the prisoners had done wrong and which prisoners had been drag-assin'. The Lieutenant in charge would start lecturing, "We ain't gonna tolerate this kind of performance. After all, we didn't invite y'all here. You cons work for the state now, and the taxpayers expect to get their money's worth."

Depending on the severity of the infraction the Lieutenant would assign each prisoner either a five-gallon, twenty-gallon or fifty-gallon bucket of peanuts to shell. The hours of shelling caused cuts and sore fingers. The prisoner sat in the hall and watched others eat supper while he went without food and continued shelling peanuts until time for the switch to be thrown to dim the lights for the night. Whether it took an inmate one night or a whole week to finish shelling, he was deprived of food every night until he finished shelling.

"If any of us committed a serious offense we could be put in the hole. It was a dark solitary confinement cell with no mattress—with only a hole in the center that served as a toilet. This was another way to control us. Even if you worked your ass off, you might still have to catch the hall depending on the mood of the guard. Prisoners lucked out on some nights when a guard would decline to make anyone catch the hall because he was tired and didn't want the hassle of standing around and then hauling convicts to the Lieutenant."

Prisoners worked hard, yet everyone occasionally had to catch the hall, except for the line leads who were the pacesetters. "We never knew when it would happen. I got it two or three times for minor offenses, but when you've worked hard all day, it seemed cruel to go without food at night."

During the first couple of months in his new company at Ramsey, Jim got to know the guys, and they all treated him kindly. "They weren't so bad at all—they were nothing like the bitchy queens I'd gotten away from in the last company. The guys in the new company would flirt with me and tease me. Of course, I couldn't wear drag, but I dedicated myself to be a sweet respectful young lady who made these men feel good."

The guards and tenders closely watched the prisoners to prevent them from getting involved in anything sexual. This company was very regimented, not at all relaxed and easy as the company of sexual deviants had been.

"In my new company, one absolutely gorgeous dark-haired convict was Hawk. He was a short-timer who was supposed to be released within a year. He was really assertive, 'Bambi, how you doing?' He'd wink at me, 'You're a cute thing, Babe.'"

Hawk and three or four of his buddies would make good-natured compliments to Jim. They teased him, and he flirted back.

166

Testosterone was raging through their bloodstreams. They reminded Jim of guys in straight bars in heated pursuit of women.

"Hawk was very masculine. I don't know if he was bisexual, straight, homosexual—who knows—in prison it didn't matter. A lot of the guys were hot to trot, but of course there were no women around. There were no such things as conjugal visits—no contact with women until the guys were released and returned to the free world where almost all of the ex-cons went back to women exclusively."

Hawk and his friends would tell Jim they were waiting for the corn to grow high so they could hide in the cloak of the tall corn crop and get it on with Jim. "I told them, 'Cornfields give me the creeps.' But I played along with their fun-loving kidding."

As the corn grew the prisoners on the chain gang would weed the fields. Eventually the corn reached seven feet high, tall enough that field bosses no longer were able to see convicts weeding inside the cornfields.

Figure 39: In the fields of Texas prison farm. Photo at left: Inspecting corn. Photo at right: Chain gang harvesting crop. [Texas Department of Criminal Justice]

Field bosses always remained on their horses outside the cornfields, creating the utmost secure situation for them. Boss never entered the cornfield where some prisoner could kill him with an aggie blade. The convicts had ten minutes to hoe all the way up one row, turn around and hoe back down the next row. Anything could happen in that cornfield—and it did.

"Each time we went back into the corn, Hawk and his buddies took a turn using me. After flirting with them for months, I couldn't deprive them now. So, they all made up for lost time. These guys were the cream of the crop, nice guys, I liked them."

As the men exited the cornfield repeatedly, Boss remained clueless to what had happened inside. By the time the prisoners got the whole field hoed, Hawk and his buddies were all spent and happy.

"There was this one little prick no one liked. He was trying to have sex too, but no one liked him because he was a negative odious character. He came to me inside the field, Hawk and his buddies told him to get lost and I turned him down. Back at the compound that little punk told the guards that we all had sex in the cornfield. Of course, he didn't mention that he tried to have sex too."

After dinner the cell doors were open, and the men were playing cards, watching television and shooting the bull. All of a sudden, the burly assistant building tender told Jim to get inside his cell. That was unusual, because the convicts still had a couple of hours before being locked in the cells for the night. The assistant tender made a couple of other guys move a large table in front of Jim's cell.

Then Evil came in. He turned off the TV and called out the names of Hawk and his four buddies—all five guys who got it on with Jim that day. He made them remove their clothes and stand at the big table while he degraded them and cursed names at them. He proceeded to beat then with a club, whip them with a large leather strap and pummel them with his fists. He went down the row repeatedly, whacking on them one after another.

"I'm sure that Evil was put up to it by the guards and administrators at Ramsey. The guards remained outside the tank's gate and ignored the violence inside."

"I was convinced that Evil was going to kill these guys. Most of them broke down during their beatings except Hawk and another guy who just took it. These guys were set up to be examples. They couldn't do anything to fight back at Evil and the system."

Jim was locked behind his cell door, unable to run out. He was pleading and crying. "Funny thing about crying—the last time I cried was back in the Dallas jail after I was sentenced to prison. I never had cried inside prison—until now as Evil was beating these guys. I felt responsible for their fate and tried to protect them by taking the blame. I told Evil, 'No, stop! I'm the one who did it! It's my fault!' But Evil cut me off, 'It's natural for a homo like you. But these fuckers know better.'"

"It was too much suffering to witness, especially when this evil hypocrite had his own boy he was fucking. It was like some silent nightmare where you couldn't scream. The guys eventually stopped responding—even with bloody noses and welts under their eyes and large marks on their arms and legs and torsos. It seemed like some horrible scene of the Gestapo in a concentration camp. It was the most brutal thing I'd ever witnessed close up. I turned away and closed my eyes, but Evil told me, 'Open your goddam eyes. You're gonna watch what the hell you caused.'"

Although the beating lasted well less than a half hour, it seemed to take forever. That night Jim fell asleep quietly sobbing.

The next morning Jim was distraught and broken. They had taken Hawk away to an infirmary early that morning suffering body damage. They also had whisked off Evil to someplace else in the prison system, and he was not supposed to return to Ramsey for at least a few days.

Instead of Jim heading out on the chain gang, the assistant tender told him to gather his stuff together.

"The powers that be had decided I was going to leave Ramsey by mid-morning. I wasn't even faking a mental problem this time. I was loaded into the chain truck. I wondered to myself what in the world they intended to do with me this time."

Chapter 23

The Walls

After the chain truck departed Ramsey, it stopped at a couple of farms to unload and pick up prisoners. Jim remained silent during the entire trip. In the afternoon the vehicle entered the Walls.

Guards took Jim to the infirmary. The psychiatrist informed Jim that the medical staff was holding him in the Walls for medical observation. Jim said nothing. After the previous night's beatings, he didn't care. Prisoners previously had advised Jim not to trust psychiatrists or social workers since they worked for the prison authorities and not for convicts. Prisoners told Jim furthermore to never trust any chaplain either. Prisoners should not tell any staff member anything they didn't want shared with administrators, because staff members were required to pass any information up the chain of command. In prison nothing was confidential, and savvy prisoners trusted no one.

Inside the Walls the administration placed Jim in the same location where he was placed a few months previously during his fake delusions. The guys were glad to see him, "Hey, Bambi! Welcome back to queens' row!" Jim was emotionally drained and stayed mum about the incidents at Ramsey.

After Jim was back in the Walls for a couple of weeks, a prisoner working in an admin office tipped him off that the prison system had decided to hold Jim in the Walls for the rest of his time in prison. "They thought it was better for everyone. The prison staff never told me that, but I did indeed end up serving the rest of my time inside the Walls. I just tried to keep my wits and get myself out of prison with as little hassle as possible."

"We queens were on the second floor. The place was just like you see in old movies." In front of Jim's cell was the walkway. It extended in front of the long line of cells located on one side of the massive lockup space. On the other side was a huge bank of windows. On the first floor below Jim were the straight guys. The Walls was a notoriously noisy place—clanging doors, footsteps on metal, people coughing.

Queens' row held sexual deviants—the more problematic cases. The prison administration seemed unable to manage these prisoners in any other way. "We saw each other every day and once in a while there'd be a bitch fight, and a couple of queens would ignore each other for a few days, but of course the queens never physically assaulted one another like other prisoners did to each other."

Every inmate in the tank was kept in a small separate single cell most of the time. Each cell had its own toilet and a sink. The cell contained a bed, mattress, blanket and pillow. All of the bedding was white with the prison's name on it.

The queens did no work and went nowhere unescorted. "We were absolutely segregated from the general population at all times."

Inside Jim's cell he read books and magazines, listened to radio and looked through any newspaper he could get his hands on. To break the boredom the queens kidded and camped around with each other.

Figure 40: Cellblock at the Huntsville Unit ("The Walls"). [Texas Department of Criminal Justice]

Once a week the queens were allowed to go outside into an emptied fenced-off section of the yard. They were able to walk around the grounds and catch some sun, but the few rays they caught were insufficient enough to give their pasty skin a healthy color. They could watch the straight prisoners from afar, but the overseers kept the prisoners separated far enough that the queens and bulls could never talk with one another outside.

Most of the time the queens ate meals in their cells. During some special nights the queens were escorted to the dining room for supper and were sequestered in the chow hall's corner away from other prisoners. "We'd announce, 'My dear, I just had this sent in from the Stork Club in New York. We'll all dine in high class tonight.'"

At night, guards would often release the inmates on queens' row from the confinement inside their separate cells and escort them down to a tiny locked TV area for the evening. "I'd get ready by splashing water on my face and putting perfume on a handkerchief to cover up the awful smells. Even though my hair was short I'd curl the strand ends. I pushed up my sleeves and pinched my cheeks like Scarlett O'Hara to give me red dimples. I'd grab my homemade hand fan, and off we'd all go prancing down the stairs like it was our big night going to a fancy nightclub."

∇

The Walls was a scary place. "I realized really quick that the Walls was restrictive territory for the worst of the worse hardened mean criminals. The inmates frightened me more than the system. The guards might have important decisions over you, but the inmates could kill you. The majority of them belonged there. You never realize it until you see it firsthand inside a prison. Some gay guy who has never experienced lockup might have a fantasy about how sexy some prisoners are—and there were some interesting ones—but in general they were the biggest bunch of do-nothing 'sloppy joes' who never achieved anything. Some would kill for a pack of cigarettes. They had this chip on their shoulder that you could clearly sense, and their attitude was a reason that business owners didn't want to hire ex-cons."

Prisoners felt a lot of hostility toward the guards, the system, the police, the district attorney, the jury and whomever else sent them there. "They had very little introspection about them being the ones who caused their predicaments. I never heard any of those guys worry about their victims when they boasted about their crimes."

Jim ignored a lot of the prisoners. Inmates taught each other the tricks of the trade for pulling off crimes—how to hot wire cars, make copies of keys using wax, pick locks with a hairpin and rob businesses. "I didn't mess around with them and refused to listen to those guys. I did my own time and paid them no attention and pretended they didn't exist. I wasn't interested. I didn't want to know them. I knew I wasn't going to be in prison forever. I'd learned my lesson. I determined early on that I'd never see any of those convicts again on the outside."

"One of the guys I'd met in the Dallas jail before prison had bragged how he robbed banks and stores. He and his accomplices stole money by taking out shotguns and scaring victims, 'Line up motherfuckers, or we'll blow your head off.' I questioned him, 'But you're facing 20 years now.' He told me, 'Yeah, but I lived high on the hog for damn near five or six years. I figured sooner or later the law would catch up with my ass.' And that was the typical mindset of a lot of the convicts."

By the 1960s the Walls had devised a system to keep sex to an absolute minimum. That included sequestering homosexual inmates to queens' row in attempt to keep them separated from other prisoners. "In effect the prison ended up depriving bulls of effeminate queens for passionate sex. So, the bulls terrorized young butch straight guys they coerced to get sex."

Getting to know Jim was difficult for most guys in prison, since the guards maintained a close watch over him. "Whenever guards escorted me throughout the Walls to some appointment, I would flirt around and try to make prisoners feel good. I would see guys whenever I went to the barber shop or the doctor or somewhere. Not just anybody could get to me. They were guarding me, because I was young and effeminate and one of the hottest properties inside the Walls. When I waited in an office or room there usually were no guards with me since the other staff members and working prisoners were supposed to watch over us. This allowed us queens a chance to talk with the straight prisoners—only talk."

Before Jim would say a word, the prisoners already were aware of who Bambi was. "I was not a loudmouth or a braggart. I was real. Some insufferable queens would treat other convicts like shit, but I could never understand that. I never told anybody that they were bothering me or raised my voice to them. I figured none of those convicts were going to be able to get at me, so why not treat them all nice?"

Jim acquired many boyfriends throughout the Walls who communicated with him through love notes that runners secretly passed back and forth between prisoners. Notes were considered contraband. Although Jim's boyfriends sent him gifts, he always needed additional items he thought were necessary for enduring prison life.

A few hours or days after Jim would return to his cell, one of the runners often would pass him a note from a straight convict he had met. "They wrote me the horniest letters telling me what they were going to do to me. They didn't sign their real names, but the names they used clued me into who wrote each letter. I made the most of my young good looks. I kept reminding myself how lucky I was that I didn't have to go to prison in my thirties or forties or fifties. It was true—I was the closest thing to a nice young lady many of these guys had seen in a long time. If I'd seen these guys outside of prison instead of inside, they would've paid no attention to me since most of them would have been in search of women only."

Reading and writing was one of the ways Jim filled up his time in the Walls. He wrote love letters back to his admirers, and the runners delivered them. Jim never had to pay the runners anything because his boyfriends covered the costs of all correspondence. "I would tell an admirer how hot he was, that he was a gorgeous hunk, a wonderful man. I would write like I was a woman and say sexual things. And I'm sure these guys would use my letters as hot jack-off material."

"My so-called boyfriends were locked up in various wings of the prison, so I didn't get to see them often. I never admitted it to anyone, but sometimes I lost track of who some of my letter writers were. Nonetheless, I wrote all of my letters with love and respect."

Possessing these letters were against prison rules. Jim always tore up his letters into tiny pieces and flushed them down the toilet. On occasion prison authorities held shakedowns throughout the Walls searching for contraband. Authorities never announced beforehand when they were planning to shake down the prisoners. They simply would open all of the doors at one time, "Everybody out!"

"We'd have to stand outside our cells on the tier's walkway while they tore up the beds looking for anything like silverware or sharp objects. They also searched for that awful tasting booze concocted by prisoners; and they searched for drugs, which I didn't know anything about at that time."

One time the shakedown crew caught Jim with tweezers he used to pluck his eyebrows. He played innocent, claiming he didn't know how they got there. "If I'd been in the general population I would've been busted; but on queens' row the guards just shook their heads and rolled their eyes and overlooked it. They figured it was typical for a bunch of crazy queens to possess tweezers in order to properly preen themselves."

When runners brought carts around with commissary, Jim never could afford to buy anything. "Nobody in the free world sent me money in prison. Nobody in the free world even knew I was in prison. I was forced to either rely on the corrections system to provide free prison issue or on boyfriends to give me commissary gifts."

"Often in my love letters I'd hint in a sweet way, 'Oh, by the way, I don't have such and such. I don't have anybody on the outside to help me.' So boyfriends sent me gifts—some I solicited and some not. I got handkerchiefs, glitter, tiny bottles of perfume and bottles of skin lotion for those terrible hand callouses I still had from working on the chain gang." Boyfriends bought some gifts for Jim from prison commissary, and they also got other items from people outside the prison that they in turn gave to Jim.

"I graciously thanked my boyfriends and always wrote them how wonderful they were. I told them that if only we could be together in the general population, I'd be able to show my appreciation in intimate ways."

The prison provided cheap tooth powder and unscented lye soap, but Jim's boyfriends would send him tubes of real toothpaste and popular scented soaps. They sent him nice plush colored towels to use instead of thin white prison-issued towels he had used. While Jim was incarcerated, the prison system stopped allowing people outside the prison to send towels into prison because the staff began finding drugs in them. Likewise, the prison required that all subscriptions to magazines and newspapers had to be mailed directly by publishers, although convicts could purchase individual limited copies from commissary.

Prisoners sent Jim a variety of small things like chewing gum, candy and even fruit, which the prison kitchens hardly ever included in meals. Boyfriends sent Jim needles and thread and even sequins they got from outside the prison.

"Boyfriends sent me white t-shirts that I would cut and hem to show off my figure. In wintertime they sent me white and gray sweatshirts. I would sew on decorations like peacocks and flowers using colored thread and sequins. On the front of a couple of my shirts I displayed my name 'Bambi' in glitter."

The prison system allowed each prisoner to draw and spend a maximum seven dollars for commissary each week, a lot of money at that time. The only prisoners who could afford to spend the maximum seven dollars a week were those who had somebody on the outside sending them money. Sometimes prisoners such as big-time robbers and financial thieves brought money with them when they entered prison.

All money belonging to prisoners was deposited into the prisoner accounting system. The prison forbade any prisoners from having real money. The prison retained the money and gave prisoners the exact same amount in an official small piece of paper currency called scrip.

Figure 41: Prison scrip, Texas. [author's collection]

It only could be used as legal tender inside prison, not outside of prison. Scrip was supposed to be used only for commissary, but convicts also utilized it for currency between each other. Some guys were able afford to buy lots of cigarettes and also use those to gamble and deal.

"The Texas prison system would issue us two free sacks of bull derm tobacco. It was a low-grade version of the brand-name Bull Durham tobacco, but this stuff was so bad we just called it bull derm—in our prison lexicon the word derm implied shit. I'd use my wilds to get my boyfriends to send me a package or two of real cigarettes each time since I never had money to buy any. They could purchase a whole carton for maybe two dollars, which was a luxury. I was careful to make a pack of real cigarettes last me three or four days. I didn't smoke as many cigarettes in prison as I did later in life. Whenever I couldn't get a pack of cigarettes I'd have to roll and smoke prison-issued bull derm."

Jim saved the bull derm sacks and collected them from other prisoners. He soaked them in his small sink to remove the labels, used yellow crayons to dye the sacks and used a needle and thread to make a bedspread from dozens of sacks. He made a rug and hung some pictures. With a couple scraps of cardboard, he created a beautiful cover for his toilet with two big bluebirds on it that he embroidered with sequins.

"The other queens did similar things. We would call our cells our houses. We'd tell each other, 'My dear, I'm going to redecorate.' We didn't have much else to do, so we'd spend months figuring out the little things that made our houses the prettiest cells in the Walls."

$$\nabla$$

"I knew that if you were smart, you didn't make friends in prison. However, I did become good friends with a roly-poly short fat guy called Peaches. He was locked up in the cell next to mine. He was a nice, pleasant, decent guy who was the same age as me. And we never argued."

Peaches' father made him take male hormone shots to turn his effeminate son into a real man. The only thing the shots accomplished was to cause a profusion of tiny thin hair almost like peach fuzz to grow all over his body. He would remove it with Nair hair remover, but once he entered prison there were no more shots and no more Nair either—only lots of tiny peach-fuzzy hair.

"Peaches' father owned a movie theater located in the Dallas Negro district of Deep Ellum, which contained various businesses and entertainment venues catering to the Negro community. At that time Blacks couldn't go into the White theaters. Peaches' family theater showed all White films, but the audience was all Colored."

"Peaches worked behind the refreshment counter selling popcorn, soda pop and other goodies. Peaches developed a taste for Black men there and started seeing them on the side. His father didn't like it one bit. He made money from the Colored community, but his children weren't supposed to associate with Negros. Those who knew about Peaches thought he was a disgrace, 'How low can you go? Not only is he a homo, but he's going with Negro men.'"

When Peaches' grandfather died, he left Peaches money in a trust, which he was able to spend each month. It was Peaches' account, but his father was the trustee.

"Peaches had several boyfriends and eventually fell for one. He had saved money, so he was able to buy his Black boyfriend expensive silk shirts and a gold watch. The two guys left the oppression of Dallas and went off to a new crib in Denver. The Colorado attitude was a lot more accepting than they'd ever encountered in Texas. The stories Peaches told us about the Colorado mountains and Denver made the whole area sound absolutely idyllic."

Peaches' father found out about him being in Denver when the bills started coming in; so he removed all of the money from Peaches' account, and all of the checks started bouncing. Peaches found out there was a warrant out for his arrest, so he returned to Dallas to clear it up. Instead, he was arrested for writing bad checks. When his father learned that all of the expensive gifts went to Peaches' Black boyfriend, he refused to bail his son out of jail, 'It'll do him good. Leave him there.'"

Authorities convicted Peaches and his boyfriend with the same crimes and incarcerated the two in separate facilities. They sent Peaches to the Walls. "There were very few liberals around Dallas at that time, and most everybody in the Texas legal profession assumed that homosexuals got what they deserved."

It was obvious that the clout of Peaches' father somehow extended from high government officials into the prison. Peaches was kept secured in the Walls and never suffered the atrocities of the chain gangs.

Peaches acquired a couple of Black boyfriends in the Walls. "When I met Peaches, Black men were all he wanted. Everything in Texas was segregated and racist. Even Texan prisoners on queens' row considered interracial relations shameful. The other guys on queens' row were really awful to Peaches, 'How could you mess around with them people, Mary? We've got a name for you honey, and it's Dinge Queen.' With my West Coast liberal attitude, I called out those guys' attitudes as moronic. If these guys wanted the freedom to fulfill their sexual desires, I thought they should have given Peaches the support to fulfill his desires since he wasn't hurting anyone."

"In the Walls, Blacks were housed in the Negro wing, and occasionally we could hear them. They took a lot of pride wearing expensive watches and stylish Stacy Adams shoes and shoes made of alligator—all status symbols. Wrist watches and shoes were the only items that convicts were allowed to buy from the free world and wear in prison."

Jim would talk with Black prisoners in the Walls primarily when they delivered meal trays inside the Walls through the slots in the cell doors. Black prisoners were the ones who delivered meals to the cells. Even in prison, Blacks were relegated to serving food to White prisoners—still in the role of servant.

"Three or four months after I was put in the Walls, we heard on the radio that President John Kennedy had been shot. The Dallas daily newspapers had published ads claiming that Kennedy was wanted for treason and was soft on communism. The guards allowed us to go down to our small TV area and watch the assassination events unfold."

"Most of the guys in the Walls couldn't have cared less about Kennedy's death. This was Texas, and everyone was sort of glad that Lyndon Johnson was the new president. They thought Johnson was down to earth and better at getting things done. They viewed Kennedy as an upstart rich guy with his own yacht and a strange eastern accent. Prisoners there couldn't relate to him and didn't think he ever had done anything for them. I wasn't surprised it happened in Dallas. I knew first-hand that Dallas was a large redneck town and certainly not liberal in any sense of the word."

Every week guards would open the cell doors and the inmates on queens' row all went down to the emptied shower room to wash up. Jim would take his shower, then wrap himself in one of his colored towels and hurry back to his cell. Then he would watch the other guys parading past him naked, the only titillation available in queens' row.

"The guy I really waited to see was Gene. He was almost 30 years old. He was kind of stupid, but very masculine. He stood about 6 foot 4 and had the biggest and fattest thing I'd ever seen. A lot of guys kidded him and called him horse cock. For months I'd watch Gene walk back from his shower as he passed my cell. At night down in the TV area I'd flirt with him. I don't think he knew what to make of me. The guards were always watching us in the TV area, so it was impossible to fool around there. Gene was straight but told me that when he was younger he and his cousin would stick things up Gene's butt. The prison authorities ended up placing Gene in queens' row because he continued to stick things up his ass—and not another man either. I kept thinking what a waste."

Gene was released from prison, but within a week he attempted to rob a post office. His gun contained no bullets. "A lot of guys were like that. They couldn't make it on the outside and wanted to get back in prison. Gene didn't boomerang back to the Walls because he had robbed a federal facility, so he was sent to a federal prison. Convicts claimed that if you were going to commit a crime, do it federal, since federal prisons were better than Texas prisons."

Some convicts that Jim talked to during his stint in the Texas prison system had served time in various prisons—San Quentin, Soledad and one guy in Michigan. The prisoners would grade the various prisons claiming that the food was better in one certain prison or the lockdowns were fewer in a different one.

"I generally tried to avoid those people. A lot of them didn't feel comfortable out in the free world. They didn't have anything there. No skills. No status. Prisoners claimed they couldn't get a decent job on the outside and were determined they wouldn't work at some shit job beneath their respect. These guys could be important in prison. If they could con a wife or some dumb broad on the outside to send money, they could be big shots, wear a nice watch, have a little control and some power. Many prisoners intimidated others. Some hardened convicts in prison were vicious dogs to everybody they ever encountered, and they deserved to be kept there."

"One older guy with us up on queens' row had been in the Walls a long time and was supposed to remain in prison for the rest of his life. This guy acted really creepy, and no one wanted to talk to him. I was scared of him, so I kept my distance. When he was a little boy, they caught up with him wandering the streets with another boy's penis in his pocket that he had cut off. There were some really strange people in prison. At that time in Texas if someone claimed insanity as a defense, it didn't matter if you were nuts or not; once convicted you were going to prison since a lot of people there at that time thought psychiatrists basically were full of shit."

"A guy in his thirties who we called Wolf was the only prisoner I ever saw who truly received psychiatric help. I never talked to him, but a couple of runners told me the poor guy was crazy as hell."

"Wolf was locked up for robbery. He was in a cell downstairs among the straight guys. He would strip off his clothes and howl like a wolf—howl at the moon, howl at visitors, howl at the staff. It was disturbing, and he got on everyone's nerves. Guys would yell out at him to shut the fuck up."

The courts sentenced Wolf to prison for close to a decade. Guards would take him out on occasion, but basically he remained in his cell for his own protection. Finally, he had done his time and was released. Jim watched through the big windows as guards took Wolf outside and placed him in a van with a sign on it identifying the vehicle as belonging to the Texas state mental hospital—and it promptly carted him off to the psychiatric hospital. The government had not sent him to psychiatric care earlier since he was required to pay his debt to society first.

$$\nabla$$

"I kind of liked one runner who seemed like a decent guy. He did miscellaneous repairs throughout the Walls. I flirted with him like I did with a lot of other runners and guys who swept and mopped our tier. This runner was a straight guy, but he flirted back."

One morning the guy was in Jim's cell repairing the faucet that had been dripping. The two ended up getting caught in the middle of a little quick sex. Guards placed both guys in solitary confinement— the hole—the dark cell with the hole in the middle.

The prison system kept Jim locked up in isolation for three days. He was worried that he might lose all of his good time—he only had a half year until he was eligible for early release. The guards interviewed him each day in the hole about why he did this, but Jim was not admitting anything. For three days he kept to the code and claimed that he and the guy were not doing anything. On the third day the guards came into the hole and revealed to Jim that the other guy had cracked in less than a day there and said it was all Jim's fault— that Jim forced him to do it.

"I was indignant and informed them that it was a mutual thing— he was the one who unzipped his pants, 'Look, I only weigh 134 pounds with a 27-inch waist. I didn't put a knife to his throat or pull a gun on him. How could I ever have forced him? He was doing it because he liked it.' And that made obvious sense to the guards." They declined to place the blame on Jim and released him from solitary confinement.

Guards told Jim they would not deduct any of his good time. "After all, wasn't that what they expected of me? Their attitude was that since I made no bones about being gay, it was in my effeminate nature to let men use my body for their gratification. Convicts who got caught with a queen were the ones who normally got in trouble, because the system assumed that we queens were doing only what our inclinations compelled us to do."

"I came back from the hole to my cell as a heroine because I didn't crack. Every time I went down the walkway everybody would smile, and they'd call out, 'Hey, Bambi! Way to hang tough, girl!'" Jim gained status and a modicum of respect for the first time in prison for his unbroken perseverance in the hole.

"The other guy was kept in solitary confinement for a few more days. Most people thought he did a cowardly thing. Even the guards resented him. He was never allowed up on queens' row again."

While the guys got their food trays delivered, guards watched over the tier in order to prevent contraband. They stood inside the shower room to prevent any hanky-panky. And they sat outside the small TV area downstairs to keep an eye on the queers.

"While we queens were down in our tiny TV room, three or four of us would sit together talking, 'Oh my dear, my new boyfriend walked by last night...' or 'Have you heard about this guy who...' or 'Did you hear about Miss Thing?' It was all harmless fun."

"We had this new young Texas cowboy to guard us—a big hunk in his twenties who had just been transferred to queens' row. He was hot—unlike most of the guards—and he was married. I couldn't keep myself from sneaking glances down at his crotch, even though I knew I could get in trouble. I noticed the guard looking at us. He and I wouldn't say anything to each other, but I'd make sure I sat right in front where he could see and hear me talking to the other queens. One night within earshot of the guard I told the other queens, 'My dear, I know how to go down on a man like you wouldn't believe.' I knew the guard was listening to me describe details of how well I could suck cock. I figured the system harassed us, so I'd just harass back. It was all a game to me trying to stir him up just for the humor of it."

That night all of the prisoners on queens' row were retiring for bed. "We always said goodnight to each other. To Peaches on one side and Miss Thing on the other, 'Girls, I'm going to dream about my boyfriend tonight.'"

Then the new guard showed up and unlocked Jim's cell door. He informed Jim there was a serious problem, and that Jim needed to follow him to talk about it. "I'm thinking, *Oh shit, he's going to beat me or something for cruising him.*' When we got to his office all the runners were gone. He first stated that he didn't appreciate me carrying on like that, and he knew what I was doing."

"I was ready to concede defeat when he grabbed my head and forced me down on my knees like he was going to pound me. Instead he told me to take it out of his pants. So, I reached in his uniform and pulled it out. He said he heard me talking about how good I could suck cock, and he wanted to find out if I knew what I was talking about—and he found out."

Afterward, the guard got tough with Jim and told him that if Jim said anything about this, not only would the guard deny it, but he would make sure that Jim lost all of his good time. "It ended up being a one-time thing. I guess he was just curious and went back to his wife satisfied. I went back to my cell floating on air. Of course, I lied about it and told the others that the guard thought I was being too loud in the TV area. They didn't ask any questions. Everybody in prison kept certain things about themselves hidden. If you wanted to talk about something then that was fine, but no one in prison ever pressed you to blab."

∇

Guys from Ramsey who Jim knew would circulate through the Walls for a week or two under observation for various reasons or to spend a couple of days while being processed for release from prison.

Gay prisoners from Ramsey sometimes were placed in queens' row. Often they would bring news with them about Ramsey.

Jim learned that Hawk had been released from prison. Back when Jim was at Ramsey, Hawk and Jim had discussed Hawk's impending release and what he wanted to do after he got out. But Jim was surprised when he heard that Hawk already had been released from prison, because Jim never saw him when he came through the Walls. "They obviously kept him in another wing of the prison away from queens' row—maybe on purpose. I was happy for Hawk. He was young and so sweet. Hawk was so brave and didn't break down when Evil beat him. Under the right direction, my direction of course, he could've been a wonderful human being."

"Another guy from Ramsey told me Evil got released from prison. The scuttlebutt was that his court case was being dismissed on technicalities. I couldn't have cared less. At the time I figured he brown-nosed his way out by beating up enough people to please the prison administration. He never should've been released. He was pure rotten to the core. There wasn't a decent thing about him. Too much fucking power given to tenders on the farms enabled that brutality."

A couple of months later a queen from Ramsey came through the Walls, "Did you hear? Hawk's coming back to prison."

Jim was shocked, "Why?"

He told me, "He murdered Evil."

"I guess Hawk found out Evil got released and went hunting for him. I'd heard that out in the free world there were bars and places where ex-cons hung out. Hawk found Evil and killed him. Evil had done awful things. I heard that Evil had done other things to Hawk. Hawk didn't forgive and forget. Hawk got his revenge on that bastard. I hate to admit it, but I was glad. Evil was someone who really deserved to be taken out of society. I sure hope the Texas prison system has changed its policies about building tenders."

"This all happened a short time before I was released. I heard the scuttlebutt that Hawk was in jail somewhere else waiting to be sent back. Another rumor floating around said there was no solid proof that Hawk was the actual killer and he might get off the hook. Whatever happened to Hawk, I never found out. And once I left prison I never looked back."

Some convicts could be very charming. Tommy was one of them. He was a runner who brought books and magazines to prisoners' cells from the prison library. During days he also worked inside the medical facilities as a medical assistant.

As Tommy rolled the book cart through the Walls, he would stop to talk about the various reading materials and to visit with prisoners. "Tommy was an absolutely beautiful man. He was about my age. He was a smart guy and had an ivy league look with short hair. He had a masculine soothing voice and treated everyone nice. The queens all had a thing for him and would ask each other, 'How'd you like to get ahold of that one?' But Tommy was straight and lived in the general population. Word among the queens was that he would not go with anybody—he didn't play that shit."

Tommy had been in prison for about a half decade already. When he was about 17 years old, he murdered his mother and father. When Jim first heard about it, he shied away from Tommy, but then Jim heard talk from other prisoners claiming that Tommy was okay. Jim found it somewhat strange how murderers in prison seemed to be trusted so much.

Tommy would come up to Jim's cell, and Jim was always gracious to him. "I started developing a crazy crush on Tommy, but I didn't flirt with him or come onto him since I'd never get anywhere with him. You never would've known that Tommy killed his parents. He and I had some interesting talks, but I never asked him why he did it." Prisoners simply didn't ask other prisoners about their crimes. Convicts were very private and didn't want to put their business on the street.

"We prisoners could earn scrip and cigarettes by letting ourselves be used as guinea pigs to test experimental drugs and pills. The prison staff sometimes would come around and ask us if we'd like to be involved in a medical experiment. During this last year in prison I figured why not, and I volunteered. Not only could I earn stuff, but Tommy was involved in administering the medical experiments to convicts. That would give him and me more to talk about."

In the lab room, Tommy distributed pills to Jim and another couple of volunteers. Tommy passed out cigarettes to them and set up appointments for each guy to return separately to give a urine sample and get an electrocardiogram.

Jim never knew what the medicine was that he swallowed. He noticed nothing strange. However, years later he wondered what the substance was that he took. "It could've been anything and literally could've killed us—just for a couple packs of cigarettes. At times prisoners would warn others don't take this certain drug or don't volunteer for that certain study. This drug might include a wild virus or that drug could be something that could cause cancer. The rumors were always flying."

When Jim returned for the testing, Tommy was again on duty as the medical assistant. Tommy's assistant was an orderly who retrieved things for him and cleaned. Tommy attached the electrodes to Jim. "His crotch was inches from my face. Tommy told his assistant to go guard the door and be on point for him to make sure no guards approached. Tommy and I had the sweetest sex. I tell you it was wonderful. It was every fantasy. I desired this guy for a long time, and it was better than I ever imagined."

"Later I found out that traditionally I also was supposed to take care of his buddy watching the door, but luckily I didn't have to do that because the next volunteer came in, and soon there were too many people around."

"Anyway, Tommy turned the machine on, and we finished the EKG. I was hoping that my heart and pulse rate wouldn't read too high."

"Tommy made me swear I would never tell anyone. I went back and wanted to scream it up and down the walkways, 'He chose me and let me have it!' I felt so good."

"Then, of course, I fell in love with Tommy. I'd see him through the windows while he worked weights outside and hung out with the other guys. We would always visit with each other when he came by my cell. I never told anyone about us. It was our own private secret. I've been vulnerable to the right men who probably could get me to do a lot for them. I was completely under his control, but I didn't dare let him know it."

"I never understood how a clean-cut perfect guy could kill his parents. One time Tommy mentioned it to me and only said it was just the way things happened. He regretted it."

"Tommy was never one of the phonies who pretended to be religious. Two good ways to get yourself a parole was either to join AA and blame everything on alcohol or to find God. So, you had these guys running around conspicuously spreading the word of God. In a mixed way I could understand them—after all, I acted the part of a preacher back in the orphanage at a young formative age. But you could tell that these cons were phonies. They would say or do something religiously irreverent when the system wasn't observing them. They'd try this crap of coming to preach to us, and we were literally a captive audience; but I avoided them and stayed away and refused to engage in any talk with them."

Tommy and Jim did nothing together again. Three or four months after their sexual union, Jim was released from prison. "I often wondered about Tommy. He was one of the prisoners I felt sorry for. I never found out if he grew old and died there or whatever happened to him. He was sentenced to life, but who knows, maybe after 25 years or so he was able to make parole. I never tried to find out. I didn't want to know about anybody I was in prison with. I was determined to move on and break away from all of those people."

Chapter 24

Getting Out of Texas

After a while, every day in the Walls seemed the same. Peaches and Jim made calendars and marked off the days, which comprised another week, which comprised another month, which comprised another year.

Since Jim's five-year sentence began in September 1962, it would expire in September 1967. However, by maintaining a clean record in prison, it was possible for Jim to get released two years early in September 1965. "I wanted to get released even earlier than my two years of good time by getting a parole, but they informed me they didn't give paroles to homosexuals, so I was out of luck with that."

"I'd been anticipating getting released since the first day I arrived in prison. I remember having dreams in prison about being out of prison and living in California. The three years seemed like a long time to be locked up and not able to get away. Freedom was approaching. For months I constantly talked about getting released. Finally I was within just a couple of months, then weeks, then days. It got worse the shorter I got. The closer to my release date the more I worried—I just hoped nothing would go wrong."

"I gave Peaches my decorations that we made for my cell. I appreciated him so much and hated saying goodbye. You don't find good friends in prison like Peaches."

Jim spent three years incarcerated in the Texas State Penitentiary System.

He was released on Saturday, September 18, 1965. The State of Texas gave each departing prisoner a pair of pants, undershorts, a shirt, a pair of shoes, a bus ticket and $50 to start a new life. "I had nothing saved up because Texas didn't pay us a dime for the work we did. We were there to pay the State of Texas in good old blood, sweat and tears."

Later in the century, U.S. prison systems paid inmates money for the work they performed while incarcerated. Prisoners might earn only a few cents an hour, but it built up enough that released inmates had some money when they left prison. "When I was in the Texas pen it provided no training to get rehabilitated and find a skilled job. We hadn't learned a damn thing in the Texas prison system except how to work in the fields. At least prison systems nowadays try to provide inmates with job skills to help boost their chances of staying out of prison."

"The other prisoners in the Walls would tell me, 'Y'all ain't gonna last long out there. It's hard for ex-cons in the free world. You'll be back here within months. You won't be able to find a job. Nobody will hire an ex-con.' Some prisoners become institutionalized in the revolving doors of prisons forever and never can be rehabilitated, but I was rehabilitated my first night in prison. I knew that ex-cons return to prison all the time—but not me. I told everyone from the beginning of my sentence that I would never be back once I left. I had learned my lesson." Jim was determined to do an about face and stay crime-free for the rest of his life.

Since Jim never told anybody on the outside that he was serving time in prison, he had no support to lean on from any relatives or friends. A prison sentence was not something that made him proud in any way. Jim's mother and sisters never dreamed that he was in prison during those three years. They seldom knew where he was anyway.

As Jim and the other inmates got ready to depart the prison that day, guards checked to make sure nobody carried out any contraband or addresses. "The prison system discouraged us from corresponding with each other. Everyone says, 'Call me, and we'll get together outside.' The prison didn't want that, and frankly neither did I. I had no desire whatsoever to meet anybody from back there. I just wanted to get away. Once I left, I tried to forget as much as I could. I didn't want to see any of them ever again."

Jim and the others walked through the prison door and hit the streets of freedom. "One guy wanted to go off with me, but I got the impression he was more interested in my $50 than in me."

At the bus station each chose their individual bus ticket. Jim lacked the extra money to get out of Texas. He declined to go to Houston because he was unfamiliar with it. He considered going to New Orleans, which would have been a wilder place and much nicer, but he didn't have the extra money to get there either. So, he chose to go to the only nearby city he was familiar with—Dallas. At least he knew where things were located in the downtown area.

Jim arrived in Dallas late in the afternoon. He viewed it as a challenge to succeed now where he failed previously. He told a cab driver that he needed a cheap place to stay, so he drove Jim six or seven blocks to a hotel. It was seedy, but Jim felt he didn't have the money to search for something better at the moment, so he paid for a room there for the night. It had a bed and a teak chest of drawers. Jim turned on the wobbly ceiling fan above the bed. "I'm lying there, and this thing is right over me making weird noises, and I'm thinking that if this fan falls down on me it'll cut me into 20 ribbons."

There was no bathroom in the room. Jim used the men's room located at the end of the hall to wash up for bed. "Since it was a weekend night, the place was hopping, busy with couples going in and out of rooms. Some of the women just stood around in their negligees, and I realized I was in some kind of house where prostitutes took their tricks they picked up. I should have realized it sooner by all the red lights in the halls. I suppose if I'd been straight, I would have been in seventh heaven thanks to the cab driver, but why the hell would I want to be in a straight whorehouse?"

Jim returned to his room and barricaded the door with the chest of drawers, thinking people might attempt to come in and rob him of the only money he had left. "I still was worried about that fan, so I turned it off, but the room got too hot—it was like an oven. So, I turned the fan back on and slept on the floor."

Jim decided long before morning that he no longer was going to stay there. He bought a newspaper, and he had a cup of coffee and a bite to eat. He was stuck in Texas until he could save enough money to get back to California. His first priority was renting a decent place to live for a short time. He found an ad in the newspaper for a rooming house, similar to a boarding house except it did not supply meals. It was advertised at a price Jim could afford, so he called, was shown the place, made arrangements and moved in. It turned out to be nice.

Only guys lived there, since at that time nobody would rent to a lone woman. Jim figured he would try it out for at least a week.

Next, Jim looked through the want ads for a job. There were lots of ads in the newspaper for low-skilled jobs. "I needed anything to stay out of prison. I found an ad for a job at the Dallas Statler Hilton—at that time it was the premier grand hotel in Dallas. The ad was for a houseman, another fancy word for janitor. Rather than thinking I was too good to be a janitor, I figured they wouldn't ask too many questions if I applied for that job. I was not about to tell them I just got out of prison. I needed money. If they eventually found out about my prison record then I'd simply move on."

The next morning on his way to the hotel interview Jim stopped in a department store with his dwindling pocketful of cash. He bought a cheap blazer to make a good impression. He started noticing new items in the store. He wandered around for a few minutes in a daze seeing all of the new goods for sale. It had been so long.

"I arrived at the hotel dressed up and was filling out the application when a guy from the personnel office came into the room. He asked me what job I was applying for, and I answered, 'janitor or houseman.' I started worrying that I wasn't going to get the job. He asked me if I'd ever worked room service. I said no, but he liked the way I looked, so the hotel ended up training me to be a room service waiter."

Jim worked at the Statler for a month. The hotel provided a uniform and a free meal every day he worked. Jim learned quickly and made a lot of money in tips, which was how he earned most of his money since actual wages were only about 80 cents an hour.

"I thought the hotel was a wonderful place. It had what they called silver service with everything served in silver-plated coffee pots and creamers and trays. I had to check each piece out of the pantry and was responsible for returning every one of them. After the guests were done with them, they'd set the items in the halls, and we'd run by and retrieve them. Since this was a very fancy hotel, nobody could just walk inside off the street and steal this stuff."

Every night, Jim would leave work and return to the rooming house. Since he was afraid the police might stop him, he stayed off the streets at night.

"I just didn't want to take any chances on anything. Before prison everything was an adventure, and everything seemed possible. I was never afraid to get in people's cars. Now in Dallas after prison, my adventurous spirit and spontaneity had evaporated. I even worried that if I hitchhiked the police would stop me and throw me back in jail. I recalled some of the characters back in prison and the horrid things some of them had done, and I thought, 'What if I meet the wrong person, somebody who deserved to be in prison?' I was like someone hunkering down in their home, watching lots of news programs and crime shows and becoming afraid that there's a criminal behind every bush."

"I found Texas men to be virile and macho and down to earth—all the things I liked in guys—even their Texas accents. Country Western singer Jim Reeves had recently died, and I remember that the Dallas radio stations were playing his number one song *Is It Really Over*. The song moved me emotionally in different ways."

Jim was determined to keep his prison experience from changing him. He would simply pick up the pieces of his life again. However, the longer he remained in Dallas the more oppressed he felt. "If they arrested me or stopped me for anything, they'd ask if I'd ever been arrested before, and I couldn't lie to them."

Jim was determined to leave Texas as soon as he acquired sufficient travel money.

Jim hoarded his tips, and when he received his second paycheck he got out of town. He had no legal requirement to remain in Texas. He was under no order. "So I boarded a bus and left Texas and never ever returned."

Chapter 25

Freedom in the Free World

On the day his bus arrived in Los Angeles from Dallas, Jim realized that dreams do come true. He had survived a three-year prison nightmare in Texas, and now the memories of sweating out long days on a chain gang and being confined in a solitary prison cell slowly began fading into his past. The past was not something he wanted to relive or talk about.

"This was one of the happiest days of my life. I loved the West Coast and was finally back home after being away far too long."

Jim primarily lived in Los Angeles during the next two years after he returned to California. He continued living paycheck to paycheck working at a string of dead-end jobs as a bus boy, dishwasher and waiter. Sometimes he cleaned businesses during nights.

"I moved in with three other guys, and we all pooled what little money we earned to pay our rent. I read books and listened to radio. The popular song of the day playing on all of the radio stations was *California Dreamin'* by The Mamas and the Papas. Here was this new impassioned song that inspired my thoughts and feelings. For three years in prison I'd been dreaming about California when I slept. Even when I was awake I'd daydream about returning to California. Now I was back in the moderate winter weather in the coastal region of Southern California."

Jim noticed right away that none of the guys his age wore crew cuts anymore, and they no longer combed their hair back on the sides of their heads. Many wore longer hair down below their ears. Jim was fascinated by the new cars on the streets and attended an annual auto show to see the new models.

"I always kept quiet about my legal past. People back then, even gay guys, would've thought my prison stint was an awful disgrace. There were certain things that you didn't talk about to anyone in those days. You didn't announce to the world that you were gay and expect them to accept it. You didn't talk about being unmarried and having a child. However, times were beginning to change."

Some of those changes were fueled by technology, racial unrest and war. The Gemini Space Program of sending two-man teams into orbit around the earth was laying the groundwork for fulfilling the late President Kennedy's call to put a man on the Moon. In the Watts neighborhood of Los Angeles, decades of racial discrimination erupted, touching off a race riot that lasted five days, killing 34 people and injuring more than 1,000 others.

While the United States seemed to be at war with itself at home, there was another war overseas that raged on. President Lyndon Baines Johnson committed more troops to Southeast Asia and kicked off Operation Rolling Thunder, which included bombing targets in Communist North Vietnam.

All of these upheavals taking place at home, abroad and in the stratosphere had no bearing or direct influence on Jim. He was a free spirit again and did not want to stay in one place for too long.

Although LA remained his home base, he traveled to other cities up and down the West Coast. He accompanied one guy to a weekend stay at a cabin in the San Rafael Mountains near Santa Barbara. Another guy took him up to Washington State on a two-week sightseeing adventure.

"I didn't go to San Diego much, but I went to Long Beach a lot. The naval base there had lots of sailors. I had a wonderful two-day affair with one sailor while he was in port. His ship was about to leave for a WestPac tour to Asia and the Western Pacific. We promised each other that I'd wait for him and he'd return to me. Of course, it ended up just being hopeful daydreaming, but oh man, it was nice."

"Before prison, I quit going back to Idaho. I decided I really didn't have a place there anymore. After prison I visited my mother only one time. She didn't say, 'Where have you been for four years? We never heard from you.' She only harped about Ruth and me being heathens and heretics. Since she and my real father Charlie put me under the hand of God before I was born, she could not give up on me serving as a minister, 'You'll never succeed in anything in life until you return to the fold and become a minister.' Eventually she realized that I wasn't going to become one."

"From the earliest days with my mother and Ross in church, I became guarded against religious beliefs and dogma—whether it was Christian, Muslim, Jewish, Hindu, Wicca, Atheist, or whatever theory or superstition or religion that people latched onto. A lot of religious people say, 'I know what it's all about and there's a God or Gods and here are all of my beliefs because my church is right. I am right.' A lot of atheists say, 'I know what it's all about and there are no god or gods.' Some atheists can be just as adamant in their dogmatic beliefs as some religious people."

"I think there's a lot more to this world than meets the eye—things that can hardly be perceived. Humans have a primal desire to understand why the world is here, what's beyond our perceptions of the world, why are we here, and what happens to us after death? Nobody knows for sure. Humans align themselves with all sorts of beliefs, especially those they're indoctrinated to while growing up. Not everybody can be right. Each person truly is guessing what 'it' is all about. I think every individual should be free to believe however they see the world—as long as they don't try to harm anyone else. I discovered that people could be upstanding through moral codes and be decent people without having to choose to believe a particular religion or tenet."

"I was the son, not of a preacher, but of preachers—four of them. Throughout my parents' ministries they never cheated anyone. And we certainly didn't live high on the hog. We struggled all the time."

"During the summers when I was young my mother required me to read a Christian bible for hours every day. She also sent me to bible vacation school—and it was no vacation either. All the kids had to attend youth assemblies all day long, and we earned points for memorizing bible passages. Then after supper we played out what we had learned that day."

"Some of the stories I learned in the Christian bible were very interesting, and I wanted to know more. I was very young when I first asked my mother about Adam and Eve and their two sons Cain and Abel. I was curious about Cain going off and getting married. Who did he marry? My mother didn't know how to answer. Now in my twenties, visiting my folks a year after prison, I questioned my mother again, and she guessed that Adam and Eve probably had other children. I said, 'You mean they committed incest?' Whenever she got stumped with contradictory inconsistencies in the Christian bible, she would fall back on the old hackneyed bromide, 'God works in mysterious ways.'"

"My mother believed that a person had to be the same denomination as she was in order to truly be saved—a whole lot of religious people believed that about their own churches at that time."

"As a kid I discovered and got interested in history and read about all the atrocities committed by various religious zealots and how sanctimonious they were. I read about religious differences being responsible for so many millions dying and the societies these people conquered around the world."

"My mother didn't have much education. Her friends and acquaintances were all fundamentalist Pentecostals. In her life she and relatives mainly listened to religious radio broadcasts by small-time preachers heard on small radio stations. This was long before the mega-corporate religious broadcasters dominated the lucrative religious broadcast industry. I remember that in my earlier years the preachers on air couldn't speak very well, but I just figured they didn't have the same opportunity for much schooling or education that we kids received. I don't remember hearing radio preachers speak about anything good or positive. Everything to them was a catastrophe. The world constantly was ending tomorrow."

"My mother voted for our country's presidents depending on what they claimed they believed about religion. She voted against John Kennedy because he was a Catholic. She claimed that Catholics and Baptists and the others were never getting into heaven. I challenged her by pointing out that the nuns and the pope did great work. She was adamant. She said that Catholics might have meant well, but they all were going to hell."

"My folks and their friends wanted the United States to be run in accordance with their beliefs. That always had been the goal of my folks and their associates. They wanted their religion taught in the public schools. They didn't want to be stuck paying for their own religious parochial schools because that cost them too much money.

They wanted taxpayers to pay for their religious indoctrinations in schools."

After two or three days, Jim returned home to California and did not visit Fannie again for about a decade.

Chapter 26

The Business Side of Going Pro

Back in Los Angeles after prison, Jim noticed a curious change that had evolved in the gay world. In the 1950s most gay men had emulated stereotypical heterosexual husband/wife relationships. One man played the masculine role and the other man played the feminine role. But now, in 1966, things had begun changing, and Jim kept encountering various masculine men who were in relationships together.

So, after prison Jim decided to butch up his act and no longer swish around. "One day I was walking down the street dressed in a pair of Levi's and a black t-shirt looking like a typical young guy. I didn't have the world's greatest body, but I was young and thin and in demand."

One driver passed Jim in the opposite direction in a nondescript late model car—not flashy, not sporty. The guy was in his forties. He turned the car around and pulled up next to Jim.

"He asked me if he could give me a lift. Well, somebody just doesn't turn around in the middle of the street and come back and ask if he can give you a ride. But I'd played that old game before, so I told him okay, I still had maybe a mile to go."

Jim was not interested in the guy, so he told him a story—that he just had arrived in town. Jim acted the part of a yokel from Nebraska or Idaho or someplace remote.

"He asked me if I'd ever thought about going to have a good time with a man. I stifled my impulse to laugh, 'No, I never thought about that.' He said, 'I suppose being new in the city, you don't have much money.' I said, 'No, I sure don't.' And he said, 'Well, I can help you with that problem. How'd you like to make a hundred dollars?' Well, a hundred dollars was a lot of money. But I said, 'I don't know. What would I have to do for a hundred dollars?' He said all I had to do was go with him to have sex in his motel room over in West Hollywood, and if I didn't like it, I could leave anytime."

Jim only personally had known one hustler previously and that was years ago in downtown LA. Jim and his friends used to see hustlers and usually looked askance at them. But now with prison in his past, selling his body seemed innocent compared to other evil horrible crimes people divulged to him in gory detail during his imprisonment.

"My friends thought we were so piss elegant, but in reality, we were giving it away. When guys would pick me up for a date, they'd buy me food and take me home where a lot of times I'd stay overnight. I was struggling and giving it away like you were supposed to do. So, in a way I was already selling it without realizing it, except it was never cut-and-dried. Nobody came up to me and told me they would pay me such and such. It was just understood that if I went out with them, they would ask me if I was hungry—and I always was—and they'd take me somewhere to eat. I was supposed to give them sex in return. I knew that, and I always was nice to all the guys who were nice to me."

Now, the guy with the hundred dollars drove to his motel and took Jim into his room. Jim wondered, *"What in the hell does he expect me to do for a hundred dollars?"* He seemed more normal than strange. He told Jim that he could stop anytime Jim wanted if Jim didn't like the scene. So, Jim assumed the guy only was lonely.

"He had me take off my clothes and lay naked on the bed as he stood by the door fully dressed, and he masturbated—just looking at me, not touching me. Then after he was done, he handed me the hundred dollars. I thought, *'This is the easiest money I ever made!'*"

They chatted, and the guy asked Jim if he liked working at low-paying jobs. Of course, the answer was no. He claimed that Jim could make a lot of money. Had Jim ever thought about going into this as a career? Jim continued to play dumb and responded, "No, not really."

"The guy handed me a card with a name and phone number on it. He said it was a callboy service. He told me to call and tell them that he recommended me as an employee. The guy got ready to leave and said, 'By the way, why don't you just stay here in this motel room tonight? The rent's all paid up.' I thought, '*Sure, why not?*' I had a hundred dollars burning a hole in my pocket, and I wouldn't have to spend it tonight on a place to sleep. I kept wondering, '*If it's this easy, why isn't everybody doing it?*' I felt flattered because he thought I had something worth selling. Here I'd been giving it away all this time. Why not make some good easy money for a change?"

It was all about money, not sex. Having money would mean Jim would not go hungry. Making money meant having a good place to sleep at night.

That night Jim called the number on the card, and a manager instructed Jim to come and talk to him the next day. The place was close to the motel, so Jim walked there since he had no car of his own. The manager who answered the door was around 25 years old, masculine and good-looking. Jim put on his butch act. The manager gave Jim a quick once-over, invited him inside and interviewed him.

"I told the manager, 'I won't lie to you. I'm not new in town. I've been away for three or four years, but I've lived here on and off for years—and I'm as gay as they come.' That fit right in with the agency's business dealings, and I could tell that the manager was growing more confident about me working for him."

A lot of the callboys the agency dealt with were bisexual hustler types who were often unreliable. They were young and many were on drugs. Most of them were straighter than not and undependable. The agency manager told Jim, "A lot of times they don't want to do the jobs. Some of them are fussy about the people we send them to. If you're going to sell it you have to make sure the guy paying for it feels at least a little appreciated. You can't go into a guy's home and give the impression that you really don't want to sleep with him because you don't care about the guy or you just want his money. You'll have to play various roles, and we might assign a few of those roles to you."

"I thought that made sense, 'I'm dependable. If I decide to do this for a career, I'm going to be professional about it. You tell me what I'm supposed to do, and I'll satisfy the customers, no matter their looks or ages, because I want to make a lot of money. The more I do, the more money I'll make, right?' And the manager agreed."

He explained to Jim how the callboy agency operated: "The difference between a male prostitute and a female is that the female can fake an orgasm. A male prostitute is expected to have a hard on, and many customers expect a male prostitute to reach a climax and cum. Even though you're young and probably can instantly get a hard on, most guys can't cum more than a half dozen times at the most in one night unless you're a Superman. In response, we'll space it out for you. You'll service one guy who wants you to cum, then for the next appointment we'll assign you to a customer who doesn't care if you cum or not. You'll have at least an hour between each assignment."

The manager expected Jim to service clients throughout LA. However, Jim had no car. So, the manager gave Jim a map of the bus system, which Jim already knew quite well.

The manager told Jim to go back to the same motel where he spent the previous night. For the first night the motel room would be paid by the callboy agency, but after that Jim would pay his own room charges. Each client would pay $50—the agency would get a cut of $20, and Jim would end up with $30. The price would be settled before Jim ever met a customer. This would be better money than Jim could make anywhere else. The manager reminded Jim that the prostitutes on the streets had no protection. In contrast, the agency had acquired many clients who had become established trustworthy customers, and the agency had analyzed exactly what those clients wanted. The manager explained that Jim would not know the clients' full names—not surprising since most gay men in those years only used first names anyway.

The manager told Jim he would give him a try and add Jim to the agency's stable. Jim was not to visit the agency again. All business between them would be conducted either at Jim's locations or over the telephone. The manager instructed Jim to call in every evening around 6:00 to obtain his assignments from the manager or his partner who was working three days in Palm Springs at a large party. He cautioned Jim to be careful about anything said over the phone, because calls could be monitored.

As Jim was getting ready to leave, the manager gave him the address of Jim's first and only customer for that night and said not to phone back that night. He explained a little bit of what the client wanted and told Jim to pretend he was straight.

Jim's customer that night was one of the agency's steady clients who had an established account, so instead of being paid in cash, Jim would receive a voucher from him, and the agency in turn would reimburse Jim.

The following afternoon the agency's manager stopped by Jim's motel room and paid him his percentage of the previous night's earnings. He told Jim the customer was very satisfied and asked Jim how he liked role-playing. Jim thought it was fun. He would even be a cowboy if that was what a customer wanted.

Jim never mentioned money to his customers. They didn't need to be reminded that they were having to pay for it. It wasn't until Jim would be walking out the door that customers would give him the money. They would slip it in Jim's pocket or might grease Jim's palm with what they called a tip or cab fare or whatever would make them feel good about paying for it. Everything was pre-arranged. Agency clients understood they had to pay up for services rendered or else. The "or else" consisted of a couple of muscle men showing up at the front door to collect.

That became Jim's life for the next few weeks. "I never in my life had so much cash. Of course, I didn't save a dime. I never socked away any money. It was all spend-it-tonight."

"I'd go downtown to shop. I certainly was able to dress a lot better now. I'd buy my working clothes at a store near me that sold all sorts of wild stuff, crazy underwear and skin tight pants that accentuated your basket down in the crotch area. I guess I'd actually call it a fag store. It was really queer. And it seemed like all the male prostitutes shopped at this store."

"One day in that store I met Hank, a real hunk of a guy—good-looking and extremely masculine. His claim to fame was his large dick. I assumed that he had recognized a brother under the skin. So, we got to talking. I was really careful about who I talked to, because you never knew who someone actually was. But he came right out with it and said he was hustling out on Santa Monica Boulevard. Whenever I would pass street-walkers, I'd sort of feel superior to them. I didn't have to do it on the street because I was a true professional. I was part of a callboy agency. I asked Hank, 'Isn't it dangerous out there on the streets?' He said he never had any problems, and that was easy to believe since he was so masculine and tough. What's more, since he was an independent worker, he didn't have to share his profits with anyone."

"In working for the agency, I serviced all kinds of guys. I met a few tricks at hotel rooms, but I'd meet most of them at their homes. Some of their places were small and tidy while others were large and well-appointed. I always played along—whatever turned on the customer and made him happy."

"I thought these guys requested me because they liked me, and they did; but clients of the callboy service paid for a variety of available men. As soon as they got tired of me, they would want somebody else and would request another different guy."

Jim had worked a couple of months for the agency when one evening he again received only one assignment for the night. The client already had prepaid his money to the bosses.

"When I arrived, I saw that I'd gotten another guy who looked like he'd only want to jack off. Easy money! He was from Holland. Mr. Milquetoast, Casper Milquetoast, the type of ineffectual ordinary harmless guy you'd never notice—there's one in every office who comes to work all the time, no personality, just fades into the woodwork. He started telling me that he was different. He seemed very cold like I imagined the Germans and Dutch could be when they were paying for sex—no romance, just coldness."

"He said I was in luck, because I had the opportunity to earn a whole lot more money. 'I want you to take off your clothes. I have my little riding crop used for striking horses. I'll give you five lashes, and for each five lashes that I give you, you'll get five dollars—a dollar per lash.'"

"I said, 'Are you crazy?' And he replied, 'No, I can be very mild. I'll do it just five times, and you can see what it's like. Then anytime you want me to stop, I'll stop; and you get to keep whatever money you earn. Some guys have made three hundred dollars or more. It depends on how strong you are. If you're a man and can take it, you could earn lots of money.'"

"So, okay, I decided to try it just once. Mr. Milquetoast hit my butt five times with the crop. I thought, *'Well, that didn't really hurt.'* So, I allowed him to string me up from a contraption from his ceiling, and I was just sort of standing there on tiptoes with no clothes on, my hands strapped to this bar. He would say, 'Okay, are you ready for another five? Make lots of money.' So, he would proceed to give me five more whacks on my butt. He then would stop and message my butt—I didn't know if that was supposed to make it feel better or what."

"He was a strange guy. He had all these five-dollar bills, and each time I received five strikes, he would lay another five-dollar bill on the bed. He seemed harmless enough. And it didn't really hurt—at first. Eventually, it began to really sting. Before long, my forehead started sweating, and I started gritting my teeth. When I had suffered through earning $75, I'd had enough and had to stop. He released me just like he said he would. He told me I could keep all the extra money I earned. He wouldn't tell the callboy service about the extra money he paid me. Of course, my ass was a mess of welts. He must have put something on my butt, because I really didn't feel a lot of bad pain—until later after I got home."

The next day Jim answered the door to find the agency's bosses looking for their cut of the extra money he earned. "Mr. Milquetoast ended up telling them after all, as though they were all testing me. I figured I was the one who had to suffer through all that pain, so fuck them. I was keeping all the money. I was mad at those fuckers for sending me to that sadist. I thought I could trust them. I told them that I simply serviced him, and that's all that happened. They didn't believe me. They said they knew what really had happened, so they fired me on the spot."

"For a whole day I was flat on my stomach. It felt awful. What really scared me afterwards was realizing that by letting that guy tie me up, I was helpless if he had wanted to kill me or something. He could have done anything. You'd think that my experiences as a kid with my stepfather Ross years before would've taught me never to do that again, but the money was a seductive enticement. Never again!"

"I was naïve and had assumed the rich life would go on forever. Sex workers think they're going to get rich, but as soon as most of them make the easy money it slips through their fingers. Only the astute ones end up saving a lot or investing their money."

After Jim lost the callboy job, he decided to go back to legitimate work waiting on tables and busing dishes. "It was hard and never paid enough money. I made more in one night as a callboy than I did in three weeks at a decent job. Working in the sex trade meant no taxes to pay, no social security deductions, no nasty jerk bosses standing over you and no one screaming at you to do this and do that. Being a callboy didn't require a guy to have a smart mind—just the ability to fulfill fantasies."

∇

A month later Jim was walking along Hollywood Boulevard when he ran into Hank the Hunk whom he originally had met at the outrageous clothing store. Hank was still hustling on the streets making loads of money. Since it was daytime Hank was off work. He primarily worked nights.

"Hank told me that he didn't have to work many hours to rake in his money. He was as masculine and sexy as ever. He really was beautiful. He and I relaxed together and had coffee. I explained my whole situation of getting fired from the callboy service and returning to restaurant work and barely living on the chintzy money I made."

"Hank asked me, 'Why the hell put up with that crap?'"

"He said, 'Move in and hustle with me. You can live free with me at the motel where I'm staying on Santa Monica Boulevard. I'll be your pimp and show you all the ropes about street hustling and you share your earnings with me. We'll knock down lots of money together. I'm a pro at it.'"

Hank learned about the sex trade from one of the best prostitutes in the business, the black sheep of his family—his own aunt. Hank did not see her much growing up. Hank's old man had no problem with her being around, but Hank's mother put her foot down. She was embarrassed by her sister and did not want her influence around the family.

Hank explained that when he left home at 18 years old, he looked up his aunt and stayed with her for a couple of months. She told him tales about her years working as a hooker before she got too old for the business. She explained the ways the business worked and told Hank all about her pimps—a real eye-opener for Hank.

Jim figured that Hank's offer to work together was the best way to make big money again, so he moved in with Hank.

"Hank was so sexy. I went complexly unglued over the guy. I had this vision of the two of us having a long-term relationship—we'd work at nights and make love during the days. Hank said that would be okay, but he said not now, that he had to save it for the customers, that we should wait until he had a night off."

"My past was truly interesting to Hank. He wanted to know everything about me, unlike most guys. On the first day living with him I ended up telling him all about being abused by my stepfather, my first homosexual experiences, getting committed to reform school, the way guys treated me and how I scraped by trying to survive the best I could. I didn't tell him about prison. I never told anyone about prison."

The motel where Hank stayed had an on-site manager who was gay. "He was the only individual getting regular sex from Hank. The manager was cooking the books to let Hank live there rent-free. Every three or four days when the manager got horny, Hank would put it to him."

The motel manager was friendly. He stayed primarily in the front office keeping an eye on everyone coming and going. That gave Jim an extra sense of safety and security. The manager loved to gossip. He told Jim that before he showed up, Hank had a hustler he pimped out for a while, and after that he had another hustler working for him. Hank made them work hard on the streets, and according to the manager they submissively followed Hank's commands.

The motel manager warned Jim that it was real hard work out there. The manager knew, because one afternoon one of Hank's hustlers had a black eye and some bruises. He claimed that one of his tricks beat him up. The manager figured it must have happened early in the morning, because the previous night the manager noticed him coming back to the motel in mid-evening, and nothing yet seemed wrong or out of the ordinary. The manager thought the hustler was a real trooper because he went right back out the next night and worked harder than ever. Jim thought to himself, *"What a dummy. I never had any problems with customers at the callboy service, because I understood how to properly treat my guys and fulfill their fantasies."*

"I knew Hank would teach me how to work the streets and would protect me. Together we'd make lots of money. Hank called us independent businessmen."

On the first night, Hank took Jim out on the streets and showed him how to stand and how to walk along the street. "He told me that if it ain't shakin' for me in one block, then I should keep moving on. Walk slow and stroll against oncoming traffic. Make clear to guys my price. Don't begin asking for low dollars—start high and let a trick feel some satisfaction in negotiating the price down."

Hank cautioned Jim to keep his guard up for cops. He said to beware of good-looking confident tricks, because those were likely to be undercover cops. Why would these guys pay for it when they could get plenty of action for free?

"Hank was aggressive and had no trouble at all. He was definitely a pro. I watched as he'd go up and tell a trick exactly what the deal was. He was a real hunk out there. He had everything going for him. The customers all wanted a hard stud like Hank. There was a lot of competition, and the streets were really busy and notorious. They were full of young men who certainly weren't doing it for nothing. The hustlers were all over Santa Monica Boulevard and also on Hollywood Boulevard and on Selma Avenue."

Almost all hustlers worked on the streets with no pimps. Jim only met one other guy who had a pimp—a 17-year-old gay guy whose pimp also had a straight female working the streets. The young gay guy felt safe with the two of them. Jim could relate since he felt safe on the streets with Hank backing him up.

Hank exuded confidence. "He thought he was the baddest son of a bitch on the street. He believed that to be a successful male hustler, you had to project an attitude that you're hot shit and the customers are lower than shit. Hank treated his tricks with disdain. He believed that hustlers shouldn't be too nice, because plenty of tricks would cheat you to get something for nothing. But I saw a bunch of creeps out there on both sides."

After an hour tutoring Jim, Hank hustled a lucrative deal he couldn't afford to ignore. The trick and Hank drove off, so Jim was on his own.

Jim just was too timid and not nearly aggressive enough. He was uncomfortable, didn't like working on the streets and was unable to muster up the courage to assert that he was there for the money. Finally, when a guy was done, Jim would absolutely have to tell him that he was doing it for money, and at that point a guy would not be terribly thrilled.

"It was a degrading thing. It was a lot different from my callboy experiences where the money was already agreed to by the agency and the client. It wasn't easy walking the streets and standing out there like a piece of meat and having people size me up and down. I was too intimidated. I felt shameful having to walk up to those guys and ask them for money. I determined that presenting yourself for sale to guys on the streets was handled more forthrightly and business-like by the bisexual and straight male hustlers out there."

On his first night, Jim ended up with only one paying customer. He returned to the motel with little money. Hank sort of schlepped it off and told Jim to go ahead and put his small amount of scratch on the dresser—Hank said he would take the majority cut of it, and Jim would have the rest. So, Jim placed his night's meager earnings there for Hank to handle.

During his second night, Jim was out on the street for five hours and still couldn't bring himself to approach anybody. "I just could not walk up to them and tell them they'd have to pay. However, one guy called me over and told me he wanted a cheap quickie. I ended up returning to the motel only with pittance to turn over to Hank."

On the third night Jim came back late. Right away Hank demanded the scratch that Jim made that night, but the money added up to practically nothing again. Hank had been drinking and flew into a rage, attacked Jim and beat him. "I didn't understand why. But Hank had learned from experience, curiously, that whores responded positively to beatings, just like his aunt claimed would happen. A normal gay guy would be repulsed and would get the fuck away if he got beaten, but Hank had this odd idea that a sex worker was a different breed, that beatings motivated whores—that a good painful lesson would drive home the reminder that their pimp was in charge of their whore asses. After a battering from Hank, his hustlers always ended up humping harder for him to live up to his dominate demands. They gave him the proper respect he demanded due to his superior position."

"Well, I wasn't his typical whore. Way back when I escaped from my stepfather's abuse, I decided that if anyone ever used violence against me again, that would be it, I would be out of there. I didn't have any money, so I decided to stay a couple more nights and keep his cut for myself."

The next night Hank directed Jim to go out. Jim's face was puffy, but he was determined and motivated. It was like he finally had caught on to the proper techniques. Jim ended up making a lot of money during the next couple of nights. "Guys took me to rented motel rooms, one took me to a run-down apartment, a couple of them wanted to do it right there in their cars and one guy even paid me a large amount to ride with him up to Mulholland Drive so he could get off and then just sit and watch the lights of the city for a while."

When Jim returned to the motel room that night, he hid the majority of his income in the socks he wore. Yet he still had plenty left over to give to Hank, who seemed satisfied with the scratch that Jim placed on the dresser for him. He told Jim, "You're catching on. You only needed a little motivation."

The following night Jim got back to the room and knew Hank would not return for a couple more hours. Jim was not about to hand over to Hank any more of his hard-earned cash. He immediately packed his clothes in his suitcase and split with all of his money.

Jim concluded that selling his body for big bucks was not something he wanted to do with his life. He had made lots of money as a sex worker, but it was not easy earnings. He abandoned that lifestyle. "I decided that the money I made was not really worth it in the long run."

Jim went back to working at low-paying menial jobs, and once again he barely had enough money to live and feed himself. Yet he was decidedly content.

A couple of months later Jim was shopping at a grocery store and ran into the gay manager of the motel where Hank lived. The manager informed Jim that Hank had skipped town.

It turned out that Hank was a U.S. marine who had been AWOL the entire time he had been hustling. A couple of military police investigators had come to the motel late one afternoon searching for Hank. Investigators tracked him down from the motel's phone number that Hank had listed on a savings account he had opened. They wanted to know where he was and also how he had gotten his hands on such a huge sum of money to stash into a secret savings account. The motel manager played dumb, covered for Hank and lied. He told the investigators that they just had missed catching Hank, claiming that he had checked out of the motel less than a week previously. Hours later in the dark early morning after Hank had worked overnight, he returned to the motel. The motel manager was waiting for him and informed him that the military police were looking for him. It took only 10 minutes for Hank to pack up and get the hell out of there.

"After working as a callboy and hustler, I had trouble responding sexually to guys. I found that puzzling. Later on I read books saying the longer you're in the sex trade the harder it is to relate to anyone, and you emotionally dry up. You have so much sex, but it's all about business, just cash and carry. You'd think it would be simple to handle that, but I found myself reluctant to turn on to other guys, even though they might be gay and sexy. For the next half year or so it gradually wore off. If I'd stayed with sex work for a long time—who knows— I even might have resorted to drugs like so many of the others."

Chapter 27

Sugar Daddies

"It struck me that there's probably not much difference between callboys and young guys who go out to bars to meet well-to-do men in a more legit form of prostitution that was both lawful and permissible—everything but cold cash."

Jim still was in his upper twenties and fairly young. Jim's favorite bar was located on one of the side streets of Hollywood. The bar played classical music and offered a variety of imported beers and wines from around the world. A lot of Jim's friends thought the bar was too uppity and preferred more typical bars with ordinary jukeboxes. But Jim liked the upscale bar because the men were older, and he thought they were more cultured.

"Whenever I left a bar with a guy, we'd end up walking two or three blocks to his car. Nobody ever parked next to a gay bar. These men usually had good jobs and didn't want their livelihoods threatened by an arrest."

Jim usually went out with guys a lot more well-to-do than himself—sugar daddies. However, he learned that a lot of them were demanding and lived their lives for themselves, set in their ways and incapable of compromising with any long-term partner. "I was always looking for the Cary Grant types—on the outside suave and debonair and put together. Although some of them were selfish, I always showed all of them my gratitude and respect."

Some of Jim's young friends at the upscale bars were kept by rich men, put on very short leashes and given little independent cash. Some rich men would let a young guy live in their homes. Others owned spare apartments where they kept their young guys available so they could drop in when they wanted to spend time with their concubines. Perhaps a rich guy had a wife or simply needed to hide the queer side of himself. Some kids discovered to their chagrin that the apartments provided by rich guys ended up available to them only while the young guys remained the property of the older guys. The kid would find out the hard way that he had to leave an apartment whenever the man said so, because the rich guy controlled the real estate since the deed was in the rich guy's name. A young guy would depart, and soon after another guy eventually would move in. "Sugar daddies usually didn't treat for an extensively long time."

Jim became more cultured by going out with the mature men. Whichever man he dated, whether he was a designer or a doctor, Jim learned from him. If the guy was a mechanic, Jim learned all about cars from him. Jim learned about buildings from an architect. One guy drove Jim all around the city pointing out the finer details of different styles of buildings, which gave Jim a good working knowledge of architecture.

"I went with an artist during one month-long visit to San Francisco. I was invited to art gallery parties, and I'd sit around with a glass of champagne in my hand being all grand. I would listen to all of these art lovers as they analyzed the pieces displayed: 'My dear, with the depth and perception, I know just what the artist is trying to say.' It was fun hobnobbing with the upper-class set, but everything seemed so pretentious. I went along pretending and made only generalized comments. I knew to never blurt out that some piece of art was ugly. I wanted to be invited back, and I didn't need any enemies in that crowd."

A lot of mature men took Jim to fancy restaurants. Whenever Jim met a guy who suggested going out to a restaurant, it was at the older man's suggestion. "With older men I never heard the dreaded words, 'Let's go Dutch.' Dutch my ass, I was dirt poor, but luckily I was a young good-looking guy at that time, and these mature men wanted my company."

Jim maintained the necessary wardrobe in order to dress up and go out with the older guys. He needed the correct clothes. He owned a dark blue blazer sport coat and various conservative dress slacks. He had a couple of pairs of high-class shoes and took special care to keep them looking brand new. "In those days there were certain rules. You could wear brown shoes and yellow and tans during the day, but after the sun went down you changed into black shoes. Nobody wore brown shoes at night."

"I wasn't with these guys to be a complainer. I was there to be their companion. They were being nice by paying my way, so I always responded in kindness and appreciation. These guys would usually pay by check or even credit card."

Richer guys took Jim to eat at high-end establishments. These restaurants were unlike the middle-class restaurants Jim worked in. "I found it always very quiet in these restaurants, and it could take three or four hours to serve a multi-course meal. I thought it was wonderful. My date and I would sit there and talk, and then a waiter would come over with another course, and we'd eat something else, and the meal would drag on. Then dessert was served, which usually was a sliver of something that tasted extra delicious but was very expensive. I assumed they ate like that all the time, but actually some of them went out only once a month or so. It all felt so good, and I was flattered."

"I learned a lot about high-class restaurants, about the best food, how to order and how various dishes were supposed to be served. With one of my dates, I ate my first Chateaubriand—it was a huge tenderloin steak that was usually served for two people. I learned the differences between T-bone, porterhouse, sirloin and New York strip steaks. I was taught all about wine lists and various points of etiquette. In the movies I'd seen champagne being served in saucer glasses, but I found out that was incorrect, that you're supposed to put champagne in a fluted column."

Jim met a millionaire earlier in his life who moved Jim into his home. Jim was walking along Sunset Boulevard on the Sunset Strip area. A car pulled up, and driving it was a 40-year-old guy. They began talking, and the guy seemed to like Jim. He took Jim to his house—a huge place in the hills with a beautiful view above Los Angeles. "I always knew if I could find a millionaire sugar daddy, he'd take care of me and my problems would be solved. Or so I thought. I discovered that just because you live with a millionaire that doesn't mean you'll get much—neither material nor spiritual. Super rich guys don't really take care of you. You're their play toy."

"Rich guys kept their toys on short reins. I would sit around his big house. He had a maid who came in. At first, he wouldn't leave me there by myself. He'd drive me down the hills and let me off, and I'd walk around wherever I wanted. I didn't have any spending money of my own. I would have to ask him for any money and explain why I thought I needed it. As he got to know me better and began to trust me, he'd have me stay at his house when he was gone. Every night he would take me to dinner at a nice restaurant. He also bought me some fashionable clothes."

At any time, these rich guys could go out and replace their toy. Plenty of other young guys were waiting in line. Jim had no real relationship security. Jim pondered if that truly was what he wanted.

"That relationship only lasted a couple of months or so. Like most young people, I couldn't settle down. That's why in my older years I understood young people. Sometimes I'd meet older sexy men who wanted to settle down with me, but in a week, two, three weeks later I'd start to feel suffocated."

"I still had a whole world before me to explore."

Chapter 28

The Summer of Love

Jim ushered in 1967 with friends at a New Year's Eve party in Hollywood. Drugs now were becoming more common with the younger crowd, and some of his friends began experimenting with LSD. They claimed that their far-out trips enabled them to obtain a great self-realization about the reality of the world because LSD expanded their minds. "I thought, *'Uh, oh. This is crazy. There's no way I'm getting involved with this.'* I was already addicted to cigarettes and was afraid if I messed around in this new drug scene then I'd become addicted to drugs too. Besides, I had enough problems in my life without that monkey on my back."

The New Year's Eve revelers attempted to get high that night by smoking dried banana peels. "A catchy song on the Top 10 rock & roll charts at that time was *Mellow Yellow* by Donovan. A rumor was going around that you could get a hallucinogenic high by smoking banana peels. Donovan's lyrics mentioned 'electrical banana,' which got a lot of people experimenting. Of course, they found out that smoking banana peels didn't do a damn thing for them."

Jim saw Timothy Leary on television, and Jim thought he seemed strange. He was a college professor who got fired for talking up the virtues of psychedelics like LSD, mescaline and psilocybin. Most of society was not ready to hear what he was saying: Turn on to the new cosmic consciousness scene unfolding at that time, tune in to the real world that normally was not perceived and drop out of traditional materialistic education in favor of mystical revelations through psychedelic chemicals.

"I couldn't make heads or tails of what that was all about."

The hippies were emerging into the forefront of young people of the day. In San Francisco the hippies were giving away free meals and clothes. "They preached about poorness as though it was divine. Don't tell me that being poor is something great. Being poor is no noble thing."

Jim kept hearing how the hippies believed in free love, peace and harmony, of being brothers and sisters. It all seemed to Jim to be a mixture of some sort of religion and good will.

On TV Jim saw flower children who handed out free flowers to strangers. At first, he couldn't figure out the flower power phenomenon. Then Jim saw some of them on the streets in LA. They were all young people wearing long baggy clothes. "I was curious and talked to them. They turned out to be nice pleasant people. They weren't like the religious sects—the Moonies or Goonies or whatever the fuck they were called who sold flowers and performed bizarre dances in airports."

"Then in the spring, LA radio stations began playing the song *San Francisco (Be Sure to Wear Flowers in Your Hair)* by Scott McKenzie. It promised that summer in San Francisco would be a big love-in. So I decided I had to go see what this was all about. Maybe I was looking for something, but it was something I needed to witness firsthand. I didn't realize that this precise time would turn out to be the optimum moment to go, because the whole thing lasted for such a very short time."

Jim quit his LA job. It was a job in which everybody there was nice, even the boss. Jim had worked there four or five months, but nonetheless he was drawn back to San Francisco for the coming Summer of Love.

When he arrived at the San Francisco bus station, the people looked normal just like Jim and everybody else in the country—all ordinary. But when he got to Haight-Ashbury, he discovered that this was the focal point of all the new transformative energy. "I saw all these strange people with long hair. For the most part they were very nonviolent, very mellow."

The first thing Jim did was go to the house in the Haight where his old beat friend Jack had helped friends move eight years previously when Jim visited Ruth and was spending lots of time in North Beach. The guys were long gone—no one knew anything about them. Instead of calling the area the Haight, people now called it Haight-Ashbury. The 1950s beat scene of North Beach had morphed into the 1960s hippie scene of Haight-Ashbury. Instead of beats wearing low-key clothes of blacks and grays, they had been replaced by hippies wearing wild colorful flower prints and psychedelic tie-dyed shirts.

Jim was uncertain exactly what the San Francisco hippie philosophy was, but there were good positive feelings all around. The hippies seemed to share everything. There was free food service in the park, a free medical clinic in the neighborhood and stores that gave away free recycled items.

Still, Jim couldn't quite figure it all out—who and what it all meant and what the different jargon being used actually meant. "It was like I had passed through some sort of time warp and landed in another time and place. But I was trying oh so hard to be broad-minded about everything."

"Of course, there were gays in Haight-Ashbury. I'd been invited to a few parties with gay people. They tended to blend in. The gay guys all wore long hair trying to be hippies too. Back then it didn't occur to most straight people during the Summer of Love to question if the person next to them was a homosexual."

In Haight-Ashbury Jim met one of the officers of the gay organization S.I.R. (Society for Individual Rights). The group published a monthly San Francisco gay magazine called *Vector*, which Jim considered just as good and maybe even more interesting in some ways than the old *ONE* magazine. SIR was very organized in San Francisco and held dances and arranged various social activities. Jim's gay activist friend invited him to his home in Haight-Ashbury and explained to Jim a lot about what was going on around them. The SIR officer took Jim to a crash pad that provided sleeping spaces on a floor for people who had no place to stay.

Haight-Ashbury was too crowded and madding for Jim, so he would walk over the hill to a quiet neighboring area called the Castro. It was a nice laid-back working-class neighborhood. Some gay people lived there. The neighborhood was barely beginning to transform into the gay mecca it eventually would become.

The Castro is where Jim met Chuck. They hit it off, and Jim stayed with him. Chuck was a sexy older guy originally from the Midwest who had seen action in the Pacific during World War II. He ended up getting a dishonorable discharge after the war for engaging in homosexual acts. His ship had made a port of call visit to the Bay Area, and he was captivated by the charm of San Francisco, so he decided to return to the city and make it his home.

"At first, we had a real hot thing going on between the two of us, but that cooled because Chuck couldn't keep it in his pants. He was playing with all the hippie guys around town."

Even though Jim began living in the Castro with Chuck, both guys would walk over to the Haight-Ashbury neighborhood at least two or three times a week. "We had a great time there. I spent a lot of days and nights in Haight-Ashbury. I wanted to stay informed about what was going on. I went to a couple of coffee houses and sat around asking people questions and listening to them strum their guitars and sing protest songs against the Vietnam War."

"Along the streets, especially in front of the bars, we'd hear these wailing electric guitars and screeching metal sounds. I wasn't used to that music. I was more comfortable with old time rock & roll. The musicians all looked strange—they all had super-long hair. They sounded strange. Everything there was topsy-turvy from the people and music I knew. As a gay guy I should have been able to accept anything and jump on the bandwagon, but I didn't trust these new surroundings."

"Hippies were dancing throughout Haight-Ashbury, and female flower children would leap forward into the air while pretending to toss imaginary flowers. It was all innocent fun."

"People around me were playing the Beatles new album, *Sgt. Pepper's Lonely Hearts Club Band*. The Beatles originally came out when I was in prison, and to me they seemed like teeny-bopper simple minds: 'She loves you, yeah, yeah, yeah.' They certainly had a lot of girls screaming in excitement at their concerts, but that just drowned out their music. I didn't realize at the time that their manager Brian Epstein was gay. It wasn't until *Sgt. Pepper* and the Summer of Love that I really began liking the Beatles."

It seemed to Jim as though everybody was visiting Golden Gate Park, grooving on the free concerts and love happenings. Allen Ginsberg had appeared there earlier in the year along with Timothy Leary, Dick Gregory and Jerry Rubin during San Francisco's 1967 "Gathering of the Tribes for a Human Be-In" with around 25,000 young people in attendance. The popular gay beat poet who wrote the famous homoerotic poem "Howl" had been prominent during the beat era in North Beach giving poetry readings. Now he still remained popular—with hippies chanting mantras for meditating. He coined the phrase "flower power," which influenced the country by instilling positive anti-war values of peace and love instead of anti-war mass violence and brute rebellion.

Performing music for the crowds at Golden Gate Park were San Francisco musical groups Jefferson Airplane and the Grateful Dead.

The top bands played at the big Fillmore Auditorium concert hall on Market Street. Long lines of people at the Fillmore would wait to get into the sold-out concerts. "I would see the shows advertised on psychedelic posters—half the words I couldn't even read because the letters looked so elastic and stretched. The posters were posted all over the city advertising bands with strange names like Moby Grape and Sopwith Camel and Deep Purple—strange, strange names. Whoever thought those posters would be worth a lot of money nowadays?"

One day Jim was walking with a hippie acquaintance who stopped at a sidewalk shop to show Jim a poster of a big spiritual music event that he had attended earlier in the year in San Francisco. It had included a performance by Big Brother and the Holding Company. Jim thought, *"Another strange band with another strange name."*

"To me the band's name sounded as exciting as seltzer water, but the guy I was with was enthusiastic. When we got to his place, he wanted me to listen to the band's new record he'd just bought. He told me the band members lived in San Francisco. Well, I heard this woman with a gravelly whiskey voice going boourwooouuu. I told him, 'That's terrible. It sounds like some old floozy singing for whorehouses—a bunch of scratchy caterwauling. Who is that old broad? She's awful.' He said, 'No, you have to listen to the whole thing. It's their lead singer, Janis Joplin. Here's what she looks like.' I was surprised at how young she looked on the back of the album."

"Before long San Francisco radio stations began playing the song *Down on Me* from the new album. She belted out the song in a coarse wailing blues style, and I actually started liking the song. Later a friend bought the album *Cheap Thrills* that contained the song *Piece of My Heart*. Then three years later when she died of a drug overdose at 27 years old, I really was disappointed. After her death all the radio stations played *Me and Bobby McGee* from her *Pearl* album, and I became an even bigger fan of hers."

On Haight Street Jim met a nice-looking hippie guy who was barefoot with no shirt. The guy was so friendly that Jim got the distinct impression that the guy was cruising him. They talked for a while, and the guy invited Jim to his apartment. Jim figured he was in for a treat.

"When we arrived, there was the guy's girlfriend. His apartment turned out to be a typical hippie pad. It had cushions on the floor and psychedelic blacklight posters and a stereo—no TV—and lots of big ashtrays for marijuana. The guy explained to me that he was a real hippie. He believed in communal living and this and that and free love and all those good things. His friends started arriving, and they all decided to drop some LSD. We all were in for a far-out psychedelic experience. I told them, 'I hate to miss out, but I've got to be somewhere in a few minutes.' And I left."

"I never really got into drugs. Eight years before in San Francisco when I visited Ruth, I smoked marijuana with Jack the beat guy in North Beach. I didn't particularly care for it. From the 1960s through the rest of my life I really didn't do drugs."

Jim liked spending time in the Polk Street area also, because it was a predominant gay area in the city before the Castro began turning into a gay neighborhood. Jim met a good-looking gay guy on Polk Street who invited Jim up to his apartment. "We had a lot of fun that evening together. He wanted me to smoke marijuana with him, so since I wanted to impress the sexy guy I said okay. It tasted terrible and stunk. Again, I wondered what was so special about it. When I was leaving to go back to the Castro, my new gay friend told me, 'Be careful, this is strong stuff.' I started walking along Polk Street loaded, and before long I was looking at cracks in the sidewalk thinking, *'I'm walking a little funny—I've got to straighten up so the cops don't stop me.'* The next minute it seemed like I'd already walked five or six blocks and crossed a couple of street lights, *'How'd I get here so fast? Man, this is so screwy.'*"

"I avoided all drugs the rest of my time in San Francisco. To me the drugs were silly. Curiously though, the true marijuana smokers were very mellow and cool. There'd be rolled fat marijuana joints among all these large ashtrays strewn on the tables. People at parties also were into psychedelics like LSD and magic mushrooms. I watched everything happen from a straight and sober vantage point and never was tempted to try any of these drugs."

Most of the hippies at these places were straight and were trying to change society. Ideal San Francisco hippies invited people into their homes, and many shared what they had. Nobody was ripping off others. It was all about peace and brotherhood. It was simple—for the most part these people had given up materialism. The hippies wore secondhand clothes. Some of them didn't even lock their doors.

"I found it to be pretty wonderful. Unfortunately, it lasted for only a quick moment in time. It seemed like overnight I noticed things starting to change. Summer 1967 vacation season began, and Haight-Ashbury started busting at the seams with people. In June schools let out across the nation, and college and high school students and even some junior high students began the great pilgrimage that summer to San Francisco. They started arriving en masse. Misfits and oddballs also pounced into the neighborhoods. Everybody was pretending to be hippies but doing poor jobs of it. They really weren't serious— they were faking it—and things turned unpleasant. These new people were filthy and couldn't care less that their garbage should have been put into trash barrels. A couple of times I saw people urinating in the street. They left the park an absolute pigsty. It was like every rule was being broken. And a lot of those new people were not nice."

"I heard that one guy on LSD jumped out of an upper-floor window because he thought he was like some superman. Abnormal freaky things like that frightened mainstream American society. Haight Street became clogged with summer tourists gawking from their cars, although they didn't dare venture out onto the streets."

Weeks prior, everything seemed to be mellow and carefree. The new social phenomenon had become a wonderful ideal. But American society proved to be an inhospitable environment for this new spiritual quest to flourish. The money-makers edged in and began to capitalize on the news coverage—the media's free publicity.

"The stores began inflating their prices. Small shops began selling used clothing for exorbitant prices—no poor person could afford them anymore. A person could end up paying a couple hundred dollars just for a fancy Sgt. Pepper coat to wear to a concert. People wore the strangest mixtures of clothes. It was like a costume party 24 hours a day."

Where there had been free concerts in the park, the entrepreneurs got involved and began charging money for concerts. The price of food in some restaurants increased sky high.

"I saw how the professional dope dealers elbowed their way into the scene and brought in hard drugs—I mean really heavy stuff like heroin. Skirmishes determined who controlled the drug supplies. I'd watch how people reacted to those hard drugs at parties, and a lot of them acted obnoxious. Sometimes I couldn't even figure out what those drugged-out people were trying to say. They were indulging in all kinds of fucked up drugs—speed, downers, prescription pills. I never heard of cocaine being around because it was so expensive at that time."

Jim would walk into parties where bowls of colorful pills were displayed like colored mints being offered. "People would come in and scoop them up. I couldn't understand people putting their trust in those pills. How in the world could they know what was in them?"

"I'd ask about a pill, and someone might say, 'Well, this is speed. It'll make you talk all the time.' I certainly didn't need that because I never was at a loss for words. Then somebody would say, 'Well, this one is a depressant or downer. It'll depress your mood.' I knew I didn't need that either—I could get depressed quite easily on my own."

"Free love was all around. I discovered that free love became a scam for straight guys to screw all the chicks they wanted. For the men it was wonderful; however, the women were still expected to serve food, get this, get that, have babies if they got pregnant and give it up to men who wanted it. These new fake hippie guys were as chauvinistic as most men in America before them."

By summer's end Jim could see that many of the people now in Haight-Ashbury seemed to be the fakes—the money handlers, the dope dealers, the prostitutes and the trendy people with fabulously expensive clothes.

The original authentic hippies began getting out of town. The new people in the area no longer held true hippie ideals in high regard. At the end of the summer some real hippies who remained in San

Francisco held a mock funeral for what they called the death of the hippie.

A couple of original hippies that Jim had gotten acquainted with fled to quiet communes in rural areas. The communal living and organic farming fit their lifestyle better than the city could. "I was tempted to go to a commune too because I kind of admired their core ideals. But I didn't want to try to fit into a commune where I'd be the only gay person living there."

Within a half-decade later, gay collectives and communal farms were organized by gays wanting to live a quiet country lifestyle. The rural gays communicated with each other through a country journal called *RFD*, named after the post office's rural free delivery service. A lot of gays referred to *RFD* by the nickname *Radical Faerie Digest*. However, before all of that evolved, Jim's life had progressed in other directions.

By the end of summer all of the new fair-weather hippies began returning home, going back to school, back to jobs, back to nice clothes, back to a middle-class lifestyle—back to The American Way.

As the summer wore on, Jim spent less and less time in Haight-Ashbury. By autumn he ended up spending most of his time with gay people in the Castro and on Polk Street. In late spring when he originally had arrived in Haight-Ashbury, he thought the answer was that all of the love there would naturally accommodate gay people into the hippie movement. "However, I found out that most of the people who reached San Francisco that summer were just as homophobic as the people they'd left back home. My gay friends grew their hair long and tried to fit it, but they told me of going to parties where these newly-arrived fake hippies didn't like gay people any more than the other people across the good nation."

After spending a half-year or so in San Francisco, Jim decided to return to LA before Thanksgiving. It had been a thrill for him to join the gentle people of San Francisco with the flowers in their hair, but now the idealism had been drained. "I'd learned all I needed to know about that scene. Even though I'd been in the midst of Haight-Ashbury during the Summer of Love, I felt too removed from the core essence of the scene. Maybe I was getting too old—after all, in less than a couple of years I would turn 30 years old."

"I departed San Francisco on an upbeat note. One of Chuck's friends had a job in theatrical stage production. Through his connections he obtained a copy of the album *Hair*, the original off-Broadway cast recording. Producers were getting ready for a run of the new stage play on Broadway in New York in the coming year. As I prepared to leave San Francisco, the wonderful music of *Hair* provided some faith in the goodness of the world. It proclaimed that Jupiter was going to align with Mars and peace was going to guide the planets. This now was supposed to be the dawning of the Age of Aquarius. I could only hope so."

Chapter 29

L.A. Bar Raid

Back in Los Angeles one night, Jim's roommate Arley struck up a conversation with a guy he met at an LA gay bar and left with him. Arley was excited about being taken to the sexy guy's crib to be alone together. Arley could tell the guy was horny. As soon as they sat down in the guy's car, the guy draped his arm over Arley's shoulder. The guy was hot to trot and immediately was anxious to know what Arley was into. So, Arley told him just what he wanted to do, and that is when a second man emerged from the back floorboard, and they arrested Arley on the spot. Arley was irritated at himself for at least not glancing at the back seat and discovering there was a guy hiding there. He had been too distracted by his seemingly excellent luck in attracting this good-looking guy.

In the 1950s and 1960s many of Jim's friends and acquaintances had been targeted by police and arrested—a common practice across the country. Some of Jim's friends had experienced police oppression first-hand, but those who had not been targeted knew others who had been arrested on trumped up charges. Some guys wore it as a badge of honor. Jim knew from experience that being gay meant he always would be taking chances.

"I went to a popular gay bar on Hollywood Boulevard one night. They had a large painting hanging on one of their walls of Barbara Stanwyck from the movie *Walk on the Wild Side* where she played a butch madam running a whorehouse. Of course, the implication was that her character was a lesbian. The women under her were straight, more or less. The painting was one of the very few things I remember about the bar. I can't recall the bar's name, but it was well known."

That night the lights went off in the bar, and the police came in with long flashlights and conducted a bar raid. They made everybody line up and hauled off the guys who looked queer to them and anyone who had been caught touching, dancing or camping it up. An undercover cop had slipped into the bar before the raid and identified the lawbreakers. "The scuttlebutt was that as soon as rookie cops got out of the police academy, the department would pick the best-looking ones and teach them how to use queer lingo and how to dress and cruise the fag bars."

"During the raid the cops seemed to zero in on the effeminate queens to take out and load into the paddy wagon—including me. I guess I had committed the great sin that night of hugging a friend."

"While the police hauled us criminals to the station, we all tried to make the best of the situation. If I had to survive some calamity, I'd much rather be with a few screaming queens who at least would have a sense of humor and make light of it: 'Oh Mary, just think of the bright side of it. We might meet Mr. Right among all those good-looking men down there.' If the paddy wagon had been hauling a bunch of masculine gay guys, those butch guys would have been fretting about their jobs or worried that their parents might find out—or that their wife might find out. Queens didn't worry about such nuisances; besides, when you're young you think you're immortal, and no matter what happens you'll survive."

"After the cops got us hauled to the jail we just waited and waited there. All the while the cops were telling us what a bunch of lousy queers we were and other crap."

The newspapers often would report homosexual arrests. Police and politicians wanted to give the public the impression that they were cracking down on gambling, prostitution and homosexuality. The cops tended to ramp up publicized busts of homosexuals during election seasons.

Most of the guys the police rounded up from the bar raid got released by the following morning either through posting bail or by someone arriving there and getting them out. Nobody had been sleepy that first night. They just sat around and talked. Two days later only Jim and one other guy remained in jail. "The jailers told both of us they were preparing to move us to the main jail for all of Los Angeles, but a couple hours later a guard released us. The cops returned our belts and shoe laces and our watches and wallets, and then we walked out of jail."

Jim still faced charges and would be required to show up at a preliminary hearing. There was one major problem—he had a record for doing time in the slammer in Texas. It all looked ominous. He was afraid that if he were convicted, which was likely, he would become a repeat offender, and he figured that might mean he would face additional time locked up. Jim was unprepared to face it all. He thought about running back to Idaho or another state when a short official letter arrived in the mail telling him that all charges had been dropped.

"What a fucking waste of everybody's time and energy."

Chapter 30

Lenora & Phil

During Jim's visits to San Francisco in the late 1960s he often would stay with one of his best friends—Lenora Cantrell. She was a straight woman in her sixties with long gray hair and a very slim body. She claimed she was a psychic.

Jim was staying at a large boarding house that housed senior citizens. He earned his keep by working in the dining room. "I'd seen Lenora eating there a couple of times. One day she walked in with a friend of hers, and the three of us started talking while I was serving them. They could tell I was gay, and they were charming. They sort of liked me. Very often Lenora's friends who lived elsewhere would stop in and accompany her to lunch or dinner. People who didn't live in the boarding house could come in and buy a tasty inexpensive meal."

Lenora was in show business. She worked as a talent agent for San Francisco area nightclubs and represented various jazz musicians. She also represented a set of curiosity acts including a transsexual singer.

"When I first met Lenora, she was representing the woman who was eating with her that day. Lenora's guest had been a showgirl for years and was a former stripper who put tassels on her breasts. She would rotate one clockwise and the other counterclockwise; I figured that took a lot of control and coordination to do; but I found it hard to believe, because at my age I couldn't imagine anybody that old ever doing wild appalling things."

Lenora and Jim became friends. Jim was always interested in anything and anyone connected to show business. Whenever he was in San Francisco and Lenora needed somebody to go out with her, Jim would escort her. Her job was to promote her clients, so she and Jim would drop in on all of the straight nightclubs. She introduced Jim to a lot of intriguing people in San Francisco. He met a lot of musicians and their managers. "It was so grand! There'd be some jazz group playing in front of a large crowd, and we'd walk right up to our reserved seats in front and sit down. It really felt special."

"Lenora and I often went to a place called Enrico's Coffeehouse, which was on the first floor beneath a nightclub called Finocchio's where all the drag shows were performed. One night at Enrico's she introduced me to a friend of hers, a famous *San Francisco Chronicle* newspaper columnist named Herb Caen. She often managed to get her name and her clients' names placed in his columns."

"Lenora and I always had a lot of fun together. We had this game we'd play—I'd pretend to be her boyfriend. We'd sit there, and I'd snap my fingers, and she'd pull out a cigarette to give to me; and I'd snap my fingers again, and she'd light it for me. That was just one bit of our fun together."

"One day Lenora asked me if I'd like to go with her to a hotel and meet Andy Warhol. I'd read enough in the press to know that he was the guy who had created pop art paintings of Campbell Soup cans and screen prints of Marilyn Monroe. I also had seen one of his movies. He coined the phrase, 'In the future everyone will be famous for 15 minutes.' I wasn't particularly interested in meeting him, but Lenora said that he had brought with him three or four of his Warhol superstars from The Factory. I thought maybe I'd get to meet his sexy hunky film star Joe Dallesandro. So I went along, but Joe wasn't there."

"Lenora introduced me to Andy, and he didn't say a word. He had these dark glasses on, this white blondish hair, and he was completely white. It was strange that he wouldn't say anything. I wasn't particularly impressed with him, but he was somebody famous, so I tried to be hip and cool."

∇

"While in San Francisco I met Phil. He took me to his nice small apartment for dinner. Phil's specialty was beef stroganoff—a real treat in those days. He never followed a recipe. He just bought the ingredients and threw the meal together."

Phil became enthralled with Jim. Phil was turning 40—about 10 years older than Jim. He was balding, and he was a little heavy. "I thought he was sweet with a nice personality. He was a wonderful partner, although kind of demanding."

Phil had a responsible job as a floral designer. He worked for a San Francisco floral company, but he was dissatisfied with that job. So he found a better job south of San Francisco in the beach town of Santa Cruz where Phil became a popular floral designer. "In fact they announced in local Santa Cruz newspaper ads that Phil from San Francisco had arrived."

He ran a small shop with his own name attached to it. He made a good income selling to rich people in exclusive neighborhoods up in the mountains above Santa Cruz. He created beautiful flower arrangements—huge expensive pieces that sold for two or three hundred dollars—a lot of money in those days.

"I loved Santa Cruz. Phil and I would stroll down the remarkable beachfront that featured amusement rides along the boardwalk. Then we'd have fun walking out on the charming old pier."

Phil still was unsatisfied and wanted to be in a top shop. After about a half year in Santa Cruz he decided he and Jim were moving again. So they packed up the dishes and essentials, stuffed Phil's car and moved down to Los Angeles.

"We arrived in LA, and in no time Phil got himself a job. He was aggressive about those things and got hired at a really good job working for a big company where he could be Mr. In-Charge and be taken seriously. We settled down near his work in Burbank, north of central LA—'beautiful downtown Burbank,' which was anything but."

The two guys had been getting along fairly well, but things started changing. "Phil decided we needed some pets. So one day he brings home two fucking Siamese cats. I'm not much of a cat person, and guess who had to take care of them? These cats made strange fiend-like caterwauling noises, and they jumped on people's backs and clawed at things."

Jim and Phil's relationship began to deteriorate, and they started arguing a lot. Jim left when Phil slapped him. He went back to San

Francisco and stayed with Lenora. Phil kept calling from LA asking Jim to come back. Jim was bemoaning the situation to Lenora asking her, "Should I give it another try? He wants to get back together."

"Lenora told me she would read her tarot cards to find the answer. I told Lenora that I needed real friend-to-friend advice, not some hocus-pocus fortune telling. She insisted that she'd discover if Phil was the man for me. I finally said okay, but I knew better than to stake my life on some card reading."

"Lenora dealt the cards and arranged them. She told me, 'I do see a man, but it can't be Phil. Phil is south of you. The man I see is to your east. It will be the true thing, and it will last forever.' But then Lenora told me the man was a tall blonde. Right away I figured she didn't know what she was talking about, because I'd always been attracted to men with dark hair, not blondes. I always thought fortune telling was fake anyway. Nevertheless, I did appreciate Lenora trying to help me in her own way."

Jim and Phil decided to try and work things out in LA. "At least Phil had missed me and hadn't replaced me with someone else. We tried and tried, but within a couple of weeks I knew it was pretty much over. The relationship was not getting any better. Finally Phil told me, 'It's not going to work. It's just over.' And I felt the same way. So we parted ways with okay feelings, but it hurt because I couldn't make it work with Phil."

Jim returned to San Francisco and stayed a couple more months with Lenora. He worked at a catering job to save up some money. He had his fill of California. None of Jim's relationships had ever worked out. Now it was spring 1969—time to move on again.

Chapter 31

First Years in Denver

J im was tired. He needed a new beginning and a new place to start over.

"In the back of my mind I remembered the wonderful things my good prison friend Peaches told me about Denver and the Colorado mountains. I'd never been there before and figured there wasn't any reason I shouldn't try it out."

Jim used the money he had saved from his San Francisco catering job and bought a bus ticket to Reno. He planned to lay over there and enjoy a day or two in the city. Then he would purchase another ticket for the remainder of his trip to Denver.

"The previous two times I'd been in Nevada I was too young to gamble. Finally, I was old enough to play the games—unfortunately. I started tempting fortune and caught the fever. Within a couple of hours I lost most of my money. Before I gambled away my entire savings, I decided I absolutely had to stop playing. I was never going to make back the money I lost."

Lady Luck cost Jim the money he needed for riding a bus from Reno to Denver, so he decided to hitchhike and save his last few dollars so he could apply that money toward his new beginning in Colorado.

After a couple of days hitchhiking the roads, Jim finally made it to Denver. It was June 1969. Right away he could sense the more pleasing laid-back quality of life that seemed to envelop the Mile High City.

Denver was a youth-oriented city full of newcomers who had moved from the older decaying cities of the East, the Midwest and the small towns on the plains. Winter weather was cold, and older people were not keen on moving to the frigid Colorado climate. Colorado's young people took advantage of nearby mountain activities—skiing, snowmobiling, snowshoeing, hiking, hunting and camping.

Many of the gay guys in Denver sported a rugged bearded outdoors look complete with jeans, flannel shirts and hiking boots. A half decade later Jim's friends claimed that the Colorado look was a precursor of San Francisco's Castro Clone look in the mid-1970s that defined the masculine gay American male—boots, jeans, t-shirts, bomber jackets and mirrored aviator sunglasses.

Singles apartments in Denver were abundant. A hefty percentage of out-gay people in Colorado lived in Denver's Capitol Hill gay neighborhood located on the eastern side of the Colorado State Capitol. As with other gay ghettos across the USA, gay and straight businesses sprang up to capitalize on the needs and interests of prospective gay customers.

On Jim's first day there he found a job at a Capitol Hill restaurant. He had enough money to rent a cheap room for a couple of weeks in a hotel across from the state capitol on busy Colfax Avenue, the main thoroughfare running east/west across the entire length of the Denver metro area.

"By this time in my life I started feeling that I needed to settle down. I'd been through it all, and I was disillusioned. I really didn't enjoy going to bars. I hated liquor. I didn't like the taste of any of it— even beer—and I thought wine was bitter. I might have had an occasional social drink with vodka when I wanted to fit in with the crowd, but it all seemed so frivolous. I rarely hooked up with any guys from bars. I'd been through all that stuff, and what did I have for it? I preferred meeting guys through other friends."

"I'd met interesting people throughout my life. Like all young people, I couldn't settle down in my earlier years. I'd meet these older men out there. They were at an age that they would want to settle down, fall in love with me and all that. I always succumbed to their charms, but after weeks I'd become disenchanted. I had adventures to live and places to explore. Traveling around was exciting—certain parts of it anyway."

"I think one of the reasons older people are attracted to younger people is that the young are impulsive. They don't have a home or material possessions. They're like mercury. You can't quite control them. When you're young you decide things on the spur of the moment. You say, 'Hey, let's go to this place, let's go to that place.' But as you get older you say, 'Gee, I think I'll do it next month, so I'll save up my money, and hopefully I'll get to go.'"

Denver was a different environment. Gay events in Denver primarily consisted of frivolities such as Imperial Court crossdressing events, the gay talent contest Mr. Jockey Shorts in search of the sexiest men, and the Mouse Awards bestowing recognition in the gay community in categories such as best bartender and best bar owner. Even though those events raised funds, they were not the type of fundraisers Jim was interested in attending.

"To me the movement was about fighting oppression head-on. Not all of us wanted to go to the gay bars."

$$\nabla$$

Jim now had been out of prison for about four years. The sweat, stink and memories of what it was like toiling under the blazing sun of a Texas chain gang were fading.

"Wonderful things in Denver seemed to serendipitously fall into place. I stayed away from the bar scene and mainly went to a couple of gay record hops and to parties in private homes. I loved Denver's gay park, Cheesman Park. It was a wonderful convenient setting for escaping to the outdoors."

Cheesman Park was located in the Capitol Hill neighborhood next to the Denver Botanic Gardens. The southern end of the park was where Denver's gay crowd congregated for fun in the sun. Its signature component was a neoclassical Greek-style pavilion and reflecting pool. The park featured small circular meandering roads and pathways that joined together almost like a figure 8.

"At most gay parks where I'd had fun, people got out of their cars and walked around looking to meet people and maybe find a relationship or simply a pickup for casual sex. At Cheesman Park men would drive around and cruise from inside their cars. In Denver I became friends with an old gay man named Francis Trebor-Davis who told me that as soon as Cheesman Park opened in 1907, homosexuals adopted the southern section of it as their own."

Older gay men described to gay historians a time back in the late 1800s and early 1900s when homosexuals cruised city parks in the USA, except instead of riding in automobiles the men cruised in horse-drawn carriages.[29] "I could imagine homosexual men in Denver around the beginning of the 1900s cruising Cheesman Park in their buggies on the park's carriageways."

Three weeks after Jim arrived in Denver, three American astronauts were on their way to the Moon for the first time ever. Jim sat at the park's pavilion in the evening looking up in the sky contemplating what it would be like for the astronauts to land and walk on the lunar surface. "As I thought about the men getting closer to the Moon, a voice behind me said, 'Do you think they'll make it?' He knew exactly what I was thinking. The guy sat down, and we chatted for a long time. We seemed to hit it off. He invited me for coffee at his place, and he was nice, so I went with him."

His name was John Koop Bergmann. Jim and John had a lot in common. John also had lived previously in the LA area. In fact some of his relatives were still living there. He was a Nebraska boy whose father had immigrated to the USA from Germany. John was a typical Aryan blue-eyed blonde, tall, chiseled, masculine, and a decade older than Jim.

"Before long, John's telling me that he loves me, and he wants to live together with me for the rest of his life. I'm thinking, *'Is he really serious? I've heard this before.'* Eventually I realized that I'd also fallen madly in love with John."

Jim ended up remaining with John, and they spent all of their time together. They furnished their place with nice living room furniture, a comfortable bedroom set, kitchen equipment and glass china cabinets. Every couple of months they would add another piece or two to their Waterford crystal collection that John purchased for Jim, which included water glasses, candy dishes, ashtrays and a small crystal owl.

"We were very content with our lives together and spent almost every night by ourselves just talking and watching television and reading. It was really nice. The only time we went out was to go to restaurants to eat quiet dinners together. Once in a while we'd invite another couple to our home, and we'd all enjoy a home-cooked meal and good conversation."

Figure 42: Jim and John in Denver.

John and Jim settled together in an apartment in the Capitol Hill neighborhood at 14th Avenue & Pearl Street.[30] Eventually they moved to Denver's Arvada suburb and finally bought a townhouse in the suburb of Northglenn.

Figure 43: John & Jim's apartment located inside an apartment building at 14th Avenue & Pearl Street, Denver.

"Before John came along, I'd never met anybody who truly loved me the way he did. He always was looking out for my well-being. I think I really matured in Denver. Now that I had John, I really did have security finally." John earned a solid income. He worked for a company called Automatic Laundry installing and repairing washers and dryers in commercial laundromats, apartment buildings and private homes.

John was old-fashioned in many respects. He preferred Jim to stay home and keep house and make everything comfortable for him. In turn, Jim spent his time doting on John.

Although they agreed on a lot, when it came to their birth families, they had different perspectives and experiences. John's mother died when he was young. "It left a hole in his heart. He always loved and missed her a great deal. I hadn't been back to see my mother in a decade. He kept encouraging me to go back to see her and re-established our relationship. I refused to go, 'You don't understand. I don't like being around her and her husband. I've gotten nothing but grief from her.' John thought I should treat my mother better. Eventually he wore down my resistance, so I reluctantly went back with John to visit her."

Figure 44: Jim, 1974. Payette, Idaho; at the home of Fannie & Fred.

237

Fannie and Fred lived on a small farm they had purchased near Payette, Idaho on the Idaho/Oregon border just northwest of Boise. They remained there for the remainder of their lives.

"My mother kept pretending that John and I were just friends, and John would go right along with the farce. Everybody seemed to like John, but they referred to us as roommates. I was miserable in the midst of all the bullshit and lies and deceptions. I didn't want to cope with it, so we stayed in a motel instead of staying in my mother's home. As far as I was concerned the trip wasn't worth it. After a day or two I was itching to return home to Denver, and we left."

Chapter 32

From Mattachine to Gay Liberation

After spending a couple of years working as a homemaker every day, getting outside the home began appealing to Jim. The counterculture movement was growing, and gay rights groups were organizing across the country. Jim decided to get involved. "I guess I could have been selfish and sat back and decided that John and I had our own life and intended to spend all of our time together with each other. But I didn't think like that and neither did John. John actually liked the idea of me doing volunteer activities—kind of like rich housewives who didn't work but got involved with charity groups and ladies' auxiliaries."

"In Denver I became good friends with Elver Barker who was an inspiration to me."

Figure 45: Elver Barker, Jim's friend in Denver.

"Back in 1954 Elver was living in San Francisco and was a member of the Mattachine Society there and served on its Board of Directors. He was fired from his job as a social worker because he was discovered to be a homosexual. In 1956 he moved to Denver and was an art teacher during the time I knew him."

In Denver, Elver maintained his contacts with the Mattachine Society in California. He continued to write for the nationwide *Mattachine Review* under the pseudonym of Carl B. Harding and prepared gay educational documents for Mattachine area councils nationwide.

In 1957 Elver Barker founded and organized the Denver Area Council of the Mattachine Society. It encompassed a ten-state area that was based in Colorado. Monthly meetings were often attended by 30 to 40 local members.[31]

Helping Elver to organize were six other charter members. A handful of Mattachine members ran the local council. Two important members were Rolland Karcher (pseudonym Rolland Howard) and Harry Bateman (pseudonym David L. Daniels)[32]—they both wrote and edited the *Denver Area Newsletter* published by the organization during all four years of the council's existence. Another vital gay member was Wendell Sayers[33] who volunteered legal advice to the group. He was a lawyer who worked in the Colorado State Capitol building and was the first Black assistant attorney general ever employed by the Colorado State Attorney General's Office.[34]

"Elver introduced me to some of the former Denver members. It was fascinating listening to them recall stories of Denver from the 1940s and 1950s."

The Denver Area Council offered discussion forums, theater parties, picnics, holiday dinners, rummage sales, guest speakers and a library. It influenced the lives of participants who discussed their anxieties and discovered that their problems were neither unique nor insolvable.

Two years after the Denver Area Council formed, it hosted the nationwide Mattachine Society's 1959 Sixth Annual National Convention in Denver. Attending were over 60 participants from across the country (and a couple of Denver undercover morals officers in the audiences observing the gatherings).

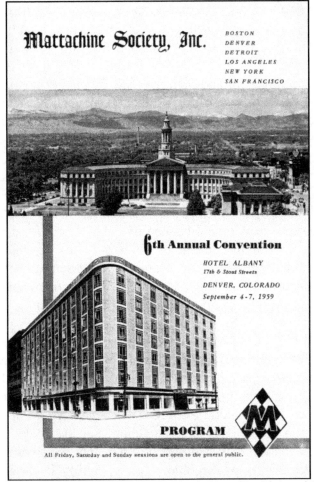

Figure 46: Front cover of Mattachine Society Program for the Mattachine 6th Annual Convention in Denver. September 4-7, 1959. [Courtesy of ONE Archives at the USC Libraries]

The convention's public relations work generated unprecedented positive press coverage from Denver's two daily newspapers—*Rocky Mountain News* and *The Denver Post*—with headlines such as "Society Probes Problem of Perversion" and "Group Seeks to End Homosexual Stigma." Mattachine's local Denver council viewed the press coverage as a breakthrough in the conspiracy of silence. As a result, the group experienced an increase in phone calls, mail and memberships.

Many newspaper readers viewed the 1959 homosexual convention as revolting and infuriating. Authorities conducted undercover operations of Mattachine members, and a month after the convention the Denver Police Department raided the organization's library inside librarian Bill Matson's apartment and arrested him. He was sentenced to 60 days in jail and a $100 fine for illegal possession of pornographic literature and pictures. *The Denver Post* published his name, address and the name of his employer. The impact was immediate. Bill Matson lost his job, and Denver's Mattachine Society faced a sudden steep decrease in membership.

A couple of years later in March 1961 the Denver Area Council of the Mattachine Society was out of business. The nationwide Mattachine Society, which originally had been headquartered in Los Angeles, had been taken over in 1953 through a power play by the San Francisco Area Council headed by "Hal" Harold Call; and they moved the Mattachine headquarters from Los Angeles to San Francisco. In 1961 the San Francisco Mattachine headquarters revoked the charters of all Mattachine area councils nationwide, including the Denver group, in order to centralize political power into its San Francisco headquarters.

Hal Call had a headstrong, long history in the gay movement.

He had been an army lieutenant in World War II's South Pacific operations battling the Japanese. Back home in civilian life he was fired from his job working for a big city newspaper, because he had been arrested in a roundup of homosexuals. After that he moved to San Francisco and joined the Mattachine Society in 1953. Shortly after that Hal and a small contingent of gay conservatives engineered the takeover of the Mattachine Society, taking it away from its original communist founders.

The new conservative leaders governed the organization cautiously in response to the hysteria of the 1950s government hunt for communists and homosexuals. Hal and other Mattachine conservatives were intent on safeguarding the Mattachine Society's primary fight for homosexuals without the Society taking on a distracting fight that might be caused by any possible revelations about the original founders' communist associations. Already, the U.S. House Un-American Activities Committee had called upon founding Mattachine member Harry Hay to testify about his communist activities; however, investigators failed to uncover his connections with the gay Mattachine Society.

Hal and the other new leaders moved the Society's headquarters from Los Angeles to San Francisco. Hal became leader/president of the Mattachine Society. In 1955 he began editing and publishing the organization's monthly magazine *The Mattachine Review*. He and friend Don Lucas created their own printing company in San Francisco, Pan Graphic Press, to prevent any possible problems with printers who might end up having a problem with homosexual content. The printing business earned money by printing the publication and other homophile publications including the lesbian publication *The Ladder*, the gay business directory *Bob Damron's Address Book* and bar owner Helen P. Branson's 1957 book *Gay Bar*.

Figure 47: Still from "The Rejected," a 1961 documentary about homosexuals aired on KQED-TV San Francisco. (at left) Don Lucas, executive secretary of the Mattachine Society and (at right) Hal Call, president of the Mattachine Society. [Courtesy Thirteen Productions LLC, New York, WNET New York]

New York's Mattachine area council had argued that Hal and Don's printing company presented a conflict of interest and accused Hal and Don of using Mattachine money to support themselves. Hal countered that he and others never received fair remuneration for all of the hours they had worked on *The Mattachine Review*. This fight is what led to the move in 1960 by Hal Call and Mattachine leaders in San Francisco to revoke the licenses and dissolve all area councils across the country (including the Denver Area Council) in order to maintain autocratic control from the San Francisco headquarters.

The Denver Area Council of the Mattachine Society regrouped, and its leaders and members formed a successor organization, calling it The Neighbors—and consequently Denver's second homosexual rights organization was in operation.

The Neighbors group ended its operations a mere few months later in 1961. During the following decade no major gay rights groups existed in Denver.

Jim was captivated listening to his friend Elver Barker explain what all occurred with Denver's first two homosexual rights groups—the Denver Area Council of the Mattachine Society and The Neighbors.

∇

Jim's move to Denver coincided with a new robust national discourse about homosexuality.

"During my first summer in Denver I found out about another gay uprising and rebellion that just had occurred—this time in New York City. I thought this one seemed a lot like the other gay public uprisings and protests and demonstrations that occurred before it: Like the 1959 Cooper Do-Nuts gay uprising in downtown LA that my friend Juan had been involved with; like the 1966 gay riot at Compton's cafeteria in San Francisco's Tenderloin District; and like the 1967 New Year's night raid of LA's Black Cat Tavern where police beat customers and employees, and in response were gay demonstrations and public protests."

The new 1969 gay uprising in New York City was at the Stonewall Inn gay bar on Christopher Street. At this storied historic event, as cops were loading customers into a police paddy wagon a rebellion erupted. Hundreds ended up protesting. Crowds threw beer cans, rocks, bricks and reportedly even parking meters at the cops.[35] The cops retreated into the bar and called for police backup. It was not until a couple of nights later that New York's riot police were able to restore order, and even then, protestors kept demonstrating for days.

The Mattachine Society of New York immediately distributed flyers encouraging homosexuals to unite in common action that asked, "Where Were You During the Christopher Street Riots?"[36] Quickly, the Christopher Street riots became known famously by one word: Stonewall.

Newspapers in New York City covered the uprising, as well as the gay publication *New York Mattachine Newsletter*. In New York's *Daily News* Sunday edition *Sunday News*, headlines read, "Homo Nest Raided, Queen Bees Are Stinging Mad." The story claimed, "Queen Power reared its bleached blonde head in revolt." *The Village Voice* weekly newspaper of New York called it the "Gay Power Riots."

The event was not a big news story across the rest of the USA.

"When it happened, I didn't see anything about it in either the national media or our local Denver media—so at first we in Denver didn't know anything about it. News of the New York riot traveled the same way that news generally traveled about previous gay riots and demonstrations—slowly. A couple of weeks after the Stonewall uprising I finally read about it in *The Advocate*, the USA's most important and widely-read national gay publication—it reprinted the Stonewall news article from the *New York Mattachine Newsletter*."[37]

As months and years passed, the Stonewall rebellion received growing attention from the gay media as well as the mainstream media, garnering increasing public awareness, more than any previous gay uprisings ever achieved. Before the late 1960s, media organizations believed they had to be sensitive to readers, listeners and viewers. In the late-1960s and beyond, the many radical changes in society became prominent topics for discussion, thus more people learned of the Stonewall story.

Mainstream Americans in 1969 were already dazed by endless riots and protests against racial discrimination and against the Vietnam War, protests for free speech, women's rights, the environment, publicity about hippies, meditation, expanded consciousness, psychedelics, LSD, marijuana, free love, men with long hair, etc. "I could feel the winds of change blowing through society. It reminded me of the Bob Dylan song *The Times They Are A-Changin'*."

Gay Power became a rallying cry after it was originally used in *The Advocate* in 1967 with a headline reading, "Gay Power Comes to Washington DC."

Stonewall ushered in a new period of gay militancy. Homosexuality was being discussed more openly. In the wake of the Stonewall uprising, older Mattachine Society homophile leaders cautioned moderation in lieu of militant riots. Younger radical liberation activists were in no mood for the more constrained gay politics of yesteryear. The homophile movement essentially passed into history. The masses of younger gays during the next couple of years began protesting in pride marches. They also joined new groups such as the Gay Liberation Front (GLF) and the Gay Activists Alliance (GAA) that initially formed in New York City immediately after Stonewall to address gay rights issues. These groups actually used the word "gay" in their names, unlike the older homophile and Mattachine terms. The new groups started demanding, not politely requesting their rights.[38]

In the radical times of the late 1960s and early 1970s, activists often worked in more than one movement, constantly transferring their experience and knowledge back and forth from one movement to another. The newly-formed gay groups also worked together with other organizations in support of the peace movement and other liberation movements of the day. Four months after forming, members of the nation-wide Gay Liberation Front joined hundreds of thousands of anti-war protesters in a gigantic anti-Vietnam War protest in Washington D.C.

Gay Liberation Front chapters began forming in other cities and college campuses across the USA. With the new momentum sparked by Stonewall, hundreds of new anti-establishment gay rights organizations formed with a huge amount of antagonistic energy. Gay organizations became more outspoken, confrontational and in-your-face. They employed the same militant political strategies used by both the anti-war and racial equality movements.

Conservatives responded. One of their derisive comments declared: "The love that once dared not speak its name now can't seem to keep its mouth shut." A 1969 Lou Harris poll showed that 63% of Americans surveyed thought homosexuality was harmful to American life.

It was now almost two decades since the first major gay rights group, the Mattachine Society, formed in 1950 in Los Angeles.

"I think Stonewall became one of the most important events in the ongoing gay rights movement. But the claims that Stonewall marked the start of the modern gay rights movement is a myth. It was a story perpetuated by the ignorance of the media through the decades.

During the 1950s well before Stonewall, I lived in LA amongst the Mattachine Society, *ONE* magazine and previous gay riots and demonstrations. I experienced the actual beginnings of the modern gay rights movement then and there in Los Angeles, so I knew first-hand that the gay movement didn't begin two decades later at the Stonewall Inn. New York has had it together better than Los Angeles in some ways. New York goes all out to celebrate the 1969 Stonewall incident every year, but Los Angeles so far has failed to annually commemorate the seminal 1950 formation of the Mattachine Society—and that's the true beginnings of the civil rights movement for gays. Nonetheless, I regard Stonewall with high esteem and respect. Stonewall's eventual media exposure to the public and its positive influence cannot be disregarded."

∇

Denver's gay movement always has been a microcosm of the national gay movement. The story of Denver's fledgling gay community in the 1970s embodied the same general dynamics reflected in the stories of so many other gay communities in major and mid-sized cities across the USA.

In January 1971 the Denver Gay Liberation Front formed—Denver's third major gay rights group. The organization began what was viewed at the time as militant gay activism in Denver. It was officially incorporated and led by Terry Mangan who signed incorporation papers. Additionally, three other Gay Liberation Front organizations formed in Colorado—Boulder, Colorado Springs and Fort Collins.

"I became aware of the Denver organization a couple of months after it started up when I saw a small stack of flyers. In those days in Denver we received all of our news either through word of mouth or by flyers. Denver didn't have any local gay newspapers at that time, and we wouldn't have one for another couple of years."

"I took a flyer home, and on Friday night John and I attended our first Denver Gay Liberation Front meeting in a room at Denver Free University. I met Terry Mangan there, but he and I really wouldn't become good friends for another couple of years or so. There must have been about 30 or more guys at the meeting. Their average ages

were around 20 years old. John and I were the only old guys there—
I was in my early thirties and John was in his early forties. That night
members planned gay liberation strategies. The group discussed
options for obtaining some office space that the entire gay community
could use as a gay social center—a gay community center."

Heads and Tales

Vol. 1   No. 1   February 12, 1971

Newsletter of the Denver Gay Liberation Front
"In the Queen City of the Plains"

COFFEEHOUSE TO OPEN FEBRUARY ~~FEBRUARY~~ 21st!

The Coffee House committee held its
second meeting on Feb. 12 and discussed
plans for the first G.L.F. coffee house
in Denver. Initially the coffee house
will be at Denver Free University, 125
East 18th Ave. on Sundays only from 1:00
p.m. to 1:00 a.m. in the now existing
coffee house. An opportunity for brothers
and sisters to meet and relate in a free
social environment will be its main
purpose.

Literature, information on upcoming
events, rapping, coffee & teas and home-
baked goodies will be provided. We have
a need for volunteers to staff and con-
tribute items to make this an united
success. The committee is also looking
into the idea of obtaining its own public
building or the possibility of forming a
living collective to maintain this. All
ideas and suggestions will be much appreciated. Come together!

COMMITTEES

There have been many suggestions for
committees (if you will) to organize and
work on projects affecting our gay com-

"Almost everything lovely in my eyes
is banned to me by law or circumstance
or impractical people.
Sometimes a long chance
and hard labor have given me a prize
but grace ought to be easy, the surprise
when need is met halfway in its advance.
Fighting to rest my inheritance
I have stayed alive in paradise,
I am not cheerful, I who always taught
others to intelligently beguile
gloomy bogey-men am myself caught
in mid-career with a freezing smile
I look at common daylight as a waste
and at the streets around me with distaste
                                        Paul Goodman

LEGAL HASSLES

If anyone should encounter legal
difficulties as a result of being gay,
they should contact the American Civil
Liberties Union at 17th & Pennshlvania,
phone: 825-5176. Mr. Robert Jones,
Assistant Dean of D.U. Law School and
lawyer for A.C.L.U. has informed us he
would be very glad to handle cases of
this type, without charge, through
A.C.L.U. in order to challenge some of

Figure 48: First edition of *Heads and Tales*, Denver Gay Liberation Front newsletter.
[*Heads and Tales*, John Paul De Cecco Papers (2001-17),
Gay Lesbian Bisexual Transgender Historical Society]

"Friday night gay lib meetings weren't convenient for John,
because he wanted to relax after working hard all week. Instead, we
attended a couple of the GLF's weekly Sunday coffee houses. They
organized encounter groups there, and people would come together
and rap—talk in an easy laid-back safe atmosphere. It promoted gay
consciousness raising. The groups also served as a nice way to find
new friends."

The Denver Gay Liberation Front did more than just organize and host meetings. The Front actively called out the State of Colorado for its discriminatory anti-gay laws, pointing out that homosexuals in Colorado were barred from voting (Colo. Revised Statutes 39-10-18) and could be sentenced to 14 years in state prison for having sex in private with a consenting adult (Colo. Revised Statutes 40-2-31).[39] The Front was determined to assert the rights of gays to live and work in a free society: "...homosexuals are no more nor less psychotic, criminal, violent, or dangerous than the general public...."[40]

The group formed committees, including a legal committee to help individuals needing legal assistance and to challenge anti-gay laws and a committee to communicate with politicians.[41]

In the early 1970s the Vietnam War was still raging and so were anti-war protesters. The anti-war movement was the strongest and most prominent of all protest movements during those years. Members of the Denver Gay Liberation Front lent time and energy to the anti-war cause.

"One weekend Gay Liberation Front members in Colorado joined other protesters in a march against the Vietnam War. Terry Mangan asked me to march with them, but John and I didn't go because spending my time protesting the Vietnam War was a low priority for me."

In November 1971 over 200 gay people turned out to join other anti-war protestors in a protest march. The gay contingent marched behind a Gay Liberation Front banner. This gay, bold assertion marked the first time ever that gays marched in Denver under a gay rights banner.[42]

Then again in April 1972 gays joined in another march against the Vietnam War—down Colfax Avenue, through downtown and to a rally at the state capitol.[43]

Gay poet Allen Ginsberg, who lived in the Denver/Boulder area on and off throughout his life, marched with the other gays behind the gay banner, joining other protesters in shouting various anti-war slogans. Along the way, Allen intoned meditation chants and mantric vocalizations. All the while he jotted down thoughts into his ever-present notebook.[44] Following the protest march, he skipped most of the subsequent rally, departing that afternoon on a flight out of

Denver's airport to travel to his next destination. That spring he was in Denver and Colorado on two or three different occasions.

Allen Ginsberg was quite comfortable protesting in Denver with the Gay Liberation Front. He had been participating in numerous anti-Vietnam War protests across the USA.

Figure 49: Allen Ginsberg speaks at a Vietnam War protest.
[Photo by Jon Sievert, Premium Archive via Getty Images]

As far back as summer 1947 Allen Ginsberg had resided for a time in Denver, working at the May Company department store while living, eating and drinking with friends Neal Cassady and Jack Kerouac around the city's downtown area. He later reflected on his Denver experiences in his poems "The Dark Corridor" and "Denver Doldrums." In 1981 Allen moved to Boulder to spend summers there teaching poetry classes and Buddhist meditation at the spiritualistic and visionary Naropa Institute[45] (later renamed Naropa University). His primary home residence, as always, remained in New York City.

About a year and a half after the Denver Gay Liberation Front formed, it began disintegrating. Members could not agree on various issues. The original Gay Liberation Front in New York had collapsed about 18 months after forming, basically due to its minimalistic laissez-faire structure. Likewise, in summer 1972 the local Denver Gay Liberation Front disbanded after 18 months of existence.

Chapter 33

Gay Coalition of Denver

Three years after the Stonewall uprising, only two gay groups existed in Denver, and neither were political groups: Rocky Mountaineers Motorcycle Club of Colorado and Metropolitan Community Church of the Rockies.

"Gay politics really kicked into high gear in Denver in late-1972. I remember that *Rocky Mountain High* by John Denver was a big song on FM radio weeks before breaking into the AM Top 40." It was on the threshold of these divergent times and favorable expectations that the Gay Coalition of Denver formed to serve the gay community.

Late in 1972 the Gay Coalition became the fourth major gay political group in Denver's history. Five gay men and lesbians founded the group: "Jerry" Gerald Gerash, a Denver attorney who primarily practiced criminal law and defended numerous gay citizens from police-initiated lawsuits; Lynn Tamlin, Jerry's partner who was a former young championship boxer from Wyoming; Jane Dundee, a Metropolitan State College lesbian who was into gay liberation; Mary Sassatelli, Jane's housemate; and Terry Mangan who a couple of years previously had formed the defunct Denver Gay Liberation Front.

The Gay Coalition ended up becoming a groundbreaking and influential force in Colorado.

"When I learned about the Coalition I immediately got involved. All Coalition work was accomplished by us volunteers. Our services to the public were pretty much free for people to use. We all had fantasies of what our group could do for Denver's gay community, and most of our hopes ended up being realized."

At the top of the Coalition's concerns were the mental health and legal rights of Denver's gay men, lesbians, bisexuals, transvestites, transsexuals and people questioning their mental and physical being. The Gay Coalition of Denver offered a wide range of services:

- Telephone help hotline,
- Mental health committee,
- Free weekly legal clinic,
- Gay alcoholics groups,
- Referrals for housing and employment,
- Speaker's bureau with activists who went out and talked with health workers, social workers, college psychology classes and churches, and
- A library filled with gay books and publications.

Gays in Denver, as with gays across the nation, encountered hostility and harassment, including physical attacks by gangs of guys hiding in bushes who jumped out and bashed gay men with clubs, sticks, bricks, chains, pipes and mace. Haters smashed car windows in parks and near gay bars. Members of the Lesbian Task Force received repeated phone threats, got their cars vandalized and even had a fence burned at one home.

The most consequential harassment was conducted by Denver police. "Denver vice squad officers were inside the bars arresting gay people for dancing together or for kissing or even for just holding hands. Denver authorities used the same old tactics of charging homosexuals with indecency."

Outside the city's premier gay nightclub, The Broadway Cabaret and Restaurant, police officer "Buster" James Snider would lie in wait to catch gay people walking from the bar to a large parking lot located across the street. He issued jaywalking tickets to hundreds of gay people crossing Broadway. Over 200 bars were located in the Broadway district, yet 80% of his jaywalking tickets were issued[46] across the street from The Broadway.[47] In summer 1984 at a departmental hearing that same officer was found guilty of sexually abusing a woman after taking over an investigation of her after she was stopped by another officer. The police department fired him for the abuse.[48] [49]

In one particular harebrained scheme in January 1973, police would park in the gay cruising areas of Cheesman Park and the State

Capitol grounds in a large Greyhound-type over-the-road passenger bus with a sign labeled "Johnny Cash Special." Undercover agents would offer gay men free tickets to a Johnny Cash concert and then would start talking about sex. Whenever guys agreed in any way to have sex, police would nab them—over 300 gay men were entrapped and arrested. That bus also showed up in other cities as well—Indianapolis and Miami in particular.[50]

In 1973 the Gay Coalition began tracking cases of police harassment, and it formed political and legal committees to approach the local Denver government.

Lawyers challenged laws and actions in court, claiming that gays were systematically targeted for arrest under various laws—lewd conduct, solicitation and men dressing in women's clothes (even though it was legal for women to dress in men's clothes).

Denver continued to enforce a repealed Colorado State sodomy law. City police persistently arrested gay men through undercover stings—plainclothes vice cops would entice gay men, and if those gay men agreed to engage in sodomy then police would make another arrest.

The Coalition was determined. It corresponded with the mayor and met with the chief of police, vice squad, city attorney, city council and the Colorado Civil Rights Commission.

"I remember how hopeful I got when Coalition leaders met with the vice squad. My earlier life was beginning to feel like a whole different time before."

Coalition members told government officials: "We do not, as homosexuals, pose any threat to the peace as criminals do. When we see the ever-rising number of real crimes and their victims, we wonder why the police department is spending so much of their time and our money to seek out and punish people who are seeking, in their own peaceful way, social relaxation and companionship.... The Coalition proposes that the only legitimate area pertaining to sexual activity for either city or state regulation is that of explicit sex in public places. We believe that courtship behavior in public is not a proper area of regulation."

The Gay Coalition challenged Denver's sex ordinance code used by police to target gay men, and Coalition lawyers proposed revisions to it. During a Denver City Council meeting in October 1973 the coalition was able to summon enough gays, lesbians and straight supporters to pack the large council chambers with a crowd so large that some of the 300 people overflowed into the halls of city hall.

"I helped the Coalition prepare questionnaires and mail them to local politicians running for public office including the mayor and city council candidates. We also sponsored Candidates' Night meetings so we could interview office-seekers."

The efforts of the Gay Coalition of Denver paid off with landmark accomplishments. Denver's Gay Coalition was recognized as one of the most successful gay rights groups in the USA. The group managed to get discriminatory laws and ordinances struck from the lawbooks and reached agreement with the police department to stop harassing gays at bars and other gathering places. As of October 1974, homosexuals in Denver were free from being prosecuted for any same-sex conduct which was not an offense when engaged by members of the opposite sex.

The gay political fight also went from the streets to TV screens. In October 1974 gay protesters picketed the local ABC affiliate Channel 9 KBTV (later renamed KUSA) in protest of a *Marcus Welby, M.D.* television episode "The Outrage," which painted gay men as child rapists.

"The National Gay Task Force had asked gay rights groups across the nation, including Denver's Gay Coalition, to organize protests against the episode. John took me to the TV station after he got off work, and I joined the other Coalition picket line protestors. We kept walking around the building holding big picketing signs."

Channel 9 aired the provocative episode anyway, but the station provided the Gay Coalition with a deal. On its public affairs program *Nine-File*, the host interviewed two Coalition members: 1) Coalition coordinator Cordell Boyce, a Harvard graduate who served as the Coalition's chief executive officer and its only paid employee, and 2) Coalition activist Marge Johnson of the National Organization of Women's Lesbian Task Force. Additionally, the station aired a 60-second public service announcement three or four times during the week. Four months later it aired ABC's 90-minute special "Homosexuals: Out of the Shadows."

Figure 50: Gay Coalition members picketing at Channel 9 TV station in Denver, 1974.
Jerry Gerash & Lynn Tamlin. [Courtesy Gerald A. Gerash]

Figure 51: Gay Coalition members picketing at Channel 9 TV station in Denver, 1974.
Cordell Boyce, Terry Mangan, & Marge Johnson. [Courtesy Gerald A. Gerash]

With initial successes and increased momentum, members of the Gay Coalition set more lofty goals.

"During our first year of operation Coalition members mainly carried out business in our living rooms and back yards and basements."

In December 1973 the Gay Coalition opened its own office in a rented space at 1450 Pennsylvania Street just south of East Colfax Avenue. Jim volunteered to work there and eventually became the office manager. Coalition President Craig Henderson provided Jim all the resources and valuable insights he needed.

"Since John worked weekdays, I was free to work at the Coalition. I arrived in late mornings and put in lots of hours throughout many afternoons."

"Sometimes people walked in and just wanted to hang out at our office for a while. Some would walk past the office a few times before they built up enough courage to come inside."

"During the weekdays most Coalition volunteers worked at their real jobs to earn a living, then they mainly donated their time to the cause at nights and on weekends."

Jim also assisted members who were organizing a Coalition prison committee in attempt to improve the lives of gay people serving time. The committee encouraged Colorado's Canon State Penitentiary to consider revising anti-gay rules there. "I worked strictly in the background to assist other Coalition activists and kept quiet about my own years in prison."

"John and I hosted a couple of Coalition meetings in our home. After one board meeting we laid out a buffet in our dining room, and everybody ate and visited."

At the Coalition office Jim answered weekday phone calls on the telephone help hotline. In the evenings the nighttime volunteers on duty answered calls, and then later in the evening they would forward the hotline to their homes and would answer phones until about midnight.

A lot of calls sought information about gay bars and business. Some consequential calls came from isolated homosexuals who used the hotline to get help with their problems.

"I remember one caller didn't want come out as gay because his parents disapproved, and he didn't want to hurt them. So I simply asked him, 'Do your parents live their lives for you?' He said that was a revealing point and thanked me. Almost every gay person I've ever known has suffered to some extent at the hands of their heterosexual parents."

Chapter 34

Denver's New Gay Press

In July 1973, a half year after the Gay Coalition began its gay activism, a small monthly independent gay newspaper *The Scene* published its first issue, ushering in an uninterrupted era of gay publishing in Denver—an unbroken string of gay publications from that time forward.

Previously, small local newsletters had been printed by the Denver Area Mattachine Society in the 1950s, the Denver Gay Liberation Front in 1971/1972 and Metropolitan Community Church in Denver in the early 1970s. But those newsletters primarily were targeted to those groups' own members and served as promotional publicity for people who were not members of those organizations.

"I was certain that *The Scene* would be successful. A year before it began publishing, the feminist newspaper *Big Mama Rag* started publishing to serve the local women's movement. I figured if the local feminist movement could succeed in publishing its own newspaper, then the local gay liberation movement should be able to succeed in publishing its own newspaper too."

The Scene reported on some significant local and national news stories, but it primarily focused on the local gay social scene, gay bar life, local gossip, beauty contests and drag shows. Featured prominently were the Mr. Gay Colorado contest, the Closet Ball crossdressing event and the annual Tobie Awards bestowing honors in categories such as Best Publication, Man or Woman of the Year Award and some campy humorous awards.

"*The Scene* was your stereotypical old bar rag, but it was all we had."

Figure 52: PHOTO AT LEFT: *The Scene* newspaper Publisher Ron Wilson—aka Jack Wilson (left) & Ron Douglas (middle) in a private commitment ceremony in Los Angeles married by Metropolitan Community Church founder & minister Troy Perry (right), 1970. PHOTO AT RIGHT: Ron Wilson & Ron Douglas at a bar, 1970. [Pat Rocco photographs, Courtesy of ONE Archives at the USC Libraries]

Publisher Ron Wilson and Jim both had something in common: They both had moved to Denver from California—Ron in March 1973,[51] four months before he began publishing *The Scene*.

In many American cities, gay bars were primary advertisers that funded gay newspapers and magazines. In turn, those bars allowed publishers to stack their gay publications near their front doors prominently available to bar customers to take home and read.

"Ron Wilson and all other gay publishers across the USA had to properly cater to gay bars and baths in order to be awarded advertising dollars. The gay bar owners banded together and arbitrarily set a minimal amount of money they made available to support the gay press."

Figure 53: *The Scene* newspaper Associate Publisher Michael Graham and Editor David Van Ryzin. [author's collection]

When Ron Wilson started publishing *The Scene*, he envisioned the paper becoming successful enough to employ a full-time staff. Instead, he ended up with only two or three volunteers helping to put out an issue of the newspaper.

"In 1975 and 1976 my friend David Van Ryzin did volunteer work at *The Scene*. He was its editor, and his partner Michael Graham was the newspaper's associate publisher. They'd meet at the newspaper's work garage and at Ron's house to get each edition ready to print. After months or a couple of years working on the newspaper, every volunteer sooner or later would burn out like so many other volunteers in so many other organizations. Eventually David and Michael resigned."

"I also helped Ron, but I did my volunteer work at home. I loved reading gay publications, so John subscribed to three or four national publications for us to read and enjoy. Whenever I came across any significant gay news articles, I'd relay them to Ron, and he'd include some of those national news items in *The Scene*."

"Since Denver's gay community was a lot smaller than the gay communities of Los Angeles and San Francisco and New York, there weren't many businesses willing to advertise in *The Scene*. During gay liberation's formative years few out-gay businesses even existed to be available to purchase ads in the gay press."

The largest chunk of ads in Denver came from the gay bars. *The Scene* focused on gay bar life, providing maximum exposure for the bars. "Yet the bars in turn paid scant amounts of money for ads in the paper. I noticed Ron using his own personal funds a lot of the time to make sure the newspaper got printed. Ron ended up depriving himself a lot in his personal life to make sure *The Scene* published on schedule."

Only a small number of contributors ever submitted any articles for publication. Some people criticized Ron for not printing articles about all of the gay organizations or for printing too few articles about the women in the gay community. Strapped for cash, all he could do was beg the critics to voluntarily submit stories and information about what was going on throughout the community, but very few people ever stepped up to the plate.

In November 1974 the Gay Coalition of Denver began publishing its own gay newspaper, *Rhinoceros*. Up until then the Coalition had been publishing a small-budget, typewritten, in-house newsletter for Coalition members. The new public newspaper presented a more professional looking image for the Coalition. "A Monthly Journal of the Gay Community" was displayed on the front-page nameplate.

The newspaper was available for free at gay bars, sold at Capitol Hill bookstores and mailed to paid subscribers. The Coalition distributed it throughout the state, including complimentary copies to libraries.

"I was a contributor and staff member of *Rhinoceros*. I organized the calendar of events and helped a little to influence the newspaper's style."

"We rejected any 'sex sells' naked advertising. We tried to watch our language so women wouldn't be offended and tried to include them as much as they were willing to get involved."

The newspaper's overall cerebral style was envisioned to set a new high standard with hard-hitting reporting and commentary. *Rhinoceros* editorials proclaimed the publication was a "gay-liberation journal" in contrast to other mere gay newspapers. Its editorials officially reflected the political views of the Gay Coalition. The editorial staff boldly printed gay articles that other gay publications in cities across the country never would dare publish.

Rhinoceros did not shrink from exposing the faults of the proverbial elephant in the room—the inordinate influence of gay bars within the gay community. Negative influences of gay bars and bathhouses in the gay community had been significant—a backdrop within the gay community that rarely has been examined publicly by either the gay press or the mainstream media. *Rhinoceros* brazenly exposed it:

- *Rhinoceros* Nov. 1974: "The bars play an overly dominant part in city gay life.... There should be more gay public social life...places where gays might meet without the tensions of cruising and alcohol."[52]
- *Rhinoceros* Dec. 1974: "Months of misunderstanding erupted in a walkout Friday, November 8 of the night employees of The Broadway Cabaret and Restaurant, Thirteenth and Broadway, described by many as Denver's most popular gay night spot. The employees described their action as a strike. Characterizing their grievances generally as "intolerable working conditions and unjust polices"...the flyer also

accused Broadway employers for not fulfilling promised wage and benefit increases.... Attempts at negotiations during Saturday failed when a letter requested by the bar owners was rejected by them."[53]

- *Rhinoceros* Mar. 1975: "The Gay Coalition brought together representatives of almost all of the area's gay groups in an attempt to focus attention on the need for community unity. Conspicuously absent was the Tavern League [an organization comprised of gay bars].... Most participants were concerned with the notable absence of any official representative of the Tavern League, although the League had been notified of the meeting. A certain amount of bitterness was discernible in one member of the audience who remarked that 'it's interesting that the group which makes its living off gay people isn't interested enough to come to this meeting.'"[54]
- *Rhinoceros* Mar. 1975: "Who will support the necessary counseling, health (physical and mental) services, civil rights, legal and other activities needed to continue and consolidate the gains already won? Clearly not the baths and bars, the major sources of gay money in the community. The sporadic contributions thus far have been undeniably helpful. But the needs are greater. Bar life as an exclusive gay outlet will probably continue as long as there are no other alternatives. There's nothing wrong with a bar, of course, unless it becomes the exclusive or near-exclusive means for gay social life. Such is the case in the Denver region. And when such a situation exists, it seems to us, that those who profit from it have an obligation to the community which reaches far beyond fair prices and occasional donations.... The burden of expense, of course will and should fall on those who can pay, particularly those who receive their money from their gay brothers and sisters. Many services now performed free of charge are services directly benefiting the bars and baths. For example, almost 80% of the calls received at the offices of the Gay Coalition are requests for information on the bars and baths."[55]
- *Rhinoceros* Apr. 1975: "Because we are believers in the possibility of a truly gay culture, we cannot ape the ways of the slick moneymakers, the gay empire builders."[56]

As with any businesses, money talked—gay publications could not criticize powerful gay bar interests and get away with it. Gay bars in most cities at that time had an inordinate amount of influence due to the large reserves of money they hauled in from gay customers. Gay publications had to tread very carefully when printing stories that put any gay bar in a bad light.

"We made sure that *Rhinoceros* gave free publicity to bars by highlighting their events. We thought the gay bars should have returned more resources back to the gay community."

"I have a negative view of owners of gay bars and bathhouses. I believe they actually never cared that much, except for the money rolling in from gay people. After all, it wasn't the bars and baths that set up the hotlines and sat there and counseled people who were depressed and threatening to commit suicide."

"Some gay bars discriminated against minorities, demanding three forms of picture I.D.s before those individuals could enter the bars. Eventually the Colorado Civil Rights Commission got involved and sent undercover investigators; and they found that minorities were indeed being illegally discriminated against in the Denver bar scene— a clear violation of the law."

"Gay bar owners proclaimed great support for the gay community, but the actual modus operandi of their support was generally limited to the bars donating a mere keg or two of beer to gay organizations during their fundraisers at bars. The non-profit community-based gay groups never made large sums of money from draft beer sales at those beer busts. Any additional income generated during fundraisers from hard liquor mixed drinks sold at the bars became profits exclusively for the bars, and none of that money went to beer bust fundraisers."

"I can find examples of bars that on rare occasions might have done something that was somewhat substantial for gay people, but most gay bar owners primarily cared only about raking in profits. The bars rarely reached into their own pockets to fund gay groups."

Gay bar owners in Denver and in other gay communities had plenty of influential bucks to use whenever they deemed it necessary to dictate terms to gay non-profit organizations.

In the 1970s the Denver Tavern League possessed an inordinate amount of behind-the-scenes power and influence in Denver's gay community. Tavern Guilds in various cities were quite capable of dealing with uncooperative publications and organizations, forcing them out of business by uniting against any particular publishing nuisance that interfered with their business model. They accomplished it by refusing to advertise in renegade publications and by refusing to allow any disloyal gay publisher to stack a publication in the bars' entryways for bar patrons to pick up. No available publication, no successful publishing business.

"We only got a dozen or so possible advertisers that were not bars that ran ads each month in *Rhinoceros*. These included a few existing small gay-owned businesses such as Ashworth's Antiques and bookstores on Capitol Hill. Even John advertised his services as a laundry equipment repairman in *Rhinoceros*."

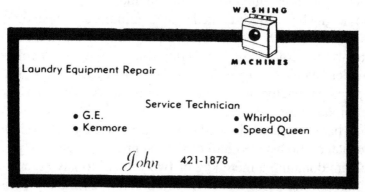

WASHING

Laundry Equipment Repair

MACHINES

Service Technician
- G.E.
- Kenmore
- Whirlpool
- Speed Queen

John 421-1878

Figure 54: John's advertisement in *Rhinoceros* newspaper, March 1975. [author's collection]

Of approximately 14 gay bars in Denver, only four were regular advertisers in *Rhinoceros*, a half dozen other bars made one or two token advertisements during the six months it was published, and the remainder of the bars did no advertising at all in *Rhinoceros*.

Gay bar owners were alarmed by *Rhinoceros'* negative stories and commentaries calling out the bars for being self-serving at the expense of the gay community. In *Rhinoceros'* third edition in January 1975 eight gay bars advertised. Two months later in March that number shrank to only two gay bars advertising, a significant blow to *Rhinoceros'* financial well-being.

"I talked to a couple of the gay bar owners. They outright refused to purchase any more ads in *Rhinoceros* or donate anything to the Gay Coalition, and furthermore, they publicly would not support either one. They believed they were being attacked and told me, 'Why should we advertise and make a newspaper available that hammers us as independent business owners?'"

As with many gay liberation groups in the 1970s, Denver's Gay Coalition constantly struggled to raise money to fund all of its projects. It was almost wholly dependent on volunteers who organized picnics, dinners, monthly dances, theatre parties, weekly coffeehouses and rummage sales. But the efforts were never enough.

The Coalition had taken on the monthly responsibilities of paying office rent, phone service and the costs of publishing *Rhinoceros.*

After only six monthly editions of *Rhinoceros*, the Gay Coalition published the last issue in April 1975.

Chapter 35

Pride, the Center & John Shepperd

The Gay Coalition of Denver forged ties with other gay groups in Colorado throughout the early and mid-1970s.

In 1974 the Coalition coordinated Denver's first gay pride celebration.[57] "We thought the last week of June would be the ideal time in Denver to celebrate a gay pride week. We had help from other gay groups like the Imperial Court. A couple of representatives from the local Metropolitan Community Church printed up flyers and gay brochures for me to hand out."

On the last Saturday in June, the week climaxed with about 50 people attending a large Gay-In celebration and picnic at Cheesman Park.[58] The event featured games, volleyball and exercise sessions, body painting artists and hundreds of helium-filled gay pride balloons.[59]

"It was all fun except for two park policemen who freaked out at our big Gay Pride banner we put up in front of the park's pavilion. They regarded the park as a family-only venue, but that section of Cheesman Park had served for years as our only outdoor gathering area in Denver."

The next year in 1975, about 500 people showed up at Cheesman Park to celebrate Denver's second annual Gay-In to celebrate gay pride.[60] "The Gay Coalition sponsored it again, and again I passed out Coalition flyers and brochures at our information table. I was able to sign up a half dozen new members to join the Gay Coalition."

The gay Catholic group, Dignity, sold hamburger picnic dinners. Gay bars donated kegs of beer for sale. Gay college student groups held Gay Olympics activities. The Imperial Court provided water balloons for people to throw at their royal dignitaries to raise funds. The day before the Gay-In, the Metropolitan Community Church of the Rockies held a rummage and craft sale at their church to raise money. All proceeds during gay pride week were donated to a special savings account to fund an anticipated new gay community center.

As in the previous year, Denver cops again were involved. A report filed with the police claimed that three gay men during the celebration had molested a 5-year-old girl. After investigating, the cops determined that the allegation ended up only to be a false complaint by someone angry at the large openly gay celebration. No charges were filed.

In 1975, planning began a year early for the next gay pride celebration, the third annual—1976; and activists began work on Denver's first official gay pride march. The person tasked with investigating how the permit system worked was Christopher James Walter Sloan whose alter-ego was female impersonator Christi Layne, an award-winning professional entertainer with experience working in multiple nightclubs in various cities.

Christi ended up paying four dollars for a generic sidewalk "civil rights march" permit and got the okay for the date. Everything was fine.

After almost a year, it finally was only four days until the 1976 pride march was to happen. The City of Denver still had not sent the permit for the pride march. At this late date Christi called the city. By this time, it already had come to the city's attention that they had a gay pride march on their hands, and the city headed by Mayor William McNichols wanted no part of it.

Christi complained, "You were supposed to send this months ago, and we need our permit."

City personnel claimed that Christi did not have a date and no arrangements for a march ever had occurred. The city denied the permit.

After getting a lead from Gay Coalition lawyers, Christi got hold of a representative in local government. However, this contact happened to work in the Colorado state government under Governor Richard Lamm, not in the Denver city government. Christi was a political novice and not yet savvy to the differences between city and state governments.

So now the Governor's office also was involved.

Christi told the contact about the problems encountered during the frustrating quest for the illusive permit. At one point Christi became agitated, "I want you to know that we're going to march on Sunday whether we have a march permit or not, so bring a lot of paddy wagons because it will be a black eye that the city will never ever forget." She made the same statement to a Denver reporter.[61]

The Governor's representative assured Christi that nobody was going to hurt the gay community. He told Christi that the staff had to go into a huddle and figure out what they were going to do. The staff member called back and told Christi that the permit would be issued. They were not sure exactly how to get it through the city, but they were making clear that this was not an option the city had.

On Sunday people were gathering for the march. In the background a car arrived, obviously carrying important people. A distinguished-looking gentleman placed the official permit in Christi's hands. Christi handed it back and requested that the official please walk at the front of the march for the first block and asked, "What about the police?" The gentleman introduced Christi to an officer in charge and explained that Christi and the gay community were permitted to walk behind him. So, a request for a permit for a sidewalk march to the Civic Center to fight for civil rights ended up being defined on the official permit as a "parade"—Denver's first pride parade.

That day over 500 marched from Cheesman Park to Denver's Civic Center Park, including Jim and John. Again that year Jim staffed the Gay Coalition table and handed out literature. During the entire gay pride week over $2000 in total funds were raised and deposited into the Gay Community Service Center Fund.[62]

∇

Up through the 1970s, gays in the USA, being outliers in American society, were unable to count on government, religion, the courts or corporations. So activists took it upon themselves to create their own institutions and support networks, which required large sums of money to operate.

In spring 1975 the Gay Coalition's newspaper *Rhinoceros* folded, the Coalition closed its office due to lack of funds, and the organization began operating again strictly through volunteer efforts. Chief among the Coalition's major problems was the negative feelings about it among Denver bar owners whose lack of support for the Coalition was consequential.

"We realized its demise was imminent, and we began searching for a fresh start. That spring the Coalition invited various gay organizations and businesses to our general membership meeting." Coalition lawyer Jerry Gerash lead the formation of an umbrella group to focus on the needs of the gay community and explore how the diverse Colorado gay groups could coordinate their efforts. About 25 gay groups worked together and formed a new gay organization they called Unity. Each gay organization contributed one person as a voting member.

Unity members identified the need in Denver for a full-fledged gay social services agency—a gay community center. The center would exist to provide services to the gay community and people in need.

Scores of people donated their time as volunteers. Unity members raised money for the anticipated community center through parties, garage sales, picnics, bake sales and beer busts. "I wasn't a member of Unity, but I volunteered at a couple of their fundraising events, and I felt pride watching their efforts."

Unity members determined that the center would require at least one paid position—a coordinator to run the daily operations. A selection committee hired Phil Nash as the center's paid coordinator who would shepherd the center's day-to-day business activities. Phil was a refreshingly new member of Denver's gay community who had moved to Denver the previous year. He guided the center with an amiable ability to bring together diverse segments of the fragmented gay community.

Jim helped Phil with a couple of the community center's organizational efforts, providing attention to the details and following through on their necessary commitments.[63]

A little over two years after the first meeting of Unity, activists finally had enough money in the Unity fund to open the Gay Community Center of Colorado. Only a half dozen years had passed since the Denver Gay Liberation Front in 1971 first discussed the options of opening a Denver gay social services center—a gay community center. Now it was a reality.

Figure 55: Phil Nash, Coordinator, Gay Community Center of Colorado, late 1970s.
[Courtesy Gerald A. Gerash]

In July 1977 center organizers began moving into the new offices at 1436 Lafayette Street, and in August the center opened its doors to serve all of the diverse people in the gay community—welcoming walk-ins, answering the gay hotline phone calls and publishing a newsletter.

The community center would use a structure similar to what the Coalition office had used. However, the new center would not act as a political organization in the way the Gay Coalition had operated. The new center conducted business strictly as a social service agency, but it did provide meeting rooms and resources for gay political groups and other gay organizations. In contrast to the old Gay Coalition, the new center, in order to survive, would refrain from tarnishing the reputations of gay bars.

At the new gay community center, a half dozen representatives from various gay businesses and organizations made up the center's Board of Governors.[64] This group of professional advisors to the center served as a check on the powers of the Board of Directors. They participated in professional fundraising and helped to select the center's first Board of Directors.[65]

"My close friend John Shepperd served as president of the Board of Governors. He was involved with Colorado's Imperial Court and Sovereign Court. He was into gay politics big time and had lots of friends. He was loyal, honorable and respected everybody."

John Shepperd and two of his close friends had opened a new gay nightclub the year before in late-1976 called The Terrace Showcase, a high-class cabaret show bar at 3737 East Colfax Avenue and Jackson Street.

John's experience with bartending and professional food service provided the necessary acumen for organizing and marketing the liquor and food. When the bar was open, he served as a host managing customers' needs and maintaining the bar's standards of service.

Figure 56: Owners of The Terrace Showcase: (left to right) John Shepperd, Michael Rickard, & Christi Layne. [Courtesy Chris Lee]

The second primary owner was John's domestic partner Michael Rickard, a banker and accountant who served as business manager. He also served as a host during business hours.

The third primary owner with the main share in the Terrace Showcase was Christi Layne. It only had been a few weeks since Christi had pressured the local political infrastructure for the rights to conduct Denver's first pride parade.

Christi was in charge of the bar's entertainment and directed three feature shows on most nights as lead performer and emcee of an ensemble cast. Christi presented a warm happy demeanor both on stage and off stage with a fun friendly attitude.

Before The Terrace Showcase began business in its newly rented building, the building had housed a rock bar. Christi and her workers used the framework of the old rock music stage to build a new glamorous show stage.

John, Michael and Christi raised funds to open the business through the help of 20 other individual investors.

Female impersonators and cast members included both local entertainers and performers with nationwide touring companies.

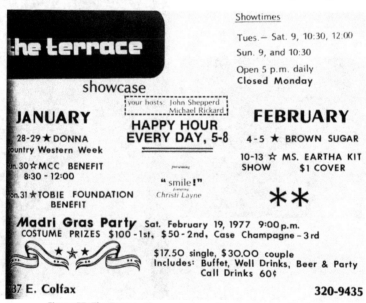

Figure 57: The Terrace Showcase promotion. [author's collection]

A newspaper review in *The Scene* proclaimed that the new nightclub's entertainment located locally in the Rocky Mountain Empire was unsurpassed by many stages on the East and West Coasts.[66]

John, Christi and Michael also used The Terrace to prominently support Denver's new gay community center, which would open the following summer. Special events at The Terrace included holiday parties, benefits for the gay center and other assorted fundraisers.

The three Terrace owners deposited all monies they raised for the center into a bank savings account. When the community center's first Board of Directors was elected, the three guys presented their donation of funds to the new organization.

Intensive fundraising was required to finance the opening of Colorado's gay community center. The largest resource in the community—gay bar owners—did not team up to donate money from their profits. Instead, raising the most money for the new center were the events held by Denver's female impersonators, the gay crossdressing subculture and the leather and biker gay subcultures. The Imperial Court of the Rocky Mountain Empire and The Terrace Showcase sponsored numerous drag shows and became prime contributors of money for the new community center. However, other bar owners only on occasion would provide space inside a club and a keg or two of beer so volunteers could raise money, but only when a fundraising group approached the bar and initiated a request to hold a beer bust at the bar. If a bar owner approved the fundraiser, it invariably would benefit the bar owner by enticing additional customers to spend more money buying more drinks. With the exception of that token support, most bar owners were unenthusiastic about providing any of their profits to help open the new gay services center.

Across the country the crossdressing crowds and the leather and biker crowds had an affinity for each other, and many of them moved around in the same circles. During the early days of the Gay Coalition of Denver, most members of the crossdressing, leather and biker groups were disinclined to get involved with Gay Coalition politics since the groups viewed themselves as social not political. That changed when Gay Coalition lawyers got Denver's anti-crossdressing law repealed, and police could no longer arrest someone for crossdressing. The groups realized the benefits of the Coalition's aggressive gay liberation politics, inducing them to start getting politically involved.[67]

"One weekend, John Shepperd invited me and John to be his special guests at a grand weekend performance at The Terrace. We hardly ever went to any bars, but we were really excited to experience Denver's big new happening. John Shepperd made the necessary reservations—and were they ever needed. The place was packed. The seating capacity of the building was limited to only 200 people. So they had to utilize reservations to manage the crowds."

The venue was huge: At one end was an expansive first floor-stage; in the middle was a large open area with guest tables; in the back of the room was the bar and behind it were spaces containing refrigerated storage and a sewing room for making costumes. Above the back bar area was a mezzanine for people to sit at tables up on a balcony and view the shows down on the first-floor stage. A third entire floor (top floor) was a more secluded private loft used as a separate cruise area for the leather and biker crowds.

The three partners had big plans to build new restaurant facilities in the building and to transform the bar into a true dinner theater; but for the first few months they would be limited to utilizing hot steam tables for special event dinner buffets.

The three guys found a seemingly friendly soul in their landlord, Chris Allison, who was listed as owner on both the deed to the property and the liquor license. On occasion he provided good advice. The landlord was well-compensated, making $2000 a month in reliable rental income from The Terrace owners. But the guy was an older, fat, cigar-smoking troll. He had no practical knowledge of the gay community. The incongruent image of this straight guy sitting at the bar among all the queens obviously would have been awkwardly peculiar. So the three Terrace owners stipulated in the rental contract that the owner was not allowed inside the bar during business hours.

John, Michael and Christi did not pay themselves because they were investing all income back into their business. Within six months after opening, they paid off (with interest) all of their other investors.

"I was impressed how the three guys were earning money hand-over-fist at such young ages—late twenties and thirties. Some of their life dreams already were materializing. They were idealistic and innocent, lucky entrepreneurs, and they were making loads of money from their exciting new business."

The landlord had little insight into how the three business owners were so successful, but he was far from dumb—he saw the crowds and realized that huge sums of money were flowing in. One day he came into the bar and informed John and his two partners that their six-month rental contract had expired, and he reminded them that he owned both the real estate property and the liquor license. It was time to renegotiate the terms of the contract for a price that he claimed was fairer to him.

He raised the monthly rent from $2,000 to $5,000 and demanded a large deposit.[68]

The three guys had failed to pay close attention to the rental lease and got caught by subtle provisions in the contract that they had overlooked. Other gay bar owners in the Tavern League came in to help by reviewing the contract, but they determined that the owner of the property and liquor license had correctly interpreted the legally binding rental contract. The three Terrace owners were out of luck.

They attempted to keep The Terrace open by holding a special two-night benefit, but it became obvious—do not prolong the misery. The three friends closed up business on a Sunday night in May 1977.

"We invited John Shepperd for dinner in our home a few weeks after the bar closed. He and his partner Michael Rickard talked that night about their experiences at The Terrace and their aspirations for the future. They were searching with Christi Layne to find a new Denver location with restaurant facilities so they could create a full-fledged dinner club." John Shepperd told Jim that the three of them had learned the hard way how vitally important it is to always have a business attorney review all contracts and provide legal counsel before signing any and all documents.

After the three guys vacated the rented building, the landlord decided he would operate his own gay bar to replace The Terrace. Now he could keep all profits for himself. The following month he opened his new bar business, which he called Going Bananas. He eagerly anticipated huge sums of money rolling in.

"I talked with John Shepperd a lot and was curious to see what had happened with the bar. One night before going home I convinced my

John to check out Going Bananas with me. I promised we'd be there no longer than 20 minutes."

The entire time that Jim and John were inside Going Bananas, only two other souls were there inside the place: 1) The new manager, John Zachariah Drummer, who published *Contact*, a short-lived Denver gay newspaper containing inconsequential cut-and-paste articles and basically no original local reporting; and 2) the owner of the property and liquor license, Chris Allison, who was sitting at the end of the bar smoking a cigar and lording over the empty space.

"I thought, '*What an oddball first impression for a gay bar.*' We didn't stay long."

The owner advertised Going Bananas in a cluelessly goofy ad campaign calling the bar a "new gay disco saloon ... for sophisticated savages." "Have you tried Going Bananas?" "Come cruise the jungle boys."[69]

Going Bananas was going nowhere. In a few short months the owner gave up his losing speculative venture, and all gay bar operations at that location ceased. The owner ended up with neither a profitable gay bar business that he successfully managed on his own nor an effortless armchair investment that earned good monthly rental income from the three reliable Terrace renters. Everyone was out of luck.

Chapter 36

Gay History Research

The 1970s was a watershed period for Jim in the sense that he found a purpose in life—becoming an architect and foot soldier in the gay liberation movement. It was as though Jim was made for the movement. He was never afraid and ashamed to live his life truthfully as a gay man. As a teenager he had been willing to risk it all on the open road rather than endure the mental, emotional and physical strain from his dysfunctional family. He learned quickly that he had to survive by his wits and cast aside any pretense of self-respect in exchange for a hot meal and a warm place to sleep. It was a price he was willing to pay to survive another day. After all of that, plus being incarcerated in a Texas prison and forced to work on a chain gang, Jim had decided to turn around his former life. Instead of remaining a helpless victim, he became an activist who placed his destiny in his own hands. With the gay liberation movement gaining momentum, Jim knew he found a cause greater than his past.

"During this time, I started researching gay history. I became friends with Terry Mangan. I respected him as a founding member of both the Denver Gay Liberation Front and the Gay Coalition of Denver. He wrote a monthly gay history column in *Rhinoceros*. He set up the Coalition's gay library. I assisted Terry and helped run the library. We were always on the lookout for donations of gay books and for money to purchase more books."

"Terry was the first true professional historian I'd ever met." Terry Mangan was known as a very scholarly and brilliant young man ahead of his time[70] with an astounding and accurate wit.[71]

Terry worked as a media librarian for the State Historical Society of Colorado. In 1975 he published a book of historic Colorado photographs called *Colorado on Glass: Colorado's First Half-Century As Seen by the Camera*, which received critical raves from *The New York Times*.[72]

"Terry's the first person who interested me in the idea of researching gay history. For years I'd read about gay history in various articles published in *ONE* magazine and in the *Quarterly of Homophile Studies* and in *Mattachine Review*. I knew gay people had always been around, but to prove it was another thing."[73]

Figure 58: Terry Mangan in San Francisco.

"In 1975 Terry moved to San Francisco to take a job with the California Historical Society as curator of photographs. Terry and I wrote letters back and forth. He asked me to research certain gay history info for his writing projects, including a book he intended to author about gay people in the Old West, which was really a massive undertaking. I would search and uncover stories from old 1800s newspapers and documents and send him what I found. He asked me to research a lead he had found about two lesbians from Aspen, Colorado in 1888 and 1889."

Terry wrote to Jim, "I have not had time to look up all the references which you sent last week. Those that I have looked into are quite interesting. They are as interesting as anything I have seen in published materials anywhere that I have looked."[74] "You have found far more than I ever supposed you could already."[75] Jim felt quite elated in his new gay activism niche.

In late June 1977 Jim visited Terry in San Francisco and stayed with him during the city's huge Gay Pride Week celebrations.

In between Gay Pride activities and Terry's work at the California Historical Society, Jim had extra time to visit with two old friends.

"I spent time with my friend Lenora Cantrell, and we went out at night to dinner while she previewed a couple of shows featuring new entertainers."

"I also spent a day with my old friend Bailey Whitaker and one of his friends. He hadn't been involved with *ONE* magazine for over a couple of decades, but he still kept in contact with his friend and former interracial partner Dorr Legg. Since those early years in LA when we first met, he had moved to the San Francisco area. He was living across the bay in a wonderful old building just a couple of blocks from the campus of the University of California, Berkeley. He had earned a Doctor's Degree in Philosophy and Communications and had become a college professor. We visited and listened to Bailey's Marvin Gaye albums, and I remember him singing along to the song *Mercy Mercy Me* and dancing. The three of us ate lunch at a restaurant on the edge of the Berkeley campus."

"As fun as Bailey was, he was also serious and erudite. I always thought of him as the modern gay rights movement's first true Black activist. He hadn't been in the forefront of the gay movement since the early 1950s, but he still had strong political views. He followed all news about the U.S. Supreme Court. He even could name every justice on the court and talk about the cases they heard. A lot of his interest undoubtedly started back during *ONE* magazine's case at the Supreme Court in 1958."

Bailey also had a mystical side to himself. He was intrigued by spiritual teacher and writer Baba Ram Dass who at various times in his life acknowledged his homosexuality,[76] his bisexuality and his celibacy.[77] Bailey talked about his thoughts of Ram Dass's spiritual manifesto contained in his book *Be Here Now*. Previously, Ram Dass had joined Timothy Leary conducting research at Harvard University on the therapeutic potential of psychedelics prior to laws being passed that made LSD and other psychedelics illegal. In the wake of their joint psychedelic studies, not only did Timothy Leary lose his job at Harvard, Ram Dass also lost his job there.

Earlier in his life, Ram Dass had not embraced any religious thoughts, "I didn't have one whiff of God until I took psychedelics."[78] Then in the late 1960s Ram Dass embarked on a path of meditative spiritual awareness and transformation visiting Hindu yogis in India in search of a new level of thinking.

Likewise, Bailey Whitaker also sojourned to India and Katmandu, Nepal in the early 1970s to spend summertime sightseeing and getting a personal up-close glimpse of Hindu metaphysical theories explored there.

"To tell you the truth, it was all a little too offbeat for me. But it was great being with Bailey again, so I listened affectionately to his heartfelt wonderment."

In the 1950s and 1960s Bailey had experienced racial discrimination and was marginalized within the gay community as a Black individual. He also faced discrimination within the Black community for being gay and proudly out.

Bailey noted that the founding of the Mattachine Society in 1950 occurred during accelerating momentum in the civil rights movement. It only was five years after the Mattachine founding that Rosa Parks in 1955 refused to give up her seat to a White person on a Montgomery, Alabama city bus. Her subsequent arrest was the catalyst for organizing the successful Montgomery Bus Boycott. Historians believe her defiance was the tipping point for the civil rights movement in the United States.

"Bailey thought the racial civil rights movement and the gay civil rights movement were more closely aligned than many Blacks and gay people at that time realized. He claimed that in fact the two movements and other minority groups all truly comprised one Civil Rights Movement as a whole."

Numerous White gays and lesbians had participated in the racial civil rights movement.[79] As a gay Black man, Bailey himself supported both the racial civil rights movement and the gay civil rights movement. He predicted their ties would grow increasingly closer together.

In the 1950s and 1960s the media covered the racial struggles much more robustly than any of the gay struggles. Bailey thought the lack of gay coverage had given an unfair advantage to the forces at work trying to weaken civil rights groups and divide groups against each other. He thought conservatives had attempted to disenfranchise gay people by pitting the racial civil rights movement against the gay civil rights movement. Conservative politicians and public figures claimed that gay people were not worthy of special rights in contrast to the bonafide rights of other minorities.

Those conservatives claimed that gay people built the gay civil rights movement by hijacking the Black civil rights movement and following the blueprint of the racial civil rights groups to make gay rights the new civil rights.

Bailey's primary dispute regarding this narrative was that it played into the conservative assertion that gays co-opted the civil rights movement—all based on the untenable premise that the gay movement began in 1969 with Stonewall, and therefore it followed the racial civil rights movement. Bailey believed it was imperative that gay people and the media understood that the gay civil rights movement really began in the early 1950s with the formation of the Mattachine Society and other early gay groups. Bailey thought it was obvious that the gay civil rights movement moved forward in tandem with the racial civil rights movement throughout the 1950s and 1960s and did not follow it.

Every June, activists celebrate the 1969 Stonewall uprising. Bailey was frustrated that activists in Los Angeles never organized big yearly celebrations around the December 1950 founding of the Mattachine Society. He thought it was crucial for activists to annually highlight Mattachine's initial transformative effect on sexually diverse people and the true beginning of the gay civil rights movement.

$$\nabla$$

"After this trip to the Bay Area, I never saw my two wonderful friends again. Lenora and I moved about the same time, and somehow we lost contact with each other. Not long after I visited Bailey he died."

After that Gay Pride Week, Jim returned to Denver, and so did Terry Mangan who spent a week in Denver. Terry brought along copies of his documents and research and deposited them in the Colorado Historical Society. Jim followed Terry's example of donating gay items to the Historical Society. Jim began searching for back issues of assorted older gay publications in Colorado: late-

1950s/early-1960s editions of the *Denver Area Newsletter* of the Mattachine Society; 1961 editions of *The Neighbors Denver Area Newsletter* and early-1970s editions of *The Scene*. As Jim found copies of old back issues, he placed some of them in the Colorado Historical Society.

During both Gay Pride in San Francisco and Terry's visit to Denver, it was obvious that Terry was despondent over the recent stabbing death of his close friend and ex-boyfriend Robert Hillsborough, killed by four teenagers in San Francisco shortly before Gay Pride Week.

Terry returned to San Francisco, and a couple of weeks later in late July he died by suicide. Since he had donated some of his documents and research to the Colorado Historical Society[80] during his Denver visit, he had ensured his hard work would not be lost.

"In 1976 we wound down activities of the Gay Coalition, and it ceased functioning. Some of the Coalition's old library collection was divided between the Colorado Historical Society and the University of Colorado. The significant portion of the collection was placed under my care for safe-keeping. When the new Gay Community Center opened in August 1977, I passed on the Coalition library's holdings to the new Gay Community Center to establish its new library. I named the community center library in honor of Terry—the Terry Mangan Memorial Library—because he originally had started the library as the Gay Coalition library located in the Gay Coalition's offices. Since I knew Terry, the best thing I could do was name the library that he helped create."[81]

A half dozen years later Jerry Gerash, Terry's close friend, his attorney and the Gay Coalition's co-founder, obtained the rights from Terry's next of kin so the historical society could publish its holding of Terry's manuscript.

Terry Mangan was now a footnote in history as far as the mainstream American media was concerned, but his life and work inspired Jim to begin earnestly researching gay history.

∇

Jim read three or four nationwide gay publications that he and John subscribed to and received by mail every month, including the most widely read gay publication in the world, *The Advocate*. Around 1974-1975 Jim came across a curious ad in *The Advocate* seeking people to do gay history research. Jim answered the ad, and it ended up having been placed by Jonathan Ned Katz in search of people who could research items for his upcoming book, *Gay American History*, which he published in 1976.

Figure 59: Jonathan Ned Katz, New York City, 1988.
[Photo by Robert Giard; Copyright Estate of Robert Giard]

"I wrote to Jonathan and told him that I had the time, and I'd be glad to do it, although I really didn't have a lot of experience doing it. So he wrote back, asked me to find some things, and from there I started in."

Jim began researching by hunting through publications such as *ONE* magazine, but Jonathan regarded *ONE* and other early homophile publications as very common sources. Once Jim realized that, he decided to read through daily newspapers. Jim began pouring through them trying to find out how old newspapers covered what he was researching.

"During my adolescent years my mother bought me all the books I wanted to read. I started reading at a very early age beginning at the orphanage, so I guess that's why I developed a natural ability to speed read. After I left home and was out on my own, I loved bringing home a dozen books at a time from a library. Then within a week or two I'd have them all read, and I'd be itching to exchange them for another dozen books."

When Jim started researching in Denver, he read voraciously through hundreds of books and decades of various newspapers. A headline or paragraph or word would jump out at him, and he would discover another obscure gay reference clue that would lead him to further research sources.

"Jonathan wanted me to do research about Baron Friedrich Von Steuben, who had taught American Revolutionary soldiers how to fight and march. He wanted to get some substantiating evidence that the baron was gay. I discovered this old book that said there was a warrant out for his arrest for molesting boys in Germany in the 1700s before he came over here to the U.S. The actual German records probably were destroyed during the two World Wars of the 1900s, but we had this book to rely on. I sent my research to him, and he sent me back more requests to find evidence about other various people and events."

"Fairly soon I was sending Jonathan all sorts of items I found. Some Jonathan used, some he didn't and some he already had."

"It's really difficult doing research about these people. I first had to learn about the different people who were well known in history. Most history books in Colorado and elsewhere were written for the most part by conservative elderly people. I never saw any of them refer to any houses of prostitution until I happened to pick up this one book, and it mentioned there was a gay house of prostitution in the 1890s, and this was from an oral interview done with an old-time madam before she died in the 1930s. And she said that right around the corner there was this other place that was a man's place, and she explained that meant guys were dressed in women's clothes. So at least in the 1890s there was at least one homosexual house of prostitution. Other people have suggested that there probably were more, but it's extremely hard to prove."

"I was looking at the old police records, and I saw all these entries for sodomy, crime against nature, and I thought, *'Oh boy, I've hit on really interesting cases.'* But it ended up that they were female prostitutes. At that time anything these authorities couldn't quite figure out, they lumped into calling it crime against nature, which of course it wasn't."

Jim also searched through years of the *Colorado Medical Journal* at Terry Mangan's suggestion.

"And then Jonathan's book came out, and I was really pleased with it. I liked the name *Gay American History*. When I had the money to call him long distance on the telephone I said, 'Surely you're going to do Volume Two.' I told Jonathan he ought to do 10 volumes of it."

After that, Jim discovered more items that Jonathan used in his next book *Gay/Lesbian Almanac* published in 1983 as the follow-up book to *Gay American History*.

Terry Mangan and Jonathan Ned Katz each had been seeking different information. "Terry had begun writing a historical book about the Western United States, and I supplied him the information that I uncovered. Jonathan was more interested in general things, so I'd send him my findings from across the USA and from other countries."

"Later I started doing gay research on my own and found many more stories. The main trouble I encountered began after I'd discovered thousands of pages of research. I found it progressively harder to remember the names and specifics of all the people and subjects of my research without my massive files in front of me to keep all those names and facts straight."

Chapter 37

Colorado Gaybreak

"**O**ne of my pleasures was listening to talk radio. I liked hearing audience members call into Denver's talk radio station and debate contentious issues." Denver's talk radio station was KGMC 1150 AM, renamed KWBZ AM in the mid-1970s. It aired only talk radio shows.

"In 1974 I began to call in regularly to the station on *The Alan Berg Show*." Alan Berg was an original shock jock before the term was invented and before that particular style became ubiquitous on the talk airwaves. Still, the shock jock term fails to adequately describe Alan Berg. Alan was a liberal outspoken Jew with a confrontational style on controversial topics. The irascible talk-show host was abrasive to callers, but many listeners had a deep affection for Alan. People listened to him curious to hear what might occur next on his show.

Figure 60: Alan Berg. [Photo by Larry Laszlo, CoMedia]

"I called in and openly declared to Alan and listeners that I was a homosexual." Mid-1970s listeners to Denver's talk station were shocked to hear Jim's frequent calls—a self-admitted homosexual on the radio—of all things. Nobody could remember hearing this type of scandalous discussion before on Denver's airwaves.

"I wouldn't call Alan's show at just any old time. I'd wait until the show would get slow when Alan would start joking and begging listeners to call him. Whenever he answered my calls, I knew he'd appreciate me bailing him out of his sluggish predicament. I'd start in, 'Hi Alan. It's your friendly homosexual.' We'd occasionally talk a bit about fashion, since I'd always been interested in fine clothes, and Alan previously owned a clothing store. But we mainly talked about homosexuality and society. Then after I'd hang up, Alan literally would be flooded with callers who wanted to discuss their opinions. Some were anti-gay, some were pro-gay and some were still trying to analyze their own conflicting perspectives."

In March 1975 Jim arranged for the Gay Coalition to be represented by two of its members as guests on *The Alan Berg Show*. One guest was Jim himself. The other was Gay Coalition lawyer Jerry Gerash, Colorado's most influential gay rights activist. As lead lawyer in the 1970s he led the legal pressure that reformed city and state laws, effectively halting government authorities from utilizing repressive laws to harass and persecute homosexuals.

"Jerry and I got the opportunity to speak on the show about gay civil rights bills being introduced in the Colorado State Legislature. It really was a radical act for us to advocate our views as gay guests on Denver's airwaves."

"We began the show, and right away it started getting scary. In the first five minutes we got four phone calls threatening us on the air. One was from a guy who said he was coming to the station with his fundamentalist religious group to kill all of us. Then other callers threatened violence and said they were going to burn the place down." The radio station called the police who arrived and protected both the station and everybody there while the show went on.

Everybody made it home safely.

In 1984, nearly a decade after the Gay Coalition incident on *The Alan Berg Show*, Alan Berg was ambushed and shot to death in the driveway of his Denver townhouse by members of the White supremacist group The Order, which had ties to the Ku Klux Klan, Neo-Nazis and Aryan Nations White nationalist movements.[82]

About three years before his death, Alan had moved from small KWBZ talk radio station to the powerful 50,000-watt KOA 850 AM. Its antenna transmitted a commanding signal from the mountains just west of Denver at an altitude well over a mile high that reached listeners across 30 states. On his show, Alan had argued with and derided White nationalist callers, angering far-right extremist groups. He had been receiving death threats and bomb scares throughout his entire radio career.

That June night in front of his townhouse, Alan instantly died from a dozen or more bullets to his head and torso fired from an illegally converted semiautomatic to fully-automatic .45 caliber Ingram MAC-10 submachine gun fitted with a silencer. One neighbor dismissed the sound as merely some chain rattling on the driveway outside.

Alan was the first on The Order's list of targets proclaimed for assassination, "It's time for a revolution in America, and we're going to get rid of minorities, feminists, gays—whoever we decide are our enemies."[83] Members bombed a synagogue. They robbed banks and armored cars of millions of dollars to fund themselves. Informants and court trial witnesses revealed that The Order also had targeted two U.S. senators. In short time The Order's leader died in a standoff with federal agents. The feds rounded up more than 60 of the right-wing militants. About a dozen individuals were convicted in federal court for violating Alan's civil rights, racketeering and conspiracy to racketeer. Most received significant time behind bars with a couple of the militants sentenced to over 100 years in prison.[84]

A poll was taken in Denver four years before Alan's death, which asked two questions: 1) "Who is the most hated media personality in Denver?" and 2) "Who is the most loved media personality in Denver?" Alan won both awards.

$$\nabla$$

Jim's 1975 experience on *The Alan Berg Show* demonstrated to him the influence of local radio. "I wanted more action for the gay community inside the Denver radio market. I learned that both San

Francisco and Los Angeles had gay radio shows—so why not Denver?"

During the 1970s and 1980s, gay radio programs across the USA served as the only alternative to the gay print media. No internet existed yet to provide news, information and discussions. The nation's few gay radio shows aired on non-profit public radio stations, instead of airing on for-profit stations. In public radio's infancy, many of the public stations emphasized "community free radio" as both a community service and a simple approach for filling up airtime. The gay programs and other community-based programs received free airtime funded by contributors who pledged and donated money to the non-profit stations. Contributors included careful and circumspect gay people, many of whom gave money to the stations without mentioning any gay programming. The gay shows on public stations generally conformed to the standard public radio format that consisted of music interspersed with information, news, interviews and features.

In the 1970s and early 1980s Denver had only one public radio station, licensed to the University of Denver, KCFR 90.1 FM. The call letters stood for Colorado Free Radio.

"I did volunteer work at the Gay Coalition with NOW Lesbian Task Force member Marge Johnson. She told me about that public radio station airing a feminist show called *Women Alive*. I listened and realized that this Colorado public radio station's programming included at least one progressive community program. So in November 1974 I got a few gay people together at the Coalition's office for a meeting to discuss a possible gay radio show. We approached KCFR. We had a business-like meeting at the station, and we answered questions. The station's managers asked if any of us had broadcast experience. None of us did. Station representatives then told us that we had to have one or two people with good broadcast experience in order to get any airtime. So we were out of luck for the time being."

A couple of years later 21-year-old Roar Poliac,[85] a likable and imaginative guy, approached good old KWBZ talk radio station to seek airtime for a gay show. The for-profit station sold blocks of airtime during weekends to obtain additional profits. Roar signed a contract to purchase a weekly hour of broadcast airtime on Sunday mornings for the Denver gay community at $125 per show. Unlike other cities with gay radio programs on public radio stations, the gay community in Denver was stuck having to pay money for airtime. After all, for-profit stations do not survive in the broadcast business by giving away gifts of free airtime.

In July 1977 *Colorado Gaybreak* became the first weekly gay radio show ever broadcast in the Rocky Mountain Region. The show's format conformed to KWBZ's general call-in talk radio format. The station's 10,000-watt broadcast could be heard by up to a quarter million people from Cheyenne, Wyoming down to Pueblo, Colorado; and in the middle of the listening area was Colorado Springs, Ft. Collins and Denver. Many listeners were homosexuals who never had ventured out of the closet and never before had overheard gay people openly discussing various aspects of their lives.

"We were excited before the first show aired. Roar Poliac put the show together, but he and a half-dozen other volunteers didn't have any on-air broadcast experience, and it showed. The general feeling among those I talked to was that the show was a real disappointment."

Roar funded the first three shows from drag shows, fundraisers and donations from gay organizations and individuals.

Others pitched in to help including Mary Kupfer and Roger Rich.

Also helping out was Gay Community Center Coordinator Phil Nash and his partner Bob Janowski, a medical doctor who was building a private practice with an eventual large clientele of gay men. As *Colorado Gaybreak* began airing, the Gay Community Center was opening its doors for business. Since Phil Nash was Colorado's only paid gay activist, he felt obligated to help the community in some way to retain its new gay radio show.

Since none of the volunteers had any broadcast experience necessary to elevate the show, funding for *Colorado Gaybreak* began drying up and despair set in. The burden of coming up with $125 every week quickly became overwhelming and too expensive to maintain.

"I just couldn't let the whole endeavor drop, so I sought out people who had prior professional radio experience, and we returned to the station and signed a new contract with station owner Corky Cartwright. We now were responsible for coming up with the $125 every week to fund the show. To pay the station for the airtime, we sold commercials and then created ads that we aired on the weekly shows."[86]

Volunteers who had kept the show going for the first three weeks breathed a sigh of relief and figured this was as good a time as any to quickly depart the show without it failing. Roar Poliac also left and formed a nationwide networking of gay broadcasting programmers he named the Gay Electronic Media Service (GEMS), a resource for gay radio and TV programmers across the country.

The first couple of reformatted *Colorado Gaybreak* shows aired through Rick Miller[87] funding the two shows. He was a young real estate agent who wrote a music column in the local gay newspapers called "Two Plays for a Quarter." After those first two weeks, a slate of businesses began advertising in earnest. Businesses and most gay bars were wary of advertising on an openly gay radio show, but the program attracted advertising from some truly brave gay business owners—including Ashworth's Antiques owned by Gordon Flaws, The Haberdashery clothing store owned by Andy Chikos and Michael Astorga, and Electric Hair owned by Larry Trostels. During the show's breaks the gay commercials aired. *Colorado Gaybreak* also aired free public service announcements for non-profit gay groups.

Figure 61: *Colorado Gaybreak* advertisement, *The Scene* newspaper, 1977. [author's collection]

In the newsletter *Dispatch* of the gay Rocky Mountaineers Motorcycle Club of Colorado, Club Dispatcher Dean Elder wrote: "This program is gay produced and sponsored by various gay businesses and organizations. It's kind of different to hear an advertisement for a gay bar on the radio."[88]

For the show, Jim assembled a new crew of volunteers from people he already knew.

Ken Watts[89] was the show's male moderator—a 21-year-old who attended the University of Colorado in Boulder. Ken stayed with Jim and John on Saturday nights and woke up early Sunday mornings to pick up many of the show's guests and explore what questions he would ask during the show.[90]

Jan Grimm[91] was the show's female moderator—a middle-aged lesbian mother. Income from her real estate career supported her family. Her activism was important, but family and children were the most important things in her life.

Writing and reading the news were 1) Jan Hoegh,[92] a staff member of the feminist newspaper *The Some Times*, and 2) Will Guthrie,[93] from Cheyenne, Wyoming where his father was a Justice of the Wyoming Supreme Court.

The moderators interviewed weekly guests and fielded phone calls from listeners. Guests talked about gay issues, and sometimes they were located in other states, so the show connected with them by long distance phone lines so local callers could talk with them. A variety of listeners called in to the talk show phone lines, and they voiced a wide range of opinions—many pro-gay and a few anti-gay.

"Sometimes we were surprised by callers with opinions that ran contrary to what we believed most gay people thought. The sentiments of our callers gave us greater insight into what common gay people in the community really were thinking."

"I also was surprised at the large amount of mail we received from the listening public. Some of it was fan mail and some of it was hostile mail that was downright threatening."

In March 1978 new station owners bought KWBZ and immediately cancelled the contract to air *Colorado Gaybreak*. By that time all volunteers who worked on the show were burned out and quite content to return to their former quiet lives absent the pressures of producing a weekly radio show.

Chapter 38

Back to L.A. with John

Jim's life in Denver came to an end at the dinner table one night a month after *Colorado Gaybreak* ended.

"John told me we were moving to Los Angeles. He didn't ask what I thought about moving to LA. He didn't say he was thinking of moving there. His mind was already made up. I tried to reason with him, that we owned our own townhouse and that we had real security for the first time in our lives and that my life had turned around in Denver with him. But he was determined, so of course I went along with what made him happy."

"We moved to the southwest LA metro area and resided in the oceanside city of Torrance."

John and Jim lived near their sisters in the Los Angeles metro area.

Figure 62: Anita, cousin Stanley, and Ruth.

Jim's two sisters Ruth and Anita along with Anita's two young sons lived together in the West Covina area on the east side of the LA metro area.

John's sister Marguerite lived with her family in Long Beach, just east of John and Jim. She had lived there for years.

"We got to visit everybody a lot. It was like John had it all planned that way."

"I still loved to get outdoors, but instead of Cheesman Park and the Denver Botanic Gardens, we had Torrance Beach and the South Coast Botanic Garden. I must say, it was so nice this time around in LA compared to the previous times I struggled in LA."

"One of the most exciting things about being in LA was being able to visit the huge gay archives collection of Jim Kepner in his apartment. At that time he called it the Western Gay Archives. I'd learned about his archives from Elver Barker who knew him from their time together at the Mattachine Society."

Jim Kepner was one of the major pioneers of the gay movement.

Figure 63: Jim Kepner on the phone at the National Gay Archives in Los Angeles.
[Courtesy of ONE Archives at the USC Libraries]

His primary contribution was amassing an unparalleled collection of contemporary and historical LGBT information. One historian wrote: "Kepner's articles record not only the past of the gay rights movement but also its soul."[94]

Jim Kepner was a highly respected man—modest, decent and polite. He lived a dedicated life of self-sacrificing meager means in pursuit of equal rights for gay people. He believed everybody had a right to sit at the gay table—that the obvious swishy queens and bull dykes were the ones who originally openly fought the oppressors of homosexuals, which paved the way for the closeted straight-acting segment to be able to sneak into gay bars and cruise known gay spots.

Jim Foshee was in awe of Jim Kepner's dedication and reputation. He had been an early Mattachine Society member and served a term as its president. As with a handful of other Mattachine leaders, Jim had been a member of the Communist Party. A couple of years before he began his gay activism with the Mattachine Society, he was thrown out of the Communist Party when his comrades discovered he was a homosexual and therefore an enemy of the people. He and the other former Communist Party members who belonged to the Mattachine Society applied their acquired knowledge and strategies learned from the party in their quest to obtain equal human rights for gay people.

Jim Kepner described himself a pack rat extraordinaire.[95] In 1942 he began combing through libraries and bookstores in search of any literature about homosexuals and transgendered people that he could uncover, especially historical information.

Jim Kepner never threw away notes and papers he obtained from any gay meetings or events. His collection grew to include press clippings, photos, pamphlets, flyers, posters, signs, buttons and any other artifacts he could find.[96] He began his quest almost a decade after the Nazis in Berlin in 1933 raided and burned Magnus Hirshfeld's large sexuality library collection and destroyed his Institute for Sexual Science. It was the world's first organization devoting some of its time and resources to homosexual advocacy. No other archives matched this German library's homosexual holdings until Jim's archive became larger than any previous or subsequent gay collection anywhere.

He memorized a virtual encyclopedia of gay history. He wrote for *ONE* magazine throughout the 1950s and served as *ONE* associate editor from 1954 to 1960.[97] In addition to writing under his own name, Jim wrote articles under pseudonyms including Lyn Pedersen, Dal McIntyre and Frank Golovitz.[98] Most *ONE* writers used pseudonyms, and sometimes a particular pseudonym was passed around and shared by more than one writer depending on the context of the article. Those various pseudonyms added a lot more apparent voices to the magazine than what actually existed.

Jim Kepner also wrote numerous articles for other gay publications and mainstream press. His early writings were crucial in crafting and promoting progressive perspectives of homosexuality and gay life into the zeitgeist of the latter half of the 20th Century. For LA's first original 1967 PRIDE organization (Personal Right in Defense and Education), Jim served as the organization's Publications Director. Along with two other volunteers he edited and produced the first year's *PRIDE Newsletter*,[99] a publication that gradually developed into the preeminent national publication *The Advocate* for which Jim continued penning articles for years.

He was a founding member of the educational organization ONE Institute—part of ONE Inc., which also owned and published *ONE* magazine. He served on its Board of Directors during various years from the 1950s thru the 1980s, including stints as its corporate president,[100] chairman and vice president.[101] He served as the first editor of its scholarly journal *ONE Institute Quarterly of Homophile Studies.*

In 1953 ONE Inc. opened its own office located in downtown LA on Hill Street. Jim Kepner and other staff members taught seminars, lectures and classes for the ONE Institute Graduate School, which was a fully authorized graduate college of higher education qualified by the State of California for students to earn a California accredited degree in "Homophile Studies."

Now back in California, Jim Foshee ended up doing volunteer work for Jim Kepner for three years as an archive's assistant. "I was so excited every time I went to Jim's archives. I worked on chores to help him out with his collection, which was organized mainly in his head."

For years Jim Kepner lived amongst his expanding collections inside his cramped apartment in Hollywood. Eventually the library's size physically crowded him out of his home. In November 1979 he moved his collection—and himself—from his apartment into a spacious storefront location at 1654 N. Hudson Avenue just off of Hollywood Boulevard, and he opened for business. He slept in the basement, which contained a small bed, toilet, hotplate, clothes and stacks of archival items.

At the new location, the newly incorporated and renamed organization proudly proclaimed on its front door, "National Gay Archives Natalie Barney/Edward Carpenter Library."

Figure 64: Jim Kepner standing outside his National Gay Archives Natalie Barney/Edward Carpenter Library at 1654 North Hudson Avenue in Los Angeles, early 1980s.
[Courtesy of ONE Archives at the USC Libraries]

Moving the archives from his apartment into the new storefront immediately positioned the archives as a bonafide professional organization. A succession of volunteers constantly showed up to help.

During the archives' first year in the new storefront it acquired a government jobs training grant to fund paid positions. The archive's Board of Directors hired Jim Kepner as its curator. After three decades of Jim's unpaid work creating the archives with little monetary assistance, he finally began receiving an income for working in his newly paid position.

"Since I'd been helping Jim Kepner on and off for three years, I applied for one of the newly created paid positions. I'd earned some impressive credentials in Denver doing the research for Jonathan Ned Katz and Terry Mangan. Those things plus my excitement and passion for research got me hired."

"Inside the gay archives, Jim Kepner and I and the volunteers were surrounded by mountains of books on bookshelves that reached from the floor to the ceiling. We were forever organizing the archive's large rows of file cabinets. Jim also began collecting audio and video recordings, and he taped audio oral histories."

"At my new gay archives job I was Jim's assistant and served as an office manager and assistant curator. I did normal administrative tasks and helped volunteers catalog materials. I also helped with fundraising and conferences. Whenever Jim was out of town speaking at conferences and honorariums and fundraisers, I'd serve as Jim's temporary archivist."[102]

"I also researched gay history on topics that Jim wanted me to delve into to see what I could dig up. Over the previous half decade I'd found all sorts of things from the 1800s and 1900s. I found stories of men living as women and women living as men. Their secrets were shockingly revealed as people prepared their bodies for burial. Of course, their supposed wives or husbands 'had no idea!' I also dug up stories about arrests and drag balls and lovers' spats gone wrong. Reporters in those days always covered all of these stories and exposes as bewildering and disgusting."

$$\nabla$$

The winds of change were picking up by 1979. About 100,000 people showed up for the National March on Washington for Lesbian and Gay Rights. The Radical Faeries held retreats in Benson, Arizona and a second retreat the following year at a campground in the Colorado Mountains west of Denver.

And for Jim and John, the winds of change in December 1979 marked a crisis in the happy, simple, secure life they shared. "One evening John told me he'd been coughing up blood from his lungs. His doctors had told him he had cancer. I put up a brave front, but I was worried. John quit his job at Stanton Laundry Repair and concentrated on getting back his health. Our finances were a mess. We got hit with the double whammy of John's loss of full paychecks and the costs of his medical needs."

"The first few months were promising, and John got better. I continued driving back and forth every weekday to my job at the archives. At night I'd come home and cook and take care of John. In spring 1980 we both realized that his health was going downhill. His sister was a nurse, so we all decided that John would move in with Marguerite and her family. She would nurse him back to health. That's what I'd hoped, even though I suspected the worse."

"Most days when I got off of work, I'd drive to Long Beach in slow rush hour traffic and spend time with John, and then I'd drive back home to Torrance. John's health kept deteriorating. Even though we didn't talk about it much, we all knew his lung cancer had spread and the end was approaching."

On July 10, 1980 John's sister called Jim. "John had died as Marguerite held him in her arms. He was 52 years old. I never felt so empty in my life. I was only 41 years old, and my life had fallen apart."

"Since Marguerite was legally John's surviving next-of-kin, she was in charge of the funeral. She was cordial and invited me to attend. I went and was accompanied by Ruth who dearly loved John. I was introduced to everyone at the funeral as one of John's friends."

"I absolutely was drained by the time everything was finished. I didn't do a thing that weekend after the funeral except lie down and think. I remembered a dozen years earlier when Lenora in San Francisco read her tarot cards to me and revealed that she saw a man to my east who was a tall blonde, and she predicted that for him and me it would be the true thing. The only thing Lenora got wrong is that she told me it would last forever. I cried a lot that weekend."

"On Monday I forced myself to restart my life."

"I continued driving John's car. Thank goodness I had the car. It was my lifeline."

John and Jim's assets were eaten up by John's medical condition. Jim was unable to pay rent for the apartment by himself, so he moved in with his two sisters in West Covina.

Jim relied heavily on Ruth for her love and emotional support. She and Jim had long talks about life. They both agreed that John must have known he had cancer back in Denver, and that was why he insisted that he and Jim move to LA to live near their sisters. Although Jim and Ruth had not broached the subject with John before he died, they both felt certain that a cancer diagnosis in Denver must have been the reason for the sudden move.

"Meanwhile, I continued to work at my dream job at the gay archives. The archives awarded me a certificate for its 1980 Volunteer of the Year Award. It was a big deal to me, and I was very proud of it."[103]

Jim's position was paid through a local government grant funded by the U.S. Government's CETA program (Comprehensive Employment Training Act), which provided federal money to support public service non-profit 501(c)(3) organizations so they could employ paid staffers. In October the gay archives applied for an extension, but within a few days Jim Kepner was informed that the grant for Jim Foshee's paid position was not renewed. Within days Jim was out of a job.

In early November Ronald Reagan was elected president. Paid positions at gay non-profit organizations may have been perfectly fine for the liberal Jimmy Carter administration and for the local LA government. However, with a conservative Republican moving into the White House, government funding for jobs in some homosexual library was one of the first things on the chopping block.

Then Ruth received an excellent job offer from San Diego that she could not refuse. It required her to temporarily move down to Coronado Island. That left Jim, Anita and her two sons remaining in the house.

Jim had saved as much money as he could, because he was afraid of coming up short.

"Anita was always borrowing money and things from me. She was concerned only about herself. I was so tired of her self-centered attitude."

"Everything again was turning out bad like usual in LA. I thought about my future and decided to return to Denver where my life had never been better. I had my move all planned. For $700 I could rent a U-Haul trailer and drive back to Denver. I had enough money saved up for a good start in Denver."

"About a week before leaving for Colorado, Anita called our home one night. 'Oh Jimmy, I wrecked your car! I hurt my arm. The police are here! I need to find a way home!'"

"I didn't have any way to get her home. Besides, she just wiped out my mobility. I absolutely had to have that car to survive in the LA metro area and to take me to Denver. I knew I shouldn't have lent her my car! She was only worried about herself and not having to go to jail. Not a word about my car or how I now was stranded. It was the most important thing I had. It would cost a couple thousand dollars to repair. Now that I didn't earn a living at the archives anymore, I didn't have any way to get that extra money."

Strapped for cash and without a car to haul his furniture, Jim ended up selling almost everything he and John owned—living room furniture, dining room set, china cabinets and lots of clothes. Jim shipped his remaining possessions by Allied Moving Company to Denver, including his bed, clothes, crystal collection John had bought him and all of the files containing his gay research.

For Jim it could not happen soon enough. "Was I ever glad to get the hell out of LA!"

Jim packed a suitcase, and in late-1980 he rode a Greyhound bus to Denver.

"I moved on with my life."

Chapter 39

Return to Denver

Moving on for Jim also meant making a sharp break with what was left of his family.

Before embarking on the trip back to Denver, he called his mother to tell her about John dying. She said she was sorry to hear the news but, "Now he'll burn in hell to pay for his sins."

When he hung up, Jim vowed never to speak with his mother again. He kept that promise to himself for the rest of his life.

"I don't know a thing about whatever happened to her after that day. Within a few months, my sisters had moved, and I didn't have their new phone numbers. The only way to contact them was through my mother, and I was determined to never talk to her again. Therefore, I never again saw or talked to my sisters."

"Back in Denver at the end of 1980, I rented a one-bedroom apartment on Capitol Hill and met my neighbor there, Jeff Sperano."

Figure 65: Jim's downstairs apartment inside this converted fourplex at 1334 Downing Street, Denver.

"Unlike LA, everything in the Capitol Hill neighborhood was within blocks of each other, so I could walk everywhere and didn't need a car."

"John Shepperd and I were thrilled to see each other again. It had been about four years since he owned The Terrace Showcase, and he had not opened another gay nightclub. He was shaken about me loosing John and being alone."

Denver's gay community, like most across the USA at the time, consisted of almost all young people. They were similar to the young people in all of the other protest movements who were advocating for all sorts of social change.

In Denver during those years it was rare to see anyone with gray hair in a gay bar. Older homosexuals were set in their ways—most of them remained in the closet or were in longtime heterosexual marriages and shied away from joining the new gay rights movement. Most gay people out in those years were young enough that they had never experienced the death of another gay person. That tragically began changing within a matter of a couple of years with the onslaught of the AIDS crisis. John's death ended up a mere foreshadow of the legion of deaths that soon was to emerge.

"My loss of John touched John Shepperd, and he was determined to help me." John was working at the high-class Brown Palace Hotel in downtown Denver where he coordinated food service and tended bar in the upscale Ship's Tavern. He helped Jim get a job at the hotel. Since Jim had experience working in restaurants and working at the affluent Dallas Statler Hilton, he was hired to work in the Brown Palace's restaurant dining area.

The Brown Palace Hotel hosted U.S. presidents, foreign kings, queens and dignitaries. Therefore it conducted detailed background investigations of all employees. Three or four months after Jim was hired, the results from his background report revealed that Jim had served a prison sentence, which he had failed to disclose to the hotel.

"I was fired on the spot. I made up an excuse to explain to John Shepperd and others why I wasn't working for the hotel anymore. I never revealed to anybody that I'd been in prison."

"A few months later I got a job working at the Denver Public Library. It was located a dozen short blocks from my apartment—a nice walking distance. Working at the library was really convenient for doing research work at both the library and the nearby Colorado Historical Society. I spent many hours researching before and after my work shifts."

Located a couple of blocks from Jim's apartment was the renamed Gay and Lesbian Community Center of Colorado. Carol Lease had become the center's new paid coordinator. Her job title quickly changed from coordinator to executive director.

As soon as Jim returned to Denver he began volunteering at the center's library.

"It was so sweet to see the library again. It contained the books and publications and historical archival materials from the old gay Coalition Library that Terry Mangan and I had assembled in the early 1970s. Now four years later I was back in Denver, and things were fine at the library."

Since the community center's opening, librarian Neil Woodward had spent over three years establishing and building the center's library. It contained the largest collection of gay materials in the Rocky Mountain region. People donated books, and others made cash donations to the library in the form of restricted funds, which the community center set aside to spend exclusively on the library.[104] Neil collected, catalogued and grew the library to more than a thousand books, gay and lesbian periodicals from across the country, gay travel guides, photo collections, press clippings and a small collection of VHS video cassettes.

When Jim arrived at the library, Neil was ready for a breather and resigned as librarian. Besides, Neil had a more dynamic venture in the offing.

Jim took over the Terry Mangan Memorial Library's day-to-day operations. He expanded the community center's historical collection and formed the community center's Rocky Mountain Gay/Lesbian Archives,[105] serving as its curator. The archives would open by appointment to community center members and for anybody doing research on homosexuality.

Jim donated some of his historical research papers to the center's library and to the Colorado Historical Society. Some documents were ones he had discovered, and others he copied from the National Gay Archives in LA and brought to Denver. He located and gathered some copies of the old Mattachine *Denver Area Newsletter* and donated audio cassette copies of all *Colorado Gaybreak* radio shows to the center's Terry Mangan Library.[106]

"Jim Kepner and I began corresponding back and forth during that spring and summer in 1981. We'd become good friends through the previous three years. I let him know of my work at Denver's new gay archives, and I told him, 'In many ways I seem to be following in your footsteps.'"

In the months since Jim had left California for Denver, the situation at the archives in Los Angeles had become more insecure. Vandals had shot out the big glass windows and doors with marbles from a high-powered sling shot. No paid positions remained—all employees lost their paid jobs in light of the new Reagan administration cutting the funding for the national CETA jobs training program. Even Jim Kepner lost his personal income and barely managed to keep the archives' bills paid. With no air conditioning during an unusually hot summer, it was like an oven in the archives both day and night. It was all beginning to wear thin on Jim Kepner.[107]

Regardless, the National Gay Archives collection in LA continued to grow. Jim Kepner sponsored several fundraising art shows and theatre parties and participated at national conferences of the American Psychological Association, the American Historical Association and the Gerontological Society of America.[108]

In Denver Jim Foshee presented his idea and proposed an itinerary to sponsor a fundraising visit by Jim Kepner to come to Denver to call attention to gay history. He asked Jim in LA, "Please Jim, I know you're modest, but I want people here to know about you, so please send an extended Bio."[109]

In June 1982 during Denver's Gay Pride Week, Jim Kepner made the trip. Denver activist Pat Gourley who previously had visited Jim's archives in LA arranged for Jim's speaking engagements. Jim Kepner stayed with Pat and his partner David Woodyard at their home[110] a half dozen blocks from North Capitol Hill.

During pride week Jim Kepner attended a candlelight demonstration at the state capitol,[111] interviewed with Colorado's gay media and visited the local feminist bookstore. He gave a talk at the University of Colorado Denver, Auraria campus,[112] weaving tale upon tale of historical political figures, rulers, entertainers, authors and ordinary people known to be homosexual or transgender.

"I was acquainted with three or four old Mattachine members involved in the 1950s Denver Area Council. So I planned a reunion for them and other old Mattachine members with Phil Nash's help." Now 20 years later, Jim Kepner and a bunch of the old members once again gathered together during pride week. They visited and reminisced about their bold audacity in those oppressive bygone days.

Figure 66: Former members of 1950s Mattachine Society Denver Area Council. (Top) Bill Reynard & Earl Gebhardt. (Front) Elver Barker & Roland Karcher. [Photo by Brian Brainerd, Denver Post Collection via Getty Images]

Jim Kepner was the only Mattachine member during pride week who had remained involved in the gay rights movement. He was astonished that Elver Barker and Rolland Karcher (Rolland Howard) and the other Denver Mattachine members had not kept up with the movement during the ensuing two decades. Their reaction to the post-Stonewall era seemed to be summed up by Elver Barker, "We always thought that if we dressed properly, people would respect us. People dress just any way now."[113]

"I had the library committee sponsor a reception for Jim Kepner at the community center, which also featured lesbian feminist activist and sociologist Phyllis Gorman. Jim Kepner made a presentation there at the center archives[114] where he gave the organization copies of *Mattachine Review*. I'd asked Jim to bring copies to Denver in order to help fill a knowledge gap that I thought existed in the community center's archives."

The next evening Jim Kepner and Phyllis Gorman attended the grand opening of Denver's new gay bookstore, Category Six, at 909 East Colfax Avenue.[115] A few months after resigning as community center librarian, Neil Woodward and his business partner Sue Doell opened the bookstore. About six months after opening, Sue left Category Six to fulfill her desire to open her own feminist bookstore, Herizons.[116] Neil's life partner Dan Otero had been involved in Category Six's creation, planning and finances since its conception. He was a Continental Airlines pilot and got locked out of his job when Continental Airline employees were swept up in a large labor union dispute with the airline; so now Dan was free to step in and become Neil's active on-site business partner.

Figure 67: Owners Neil Woodward and Dan Otero at Category Six bookstore
in a Christmas advertisement in *Out Front*, December 1984.
[Denver Public Library, Western History Collection, WH2383 OV box; and *Out Front Magazine*]

Before Category Six opened, there were few places across the USA with decent selections of books about sexually diverse people. The guys ended up operating the store together for years—first on Colfax Avenue and then on 11th Avenue between Ogden and Corona Streets.

Neil's years of experience organizing the community center library plus working as a librarian at the University of Denver and the Denver County Jail helped to prepare him well for the new business venture.

During the first few months in business on Colfax, Denver police entered Category Six to hassle the business for pornography and its associated seedy elements; but officers instead learned that Category Six bookstore was not in the porn trade business but rather was a legitimate storefront dealing in serious GLBT literature for a respectable clientele. So the cops ended up working with Category Six, the Money Express check cashing center next door and other businesses in the block to minimize crime in the area. The relationship between gay people and police now was improving bit by bit.

$$\nabla$$

"I met interesting characters during my second stay in Denver. I remember my good friend Martha Brummett was involved in the intriguing politics of the community center; and I remember a guy working on the center's hotline who I shared tips with on how I helped callers at the Gay Coalition; and I remember a woman who was a member of the lesbian musical band The Rubber Husbands, which entertained crowds at various venues in the area. All nice people."

"I also had a neighbor who was this wild young biker guy into leather and whips and bondage who rode with the gay Rocky Mountaineers Motorcycle Club."

The biker club began in Denver a year before Stonewall happened. The club billed itself as a social and philanthropic group. Members rode motorcycles on the highest roads in the continental USA.

People from Colorado and across the USA, Canada, Europe and Australia would join the club's runs, hitting the roads on motorcycles for fun and freedom. Its most popular biker event was the annual Golden Fleece Run (GFR) each 4th of July weekend when the bikers partied hard in secluded mountain forest lands.

In a column in Denver's gay newspaper *Out Front*, club member Charlie Donalson wrote about the Golden Fleece Run: "It is felt that those attending GFR are also seeking something, whether it be a vacation high in the Colorado Rocky Mountains (with over a hundred men of like mind), or the brotherhood of seeing people again after a year of club activities in their own states, or for some a taste of the wilder and often intense sex that does occur between these mature and involved gay leather men."[117]

Figure 68: Rocky Mountaineers, 1981. [Courtesy Christopher Sloan]

The Rocky Mountaineers also sponsored other popular runs—including its Shakedown Run and a Poker Run. Every September members rode in the club's autumn Aspen Road Rally up into the high country to spend time among the mountainside panoramas of Aspen trees turned golden yellow.

The club had it together so well that it was able to raise enough money to eventually purchase (free and clear of any mortgage) its own 40+ acres of private rustic mountain land that bordered federal government land. The parcel, Camp Jason, served as the club's private domain for holding outdoor parties and blowouts. The club also made the land available to other gay community groups to use.[118]

"In general, I loved the good-natured people I knew in Denver. It was so good to be back. I still mourned the loss of John, so I didn't date or go out to the bars or get romantically involved with anybody. I just didn't feel like it. I could count my friends on the fingers of one hand, but my life was cozy and safe now that I was back in Denver."

Chapter 40

Pink Triangle Radio

In the early 1980s, Jim was itching to do some more gay radio. "A couple of us mulled over putting together another local gay radio show."

"I wanted us to make another visit to Denver's only public radio station, KCFR. Eight years after originally asking the station to air a gay show, I decided we needed to inquire again about the station airing a gay show. We now met the requirement that someone had to have broadcast experience in order to produce a gay program at the station. So in mid-1982 we approached them." KCFR Station Manager Max Wycisk explained that KCFR had matured and evolved into more sophisticated programming that included classical, jazz and National Public Radio programs. A gay radio show would not fit into the station's upscale format. Colorado Public Radio in Denver would not consider airing a gay program.

"We were out of luck again at Denver's only public radio station, this time for another reason. So we regrouped and brainstormed and looked back a handful of years."

After *Colorado Gaybreak* went off the air in 1978, the gay radio show *Gay Spirit* aired for about a year on Colorado's public radio station in Boulder, KGNU 88.5 FM. The station broadcasted with a weak 1300-watt signal that sometimes generated poor reception in Denver, 30 miles to the station's southeast.

"Carl Armon and Ginny Oman produced *Gay Spirit*. Carl was highly respected and well-liked. We never met Ginny. After *Gay Spirit* went off the air, no gay shows aired on any Colorado broadcast stations for the next four years."

In late 1982 Jim and other activists decided to follow Carl Armon's lead, and they inquired about producing a new gay show at KGNU and approached Program Production Coordinator Fergus Stone. The Boulder station gave approval to the group to air the new weekly gay show, and the gay group began broadcasting the show beginning the first week of 1983.[119]

The gay production group decided to call the show *Pink Triangle Radio*. The volunteers of Pink Triangle Radio told nobody at the station about any significance of the name.

Figure 69: *Pink Triangle Radio* promotion.

After a few months, a KGNU staff member came into the station during the gay show. The previous week she had attended rehearsals in Boulder for the stage play *Bent*, about the 1930s/1940s Nazi persecution and deaths of homosexuals and the internment of thousands of homosexual degenerates in concentration camps where most were worked to death—all in the Third Reich's attempt to eradicate homosexuality in Germany. She was surprised to learn during the play's rehearsals that concentration camp prisoners wore triangle badges sewn onto their clothes to identify them: Jews wore two yellow triangles that formed the Star of David; political prisoners wore a single red triangle; criminals wore a single green triangle and homosexual men wore a single pink triangle. She never had known that homosexuals had been sent to concentration camps. As soon as she understood about the pink triangle in *Bent*, she thought of *Pink Triangle Radio*. She told others at the station about the origins of the pink triangle, and people at the station perceived and understood the historical tragedy that had occurred in the lives of homosexuals.

Two Denver businesses donated money weekly to underwrite the show: 1) Category Six gay bookstore owned by Neil Woodward and Dan Otero, and 2) Papplemousse card shop and novelties, owned and operated by young entrepreneur Steve Fox and his partner Michael Creeden.

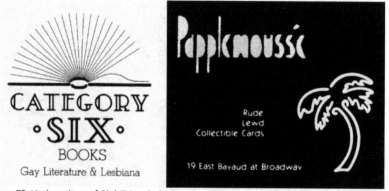

Figure 70: Underwriters of *Pink Triangle Radio*—Category Six books & Papplemousse card shop.

Jim and Lisa Miller[120] worked on the show every week doing reports and other voice work. Occasional contributors to the show included Dawn Tagerson, Jay Klausenstock, Jerome Perlinski and Mike Corbin.

"Every week a couple of us *Pink Triangle Radio* staff members drove the 60-mile-long roundtrip to and from Boulder. We carried with us the weekly shows on audio tape reel, which we had pre-recorded and produced and edited in a living room in Denver."

"One weekend I inadvertently left a couple of scripts at KGNU. They ended up mistakenly discarded into the trash barrel with other items supposed to be thrown away next to that barrel. After that I insisted that we stamp all scripts and record albums with the words 'Pink Triangle Radio' so they wouldn't get lost. We continued that practice long after the show ended. Whenever we purchased any new gay albums, we stamped them since we thought we might revive the show someday elsewhere, which never ended up happening."

For the show's opening and closing and for bridges between the program's segments, the show used the electronic moog synthesizer classical music of female transsexual Wendy Carlos. She had won a number of Grammy Awards and accolades for her innovative music.

Pink Triangle Radio's magazine format included coverage of local Colorado events, interviews with elected politicians and candidates, talks with local gay activists, local investigative journalism, gay and lesbian music and interviews with gay and lesbian musicians. It also included national gay news reports from National Public Radio about the new disease AIDS along with local AIDS coverage reported by the *Pink Triangle Radio* Staff.

KGNU's reception could be heard in Denver, although it was sometimes less than desirable. KGNU also was relayed and retransmitted to various towns throughout Colorado. "We learned that fact one day during a broadcast when a caller from a small town up in the middle of the mountains wanted to know the name of a gay song we just had played—it was *Castro Boy* by Danny Boy and the Serious Party Gods." The song was a raunchy, high energy, gay novelty takeoff of Frank Zappa's song *Valley Girl*. His lyrics "gag me with a spoon" became Danny Boy's "gag me with a dick." That and other lyrics about unconventional sexual activities throughout the song caused significant problems for airing it. "We certainly performed some heavy editing on that song to get the thing cleaned up enough for public broadcast. The caller from the mountains told us he listened to KGNU and *Pink Triangle Radio* on the town's cable system. That was a surprise to us. None of us on the show were aware that KGNU's actual reach across Colorado was so large."

The staff of *Pink Triangle Radio* exchanged tapes of the show with over a dozen other gay radio show producers across the USA. Sometimes *Pink Triangle Radio* would re-broadcast segments from their shows, and sometimes their shows would re-broadcast segments from *Pink Triangle Radio*.

During the 1983 broadcasts of the show, Jim utilized his vast collection of historical research he had uncovered. He produced gay history radio features about early gay leaders, homosexual musicians, writers, entertainers and people in history who lived their lives secretly as members of the opposite sex, including women who served as men in the U.S. Civil War. History spots included reports about Bayard Rustin, Lucy Hicks and Tony Jackson.

The show featured interviews of Jim's mentors: 1) He brought in National Gay Archives curator Jim Kepner to discuss gay history, and 2) Jim interviewed book author Jonathan Ned Katz who talked about his new gay history book *Gay/Lesbian Almanac*, the follow-up to his groundbreaking book *Gay American History*.[121]

Jim produced a feature about early gay recording artist Rae Bourbon[122] whom Jim had first heard three decades previously in 1954 at Bunny's home during Jim's first trip to California when he ran away from home as a 15-year-old. Now decades later Jim found and purchased a couple of Rae's records, which were very rare and difficult to find in the 1980s before internet sales transactions became universally available for people in search of old obscure phonograph records.

$$\nabla$$

A gay newspaper or magazine can get away with reporting gay bar incidents as long as the story does not place a gay bar in a bad light. If a report portrayed a gay bar as victimized, then it probably would pass muster, such as the attempted robbery at Denver's Tool Box gay bar or the shooting at Mike's gay bar. However, gay newspapers and magazines were beholden to their gay bar advertisers and could not get away with reporting a controversial story that might put a gay bar in a negative light.

One such story that *Pink Triangle Radio* broadcasted was about employees who were suing the Denver gay bar, David's, at the federal government's National Labor Relations Board. In contrast to gay publications, gay radio shows were able to independently report such stories, since airtime for public radio gay shows were funded through numerous small contributions made to non-profit public radio stations—money given to stations directly by listeners rather than money earned through advertising paid in large part by gay bars. Thus, *Pink Triangle Radio* was free to produce hard-hitting investigative stories about Denver's gay bars, including the case of David's bar before the NLRB (a case that the employees won, and the bar owners lost). Gay bars simply were unable to dictate *Pink Triangle Radio*'s news coverage in contrast to the way they dominated business decisions for the rest of the gay press. The way public radio gay shows were funded made those radio shows directly accountable only to station contributors, not to advertisers such as gay bars.

Phil Price founded, owned and published Denver's gay newspaper *Out Front* starting in April 1976. At the beginning of 1980 Phil Nash resigned his position as coordinator of the Gay Community Center of Colorado and became the lead contributing writer for *Out Front*. "Both Phils were friends of a couple of us who worked on *Pink Triangle Radio*. Whenever we saw one another the main topic of conversation inevitably ended up being gay related."

"Phil Price and we helped each other. We interviewed Phil on *Pink Triangle Radio*. He printed small news items in each edition of *Out Front* promoting musicians or features that were being featured on our next radio show."

"Phil Price and we would discuss the difficulties that we encountered in selling and producing advertising placed in various gay media outlets. Phil sold ads for *Out Front*, and we had sold commercials a half dozen years previously for *Colorado Gaybreak*."

Unlike *Pink Triangle Radio*, which was aired on a public radio station, the old *Colorado Gaybreak* show was funded by advertisers on a for-profit station. Therefore, *Gaybreak*'s staff could not speak out negatively about advertisers, including the gay bar advertisers.

"We clearly understood the dynamics that required Phil Price to proceed with caution when reporting about any gay bars that advertised in *Out Front*."

Figure 71: *Out Front* founder and publisher Phil Price. April 1983. [Courtesy *Out Front Magazine*]

The gay Denver Tavern Guild summoned Phil on at least a couple of occasions to declare demands. Phil explained his thoughts in an interview on *Pink Triangle Radio*:

"I don't like the control that my advertisers have over my editorial policy and concerns. In the final analysis my advertisers are the ultimate censors of *Out Front*. I have to walk a very fine line editorially between approval and disapproval. If an advertiser dislikes a particular piece, he can withdraw his support, and indeed some have on occasion if they were upset at a particular article. So, I don't like that."

"One thing that I always have to keep in mind—and that's that *Out Front* is a business. And as unfortunate as it is, I cannot bite the hand that feeds me. I nibble on it a little bit, but I never bite too hard."

"I was called in front of the newly formed Tavern Guild several weeks ago to discuss perhaps putting more coverage of bar activities in the paper. And any reader of *Out Front* will notice that recent editions do in fact have more coverage of what's going on in the bars, and unquestionably, this is a result of that meeting. But I think people like it. I've had a lot of really good comments from people who enjoy seeing their pictures, pictures of their friends, the bar personalities in the paper. *Out Front* can't be everything to everyone. We try to present a very well-balanced format with national news, feature articles, bar news, columnists. We just can't be everything to everyone—but we try."[123]

"I always thought of Phil Price as a real decent guy and a very savvy business owner."

Chapter 41

Politics of AIDS

The major disease of the late 20th Century made its debut in the media on May 18, 1981 in the gay newspaper *New York Native*. The newspaper's medical writer Dr. Lawrence D. Mass received a tip about an exotic new disease that had hit the gay community in New York City. He interviewed an epidemic intelligence officer from the federal government's Centers for Disease Control who happened to be in New York at the city's Department of Health. The CDC officer claimed that the rumors of an exotic new disease were unfounded for the most part. However, he did say that recent incidental infections of amebiasis or a possibly more virulent strain of the protozoa-like organism pneumocystis pneumonia had been reported in four or five men who were said to be gay, and one had died.[124]

Less than three weeks later on June 5 the CDC itself published its own report confirming the new disease in its publication *Morbidity and Mortality Weekly Report*. That day and the next day the Associated Press, *Los Angeles Times* and *San Francisco Chronicle* picked up the story and ran articles about the CDC's report of the new disease. A month later on July 3, *The New York Times* published its first article about the new disease.

Researchers were unsure if the cluster of cancers, lung illnesses and other opportunistic infections were the same disease, how it all was contracted and what exactly caused these illnesses. Researchers and the media were not even sure what to call it, originally referring to it as GRID (Gay Related Immune Deficiency) or simply calling it Gay Cancer. The following year in summer 1982, health experts gave an official name to the new disease—AIDS (Acquired Immune

Deficiency Syndrome), which replaced the name GRID since the syndrome did not strike only gay men.

In 1982 the first case of AIDS was diagnosed in Colorado.

Prior to the AIDS epidemic, gay activists primarily dealt with less challenging problems of helping people come out or helping them solve personal dilemmas. Those issues suddenly gave way to the new crisis. Agonized individuals mobilized to take care of friends and strangers who were dying at an unusually young age. The focus of gay activism now shifted. All other concerns took a back seat to the new terror. Who would be next to receive the death sentence? Who would end up dead in one, two or three years?

Instead of raising money for general gay causes, all fundraising attention now got redirected to the new major deadly emergency. Most gay people and gay organizations felt compelled to donate more of their money than ever to AIDS activism to care for the sick and dying.

"We broadcasted various reports covering the developing AIDS story on *Pink Triangle Radio*. In October 1983 we reported details of how the Gay & Lesbian Community Center of Colorado was using funds raised for the Colorado AIDS Project. We thought this was significant enough that the critical report deserved wider circulation, so we shared the text of our report with Phil Price so he could print it in *Out Front*—the only thing we requested of Phil was that the news article contain no byline. The story ran in *Out Front*[125] and aired on *Pink Triangle Radio*[126] within a day of each other."

The AIDS funding news story caused a stir among gay people and prodded the gay Denver Tavern Guild to get involved in gay politics once again after almost a decade since the gay bars had tangled with *Rhinoceros*. The old gay Denver Tavern League had disbanded after opposing the Gay Coalition in 1975 and recently had formed again under the slightly renamed Denver Tavern Guild (DTG). As reported in the community center's monthly *Colorado Gay and Lesbian News*: "One of the first acts of the DTG when it re-formed was to send a letter to gay publications in town threatening to pull their advertising revenue if there wasn't more coverage of their bar events."[127]

A couple of weeks before the AIDS funding report was aired on *Pink Triangle Radio* and printed in *Out Front*, the gay community had held a giant AIDS fundraiser called A Celebration of Hope at the

Paramount Theatre in downtown Denver. Few tickets for the 1,200-seat fundraiser had sold, and Denver Mayor Federico Pena was scheduled to attend. To prevent the gay community from being embarrassed by low gay support and turnout in front of the mayor, bar owners of the Denver Tavern Guild purchased blocks of tickets so they could actively push customers to buy the tickets in order to help fill an otherwise empty theater. "Gay Tavern Guilds across the country often used their money and influence for the benefit of their businesses and their profits. However, in this instance the Denver Tavern Guild was attempting to use its money and influence for the good of the gay community."

The Denver Tavern Guild presented the Gay and Lesbian Community Center of Colorado with a check for the total amount of over $7,000 raised from A Celebration of Hope. A couple of weeks after the fundraiser occurred, the news report about AIDS finances became public. The report detailed a vote at the community center that allowed it to take up to 15% of AIDS funds and channel that money into the center's general operating expenses as it deemed fit.

Of the $13,000 raised for the AIDS Project, the center spent approximately:

$3200 for brochures,
$2400 for coordinator's salary,
$500 for space rental,
$700 for supplies and postage,
$850 for front money and
$100 for direct patient support.

In the center's 1984 budget, the AIDS Project would pay for its office, one of the community center's two phone lines, photocopying, supplies, participation in a gay/lesbian health fair, slide show updates, video tapes and more.

Celebration of Hope organizers claimed the community center mislead them to believe that the money raised would go primarily to people with AIDS, not to excessive administrative costs.

"Everybody I talked to thought that only $100 spent for direct patient support was way too little financial support going to people with AIDS, considering that the community center spent about $8,000 on various administrative costs."

Organizers of A Celebration of Hope ended up having to placate angry participants who had attended the fundraiser. The Hope committee asked the community center for assurances that half of all money raised for the Colorado AIDS Project would go to provide direct assistance for needy people with AIDS. They also wanted the center to release public financial reports.

The Gay and Lesbian Community Center was obstinate. Nope, the center was not about to let outside groups dictate how it would spend any restricted funds donated to the center.

The center's Board of Directors decided that the community center leadership was most familiar with the financial needs of the AIDS Project. The center would continue making all major decisions regarding the AIDS crisis. The center's directors refused to accept the $7,000 Celebration of Hope funds, since the donation contained stipulations that the contributions were restricted for certain specific uses. The center claimed that it had to research all legal issues related to restricted donations before proceeding any further. "I remembered that in the past the center had accepted various restricted donations, including restricted donations used only to purchase books for the center's library."

"Gay people I knew balked at donating any money and contributions to AIDS that would be funneled through the Gay & Lesbian Community Center. Bar owners said they polled their gay customers and found no support for the center."

The members of the community center who paid at least $15 for a year's membership were eligible to vote for the candidates they wanted on the Board of Directors. The Board of Directors defined the center's general policies, and it hired and supervised the paid executive director who implemented those policies and ran the day-to-day activities of the center.

Part of the structure of the community center was the important Board of Governors—gay business entrepreneurs, bar owners and community groups that provided oversight, advice and a check over the powers of the Board of Directors.[128] However, currently there was a major problem. The gay businesses and bars of the Board of Governors had voted to dissolve itself four years previously after the Governors accomplished its first original goals two years after the center opened.

"I thought it was unfortunate that the gay businesses and bars had discontinued their influence." Now, instead of a Board of Governors working as a powerful integral component within the community center organization, the bar owners were relegated to fighting a public and negative battle against the center as outsiders under the banner of the Denver Tavern Guild.

The guild voted to raise no more funds for the community center until the center accepted AIDS funds with two main stipulations: 1) donors would be able to dictate how their donated money would be used and 2) the center must regularly release public financial accounting reports. A couple of weeks later the community center acquiesced to the ultimatums of the Denver Tavern Guild. The guild officially announced the end of its boycott against the center, but the guild made no more substantive efforts to raise any significant money for the community center and its AIDS Project.

"After I attended my last community center membership meeting, the center began running out of money, mainly because people just weren't supporting it anymore. Hardly anyone wanted to donate to the center." In response, the community center's leadership decided to "borrow" money from the Colorado AIDS Project to fund the center's general operating expenses.

The center ended up going over $10,000 in debts to keep itself solvent, which included over $7,000 it withdrew from Colorado AIDS Project funds.[129] Directors were confounded about how they would be able to repay the loans back to the AIDS Project.

By June, the center was completely out of money to run the Colorado AIDS Project, so CAP separated from the community center and became its own fully-independent organization. It moved into new offices and within a couple of months had built up $11,500 from newly enthusiastic donations.

By mid-July with a worsening financial crisis, the center's Board of Directors forced the resignation of the center's paid executive director who quit reluctantly. Then the majority of directors resigned. Only two directors remained on the board.

Immediately after the center's radical leadership shakeup involving exiting board members and in particular the executive director, the Denver Tavern Guild promptly donated a check to the community center. It totaled over $1,000 to pay two months back rent owed to the center's landlord. In the following months the 7-year-old community center started repaying its debts and rebuilding through the efforts of a skeleton crew of dedicated volunteers—only volunteers, no paid staff members.

The Tavern Guild had made a couple of controversial missteps during its dispute with the center and suffered public image damage. So, the Tavern Guild embarked on a positive public relations campaign in attempt to put its best foot forward. The Guild's president stated, "The center is an important and viable part of the community, and we never ever wanted to see it go under. We can't afford to lose it. It's a moral responsibility for us, even though many of our customers aren't the type of people who would use it."[130] Jim thought, *"Yes, but people who need the center's help now could become your bar customers in the future."*

Through its PR initiative, the Denver Tavern Guild publicly talked up how it perceived its good will toward the gay community. It bragged about its involvement with the Colorado Gay Rodeo Association that year. The guild proudly released its financial report in August 1984—it revealed that its largest expenditure of over $800 was spent to provide free shuttle-bus transportation[131] to haul crowds from the rodeo and place them in the gay bars in town for what gay bar owners labeled "Denver's biggest party."[132] This strategy reaped nice additional profits for bar owners.

Chapter 42

Last Years

The weekly *Pink Triangle Radio* program ended in December 1983. It had aired on KGNU for that entire year. In mid-year Fergus Stone resigned his leadership position at the station, and new Station Manager Greg Fisher assumed general control of the station. "During the year that *Pink Triangle Radio* aired, KGNU management never questioned or second-guessed any of our production or editorial decisions."

"With no radio show to work on every week, I had a lot more free time on my hands. So in February 1984, I took time off for a month-long research trip around the country. I took my portable Walkman cassette player and earphones with me. I remember that I listened over and over to the long 9-minute version of Soft Cell's *Tainted Love/Where Did Our Love Go*. Very trance-like."

Jim departed Denver to research through the northern states and then to the East Coast. His furthest eastern destination was Washington D.C. where he spent two weeks researching at the U.S. government's National Archives and the Library of Congress. On the trip back west he took the warmer southern route and stopped in Arizona to do historical research about Native Americans. Jim felt wonderful basking in the warm Southwest desert weather.

"Then I was off to Los Angeles and San Francisco. In LA I visited Jim Kepner for a few days at the National Gay Archives. I donated a few of my research papers to Jim and the archives." At the visit's end, Jim Kepner took Jim to Los Angeles Union Station to catch a train to San Francisco. There they happened to run into "Hal" Harold Call, Jim Kepner's friend from the old Mattachine Society. Hal was the member who took over the Mattachine Society from the original founders and moved its headquarters to San Francisco where he lived.

Coincidentally, Hal and a friend were catching the same train back home to San Francisco that Jim was riding.[133]

"During the whole train ride Hal Call and his friend and I talked non-stop. Hal's favorite word seemed to be cocksucker. He was opinionated, but I found our conversations really stimulating."

"By the time I met Hal in 1984, he had racked up a long mixed history in the movement. During my stay in San Francisco I visited a couple of times with Hal at his gay erotica bookstore and peepshow business he owned."

"I remained in San Francisco doing research for a week. Then I returned to Denver and its cold weather."

Figure 72: Jim in San Francisco, 1984.

"Denver had been a wonderful place to live. My first years in Denver had been a period of growth and maturity and true love. My second span of years in Denver was a healing time as I dealt with John's death. Now, after four years back in Denver I knew it was once again time to move on."

In summer 1984 Jim moved to the small city of Yuma, Arizona in that state's southwest corner—located on the tri-border area of Arizona, California and Mexico. A couple of Jim's close friends from Denver had moved to Yuma and were living there, including Jim's good friend Jeff Sperano who had lived in the same Denver fourplex apartment home where Jim had lived.[134] Jim was enthusiastic about leaving the cold weather of Colorado and basking in the hot desert climate of Arizona.

Throughout most of the next two decades—during the last years of Jim's life—he lived mainly in Arizona. Now that he was living nearer his old stomping grounds in California, it was fairly easy to visit Los Angeles and San Francisco a few times during the 1980s and 1990s. Although he attempted a couple of times to return to California to live, he ended up being disappointed with California and returned to Arizona.

In late autumn 1984—a few months after he left Colorado—Jim spent a week back in Denver for one final time. He tied up a couple of overlooked gay research items and took the opportunity to visit friends back there. Although Jim had moved from the city only a few months previously, he now encountered a profound change in the psyche of gay people there. AIDS had begun to significantly hit gay men in Denver.

"My friend John Shepperd had the HIV virus, and it already had progressed to full-blown AIDS. He was the first person I ever personally knew with the disease. I went to see him, and we visited. His health had forced him to stop working at the Brown Palace Hotel where he'd gotten me a job. He never would open up another glitzy show bar like The Terrace Showcase. A few short months later in March 1985 my close friend John Shepperd died."

"After my 1984 autumn research week in Denver I returned to Arizona and hunkered down there for the approaching winter."

"In Arizona I discovered quite a number of gay history items about Native Americans. One of the members of Jim Kepner's archives

Board of Directors was Walter Williams. He was a professor of anthropology, history and gender studies at the University of Southern California. Jim Kepner put him in contact with me because Walter was writing a book about Native American androgynous gender-variants—'two-spirits' and 'berdache.' So I sent him some of my American Indian research for his book."

Walter Williams' book *The Spirit and the Flesh: Sexual Diversity in American Indian Culture* was published in 1986. Among Jim's contributions to Walter's book were two stories of handsome young Indians among the Blackfoot and Crow Indians. One Indian in the 1840s dressed as a woman and did chores with the tribe's women. The other was a teenage Blackfoot male in the 1880s who flirted with a cowboy as the cowboy pinched and patted the Indian while the two explored whether the young Indian would be the cowboy's "squaw" or "brave."

Alas, Jim was becoming restless again. The last time he lived a settled fulfilled life was when he lived with John. Now a few years after John's death Jim was yearning to reconnect with his fellow activists and friends in California. He hit the road again in attempt to fill the emotional emptiness that lingered since John's death.

In late 1987 Jim moved from Arizona back to Los Angeles. He stayed with Jim Kepner and did some volunteer work at the archives. A few weeks later he moved in with David Van Ryzin, his old friend who had been editor of Denver's old gay newspaper *The Scene*. David was now running and operating a marketing company in LA that printed flyers and handbills that advertised various businesses. Jim went to work for him. Jim, David and David's partner Michael Pyle distributed the advertisements to homes in strategically targeted LA neighborhoods from San Fernando Valley in the north to Newport Beach in the south. "I always had walked a lot, so this job was exactly what I liked. Very healthy."

"Sometimes the three of us drove by the archives during our business trips, and we'd stop and visit with Jim Kepner and help him out in small ways. In Jim's tiny living space in the archives' basement, a flimsily-erected shower spout had been out of order for months. Jim had tried patching the plumbing, but that didn't do any good. Since the archives had a chronic shortage of money, he wasn't able to pay a plumber to work on it; so Jim was confined to cleaning himself from a small bucket with a sponge and soap. During one of our visits to the archives, David diagnosed the plumbing problem and fixed it for Jim."

Eventually Jim Foshee grew tired of California again and moved back to Arizona. He ended up reinventing himself as he had done three or four times previously in his life: In the 1950s as a starry-eyed teenage runaway hoping to hit it big in Hollywood; then on the streets trying to survive; then a doting domesticated partner when he found the man of his dreams; and then an activist when he found a cause worth living for. Now after the loss of John he settled down to live a quiet life as a respected researcher in academia.

In 1988 Jim began taking college courses at Arizona Western College in Yuma where he worked as a library clerk alongside his friendly co-worker Rickley Prewitt. A year later he moved to Flagstaff where he attended Northern Arizona University and worked at that university's library.

"During my studies in Flagstaff, I worked as a research assistant in the NAU history department. I assisted Dr. William Roosen who was Regents' Professor of History. He wrote about homosexuality in European history. I researched French and English history to find information about 18th Century Europe[135] for a book the professor was writing. I also helped prepare materials for the professor's classes."

Dr. Roosen noted: "Jim was doing the quality of work normally expected of a graduate student.... Jim searched diligently in such newspapers as Defoe's *Review* and *The Athenian Mercury* to discover references to France, sports and sexuality. He appears to have found virtually everything which existed on these topics because he reads very carefully. In fact, I have never known anyone who is as willing to spend such long hours reading microfilm as he is."[136]

Jim worked for other professors and eventually earned a reputation among university staff as a top-notch researcher. Jim also worked doing research for NAU's Center for Colorado Plateau Studies in Flagstaff. Eventually he worked as a marketing researcher for Nautical & Aviation Publishing Company of America researching and locating potential markets and sources across the USA for the company.

In 1990 he transferred again, this time to the University of Arizona in Tucson where he worked for four years in the university's main library and in the Science-Engineering Library. In Tucson he did research for University of Arizona professors and staff members.

Then in 1994 Jim tried living in California one more time. He moved to San Francisco on a limited income. The high cost of living in the city and the suffering and homelessness on the streets was too disheartening. "I was getting too old for that shit anymore, so after a couple of months I got out of San Francisco and returned to the warmth of Arizona for good."

$$\nabla$$

"Jim Kepner and I kept in contact with each other throughout our years of friendship. We exchanged sexy Christmas cards containing humorous sexual double-entendres."

Eventually Jim Kepner's huge collection, known since summer 1984 by a new expanded name, International Gay and Lesbian Archives,[137] merged with the library collection of ONE Inc. After the merger, the archives finally achieved permanent stability upon moving into one of the buildings of the University of Southern California's library system. It became the largest gay archives in the world—the esteemed "ONE National Gay & Lesbian Archives at the USC Libraries."

Jim Kepner died in November 1997. He was a man whom Jim Foshee respected above most others. The death was another sorrow in Jim Foshee's aging life. The following May Jim attended a memorial celebration for Jim Kepner in LA held at the Academy of Motion Picture Arts and Sciences' Samuel Goldwyn Theater in commemoration of Jim Kepner's life and his decades of dedication to the LGBT movement. "I felt really wonderful that evening visiting old friends and early gay activist acquaintances among the crowd whom I'd met through Jim Kepner."

Jim Foshee had been anticipating the turn of the century and the new millennium, but the new century was not kind to Jim. A lifetime of cigarette smoking took its toll. Jim was diagnosed with chronic obstructive pulmonary disease (COPD). During the last couple of decades of his life, Jim had lived intermittently in Yuma where his close friends also lived. He retired in Yuma and lived off a small monthly Social Security disability check. During the last five years of his life he stayed mainly in the safety of his little one-bedroom apartment in Yuma. He busied himself with his computer, cable TV, gay research and the new internet phenomenon. Jim realized the end of his life was approaching. He had been hospitalized three times. At the end of December 2005 an emergency ambulance crew rushed him to the hospital. One of the paramedics stuck himself with a needle he had used on Jim, and as a precaution Jim was tested for the HIV virus. The results showed that Jim was negative for the virus, and the paramedics crew breathed a hefty sigh of relief.

Jim barely made it to 2006. In Yuma on New Year's Day 2006 at the age of 66, Jim died. He had wanted to be cremated, but since his written will did not specifically stipulate that wish and since no next of kin had been found at that time, Arizona state law required that Jim's body be buried in Yuma. The following week Yuma County government buried James David Foshee in a pauper's grave in Yuma, Arizona.

Afterword

The goal of a biographer is to get as close to the truth as possible. In interviews, the recollections and memories of people are sometimes unclear or mistaken. Also, people sometimes fib.

I researched numerous documents to fill in details and to verify claims by interviewees to prevent inaccuracies from slipping into this book.

Historians and biographers who write about famous people have multitudes of available sources and documents on which to rely such as numerous interviews, plentiful public records and abundant archival materials that enable validation of facts. On the contrary, when writing a biography about an unknown private citizen, often a writer/researcher encounters a difficult time finding the few obscure independent records and credible sources that exist. In many cases that means the statements and interviews of private individuals must be taken at face value.

Governments and institutions are not always forthcoming in providing documents in their possession, and they often hold back in releasing records. State laws often forbid release of certain files, documents are excepted from open records public information laws, and old records cannot be found because in earlier decades old files were cleared away and destroyed to make room for newer pertinent files. Denials to provide documents often cause important elements of history to be missing in biographies.

This book has gone through many reiterations and editings. As new information and documents were researched and discovered, sections of the book would alter. Some stories and events in rough draft form did not advance into the final biography.

∇

Additionally…

Language and colloquialisms used by coalitions of sexually diverse people are fluid and evolving, and they change through successive decades. In this book, I generally use the terms in fashion during the various time periods covered in these pages.

Research by Jim Foshee

In the 1970s, 1980s and beyond, Jim conducted his gay research. When he died he left behind thousands of pages of extensive research of gay history from the 1800s, early 1900s and beyond.

His research included in-depth research about: women who married woman; men who married men; gay cowboys; cowboys who were girls and women; women's colonies; the Boys Secret Society; miners; hermits; hobos and tramps; same sex kissing in public; early laws; medical reports; women outlaws; military stories; prison and jail stories and statistics; Native Americans; Clear Creek, Colorado in 1859; the Bird Cage Bar; Boise sex scandal; Portland sex scandal; the bicycle girl and the mermaid; Oscar Wilde in the USA; Walt Whitman in Colorado; early Denver gay activist groups including the Denver Area Council of the Mattachine Society and The Neighbors; and others.

A.J. Baker, Albert Cashier, Archie Venable, Babe Bean, Baron Friedrich Von Steuben, Bayard Rustin, Birdie Bean, Mable Edison, Bert Martin, Billy Johnson, Charles Miller, Charles L. Newcum, Charley Parkhurst, Ed Donovan, Charley Vosbaugh, Charlotte Cushman, Cornhole Johnny, Cowboy Jack, Cowboy Miller, Dr. Faker, Ellis Glenn, Eugene Fields, Frank Gray, Frank Hall & F. Stevens, George (Mary) Miller, Helen Potter, Jack Hill, Billy Le Roy, Jenne Bonnet, Jessie Kemble, John Ryan, John Yearnshaw, Laura Deforce Gordon, La Vengadora, LeDuc & Gillin, Leon Belmont, LeRoy & Boynton, Ora Chatfield & Clara Dietrich, Mary Delay, Mary Fields, Milton Matson, Miss Mary Martin, Mountain Charley Hatfield, Mrs. Nash, Nellie B. Hewitt & Columbia Anna Robbins, Nicholai De Raylan, Pearl Hart, Percy Pincer, Sam Pollard, Senorita

Ramona Perez, Thomas Maxwell, Tom King, Wild Bill Hickok, William Breakenridge, William H. Cleery, William Horace Lingard, William Wallace, Willie Mathews, and others.

Gay entertainers: Annie Hindle, Ella Zoyara, Grace Leonard, Julian Eltinge, Leon & Kelly, Rae Bourbon, and Tony Jackson.

Acknowledgments

I offer my sincerest thanks and deepest gratitude to all of the people who helped me in so many ways with this book.

- Ruth Foshee, who provided me with invaluable information about her brother Jim Foshee and their family. She also gave me many old family photos of Jim.
- ONE National Gay & Lesbian Archives at the USC Libraries in Los Angeles: Lead Archivist Loni Shibuyama; Library Supervisor & Operations Manager Bud Thomas; and Reference & Instruction Librarian Michael Oliveira.
- The Center on Colfax/GLBT Community Center of Colorado: LGBT History Project Founder/Coordinator David Duffield.
- Denver Public Library, Western History Department: James Jeffrey, Coi Drummond-Gehrig, James Rogers, Kili Schmid, Roger Dudley, Hannah Parris, Katie Rudolph, Bryan Trembath, Martin Leuthauser, Janice Prater, Abby Hoverstock and all others there who were helpful to me but whose names I failed to write down.
- Hart Research Library at History Colorado (formerly named Colorado Historical Society): Library Director Kerry Baldwin and Reference Librarian Sarah Gilmor.
- *Out Front Magazine*: Publisher Jerry Cunningham & Editor Addison Herron-Wheeler.
- CoMedia: Larry Laszlo.
- GLBT Historical Society of San Francisco: Registrar Collections & Exhibitions Ramon Silvestre, Executive Director Terry Beswick, Assistant Archivist Patricia Delara and Managing Archivist Joanna Black.
- The Tangent Group: Stephen Allison.

- San Francisco Public Library: Christina Moretta.
- Texas Department of Criminal Justice: Jeff Linderman, Joshua Lippold, and Jerry Holdenreid.
- Idaho State Archives/Idaho State Historical Society: Alisha Graefe, Rachel Hollis.
- Thirteen Productions LLC: Jennifer Bertani.
- Estate of Robert Giard: Jonathan G. Silin.
- Décor Art Galleries: Lynne Crandall
- Pioneer gay book editor: Michael Denneny who provided valuable advice.
- Beta readers and professional historians who reviewed the manuscript and gave me feedback: Bud Thomas, Gary Dean, Jonathan Ned Katz, Lois Church Wygal and Ramon Silvestre.
- My publishing consultant: Brian Schwartz.
- Cover designers, cover technology contributors: Tatiana Vila, Marty Olson & Steve Fendt.
- And last but not least, my editor Barbara Edwards who provided indispensable review and advice.

To all of the people who were an integral influence with their help on this book — Thank You, all.

Notes / Bibliography

[1] Foshee, Jim; gay history audio report of Rae Bourbon, *Pink Triangle Radio*, Oct. 22, 1983, *Pink Triangle Radio* recordings [ONE National Gay & Lesbian Archives at the USC Libraries]

[2] Zagria.blogspot.com/2010/06/ray-bourbon-1892-1971-performer.html#WrRC7GWwBEI (date of access Jul 2, 2017)

[3] Riddle, Randy A.; "Don't Call Me Madam, The Life and Work of Ray Bourbon" Oct 2009 www.coolcatdaddy.com (date of access Jan 13, 2018)

[4] Sakk0; "Rudolph Valentino in Blood & Sand—Say Goodbye", Aug 2011, www.YouTube.com (date of access Aug 18, 2018)

[5] Centers for Disease Control and Prevention, NCHA Data Brief #114: "Trends in Out-of-Hospital Births in the United States," Mar 2014

[6] Bryan, Clifford; *The Idaho Industrial Training School: 1903-1970 (Idaho Youth Services Center) St. Anthony, Idaho, A New Social History Investigation*, published by Idaho State University Pocatello, Fall 1980, 47-57 [Idaho State Archives; Boise, Idaho]

[7] Legg, W. Dorr; *Homophile Studies in Theory and Practice*, (San Francisco CA, ONE Institute Press, GLB Publishers, 1994), 31

[8] Kepner, Jim; *Rough News—Daring Views*, (Binghamton NY: The Haworth Press, 1998), 11

[9] Rowland, Chuck (pseudonym: Freeman, David L.); "How much do we know about the Homosexual Male?" *ONE* magazine, Nov 1955, 4 [ONE National Gay & Lesbian Archives at the USC Libraries]

[10] Jones, M.A.; FBI Memorandum, "Subject: The homosexual magazine published by ONE Inc. 232 South Hill Street Los Angeles 12, California" Feb 10, 1956, 3 [ONE National Gay & Lesbian Archives at the USC Libraries]

[11] Jones, M.A.; FBI Memorandum, "Subject: The homosexual magazine published by ONE Inc. 232 South Hill Street Los Angeles 12, California" Feb 10, 1956, 1b,7,8 [ONE National Gay & Lesbian Archives at the USC Libraries]

[12] 241 Federal Reporter, 2d Series, "ONE Inc., Appellant v. Otto K. Olesen, individually and as Postmaster of the City of Los Angeles, Appellee, No. 15139," 772

[13] 78 Supreme Court Reporter, 3 355 U.S. 371 "ONE Inc., petitioner, v. Otto K. Olesen, individually and as Postmaster of the City of Los Angeles, No. 290," 364

[14] Kepner, Jim; "Introduction" *Rough News—Daring Views*, by Kepner, Jim (Binghamton, NY: The Haworth Press, 1988), 2

[15] Timmons, Stuart; *The Trouble with Harry Hay* (Boston MA, Alyson Publications, 1990) 167

[16] Jennings, Dale; "To Be Accused, Is To Be Guilty" *ONE* magazine, Jan 1953, 10 [ONE National Gay & Lesbian Archives at the USC Libraries]

[17] Legg, W. Dorr; Introduction, *Homophile Studies in Theory and Practice*, (San Francisco CA, ONE Institute Press, GLB Publishers, 1994), 3

[18] White, C. Todd; www.tangentgroup.org "ONE Incorporated First Official Board Meeting and Election of Officers Minutes, Nov 1, 1953" (date of access Apr 14, 2018

[19] Advertisements, *ONE* magazine, Jan-Jul 1953 [ONE National Gay & Lesbian Archives at the USC Libraries]

[20] Cowlishaw, Howard C., M.D.; "Readmission Note", State Hospital South, Blackfoot, ID, Apr 2, 1959 [author's collection]

[21] Kepner, Jim; *Rough News—Daring Views*, (Binghamton NY: The Haworth Press, 1998), 99

[22] The name Cassie is a pseudonym.

[23] Frank, Nathaniel; *Unfriendly Fire: How the Gay Ban Undermines the Military and Weakens America*, (New York, NY, Thomas Dunne Books, St. Martin's Press/Griffin, 2009) 1-10

[24] Ginsberg, Allen; "Howl," *Howl and Other Poems*, (San Francisco, City Lights, 1956)

[25] Cowlishaw, Howard C., M.D.; "Readmission Note," State Hospital South, Blackfoot, ID, Apr 2, 1959 [author's collection]

[26] Police Reports, General Offense Reports, Dallas Police Department, Aug 30-Sep 4, 1962.

[27] Certified Copy of Judgment and Sentence, Criminal District Court No. 3, Dallas County, The State of Texas vs. James David Foshee, No. D-8509-HJ, Sep 26, 1962

[28] Public Information Disclosure Sheet, "Basic Information Relating to Offender (Inmate) of Texas Department of Criminal Justice," Foshee, James David, ID# 169011

[29] Kepner, Jim; Oral History Interview of Jim Foshee, Jan 9, 1988 [ONE National Gay & Lesbian Archives at the USC Libraries]

[30] 1376 Pearl Street, Apt. 210, Denver, CO (Polk's Denver County Colorado City Directory 1969-1970) [Denver Public Library, Central Library, Western History/Genealogy]

[31] Mangan, Terry; Interview of Harry Bateman (pseudonym David L. Daniels) 1974 [Terry Mangan papers/John Paul De Cecco papers (2001-17), GLBT Historical Society (in San Francisco)]

32 Foshee, Jim; "List of some 1950s original members of Mattachine Society Denver Area Council" includes 12 members' names, addresses & phone numbers (including Rolland Karcher & Harry Bateman); compiled 1980 by Jim Foshee [author's collection]

33 Foshee, Jim; "List of some 1950s original members of Mattachine Society Denver Area Council" includes 12 members' names, addresses & phone numbers (including Wendell P. Sayers); compiled 1980 by Jim Foshee [author's collection]

34 Marcus, Eric, "Wendell Sayers," Oct 19, 2016, *Making Gay History* podcast, makinggayhistory.com radiopublic.com/making-gay-history-GqRA95/ep/s1!f76e2 (accessed Mar 27, 2017)

35 Leitsch, Dick; "Police Raid on N.Y. Club Sets Off First Gay Riot," *The Advocate*, (article reprinted from New York *Mattachine Newsletter*), Sep 1969

36 Flyer of the Mattachine Society of New York, "Where Were You During the Christopher St. Riots?" 1969 [Manuscripts and Archives Division, New York Public Library]

37 Leitsch, Dick; "Police Raid on N.Y. Club Sets Off First Gay Riot," *The Advocate*, (article reprinted from New York *Mattachine Newsletter*), Sep 1969

38 "What Is Gay Liberation Front?" [Gay Liberation Front, Vertical File, Tamiment Institute Library, Elmer Holmes Bobst Library, New York University]

39 Untitled report of the Denver Gay Liberation Front, 1971 [Terry Mangan papers/John Paul De Cecco papers (2001-17), GLBT Historical Society (in San Francisco)]

40 *Heads and Tales* newsletter of Denver Gay Liberation Front, Vol.1 No.3, Mar 12, 1971, 3 [Terry Mangan papers/John Paul De Cecco papers (2001-17), GLBT Historical Society (in San Francisco)]

41 *Heads and Tales* newsletter of Denver Gay Liberation Front, Vol.1 No.1, Feb 12, 1971, 1 [Terry Mangan papers/John Paul De Cecco papers (2001-17), GLBT Historical Society (in San Francisco)]

42 Denver Gay Liberation Front report about the group's participation in Denver anti-war march [Terry Mangan papers/John Paul De Cecco papers (2001-17), GLBT Historical Society (in San Francisco)]

43 "Gay Contingent Is Being Organized for Anti-War March—April 15th" *Denver Gay Liberation Newsletter*, Vol.1 No.1, Apr 8, 1972 [Terry Mangan papers/John Paul De Cecco papers (2001-17), GLBT Historical Society (in San Francisco)]

44 Ginsberg, Allen; "Colorado Collation—Vernon Memo: Notes, addresses, and poems" Apr 8-May 28, 1972 [Ginsberg (Allen) Papers, Manuscripts Division, Stanford University]

45 Author's interview of Allen Ginsberg at Naropa Institute, *Pink Triangle Radio*, Aug 27, 1983 [*Pink Triangle Radio* recordings, ONE National Gay & Lesbian Archives at the USC Libraries]

Banned from California

[46] Full Disclosure: The author of this book, along with partner Rick Miller and another friend were issued jaywalking tickets at the same time after all three jaywalked together across Broadway in front of The Broadway gay bar.

[47] "Jaywalking" *The Scene*, Mar-Apr 1976, 15 [Denver Public Library, Central Library, Western History/Genealogy]

[48] "Anti-gay Cop 'busted'" *Out Front*, Aug 31, 1984, 6 [Denver Public Library, Central Library, Western History/Genealogy]

[49] Valanzuela v. Snider, U.S. District Court for the District of Colorado, 889 F. Supp. 1409 (D. Colo. 1995), Civ. A. No. 85-K-1845, June 20, 1995.

[50] Anderson, Lee; "Denver free" *The Advocate*, Nov 6, 1974, 4 [author's collection]

[51] Interview of Ron Wilson, *Colorado Gaybreak* recordings, Nov 6, 1977 [Denver Public Library, Central Library, Western History/Genealogy] -and- [ONE National Gay & Lesbian Archives at the USC]

[52] "Feature. Profile: Colorado Gays Emerging from the Closet" *Rhinoceros* monthly newspaper of the Gay Coalition of Denver, Nov 1974, 10 [author's collection]

[53] "Broadway Emptied Due to Walkout" *Rhinoceros* monthly newspaper of the Gay Coalition of Denver, Dec 1974, 1 [author's collection]

[54] "Representatives of Denver Gays Meet" *Rhinoceros* monthly newspaper of the Gay Coalition of Denver, Mar 1975, 1 [author's collection]

[55] "Editorial" *Rhinoceros* monthly newspaper of the Gay Coalition of Denver, Mar 1975, 3 [author's collection]

[56] "Editorial" *Rhinoceros* monthly newspaper of the Gay Coalition of Denver, Apr 1975, 5 [author's collection]

[57] "Gay Pride Week" *Gay Coalition of Denver Newsletter* #13, Jul 1974, 4 [Hart Library, History Colorado (formerly named Colorado Historical Society)]

[58] Marcus, Aaron B; "PrideFest: A History of Denver's Gay Pride Celebration" *Colorado Heritage*, May/June 2013, 26 [History Colorado]

[59] "Gay Pride Week" *Gay Coalition of Denver Newsletter* #12, Jun 1974, 1 [Hart Library, History Colorado (formerly named Colorado Historical Society)]

[60] "Local Gay-In Is Big Success" *The Scene*, Vol.3 Issue9, Jul 1975, 9 [author's collection]

[61] Duffield, David; oral history interview of Christi Layne, Colorado LGBT History Project, Apr 27, 2015

[62] "The Gay Pride Parade" *The Scene*, #51, Jul 1976, 24 [author's collection]

[63] Nash, Phillip A; letter "To Whom This Concerns" Mar 25, 1980 [author's collection]

[64] Interview of Phil Nash, *Colorado Gaybreak* recordings, Jan 8, 1978 [Denver Public Library, Central Library, Western History/Genealogy] -and- [ONE National Gay & Lesbian Archives at the USC]

[65] J.Y.; "Board of Governors Disbanded" *Gaynin'* newsletter of the Gay Community Center of Colorado, Vol.2 Issue11, May 1979, 2 [author's collection]

342

[66] Johnny Gay Seed, "The Gay Stage" *The Scene* Apr 1-21, 1977, 34 [Denver Public Library, Central Library, Western History/Genealogy]

[67] Gerash, Gerald A.; "On the Shoulders of the Gay Coalition of Denver" *United We Stand: The Story of Unity and the Creation of The Center*, Phil Nash, editor; a publication of the GLBT Community Center of Colorado, Jun 3, 2016, 5 www.lgbtqcolorado-org/programs/colorado-lgbtq-history-project/research-resources/Unity-1975-1977/ (date of access Dec 11, 2018)

[68] Author's interview of J.W. Christopher Sloan aka Christi Layne, June 2018 [author's collection]

[69] Advertisement, *Contact*, Issue #10, circa June 30, 1977, 4, back page [Denver Public Library, Central Library, Western History/Genealogy]

[70] Interview of Jim Foshee, *Colorado Gaybreak* recordings, Aug 18, 1977 [Denver Public Library, Central Library, Western History/Genealogy] -and- [ONE National Gay & Lesbian Archives at the USC]

[71] Gerash, Jerry; "A Tribute To Terry Mangan" Speaking Out (Letters to the Editor), *The Scene,* Aug 5-Sep 2, 1977, 18 [Denver Public Library, Central Library, Western History/Genealogy] -and- Gerash, Gerry (sic); "Letters" *Out Front*, Aug 19, 1977, 4 [Denver Public Library, Central Library, Western History/Genealogy]

[72] Cansino, Yannek Kenneth; "Historian Terry Mangan Takes Life" *San Francisco Sentinel*, Jul 28, 1977, 2 [author's collection]

[73] Kepner, Jim; oral history interview of Jim Foshee, Jan 9, 1988 [ONE National Gay & Lesbian Archives at the USC Libraries]

[74] Mangan, Terry; letter to Jim Foshee, May 5, 1977 [Terry Mangan Collection, Hart Library, History Colorado (formerly named Colorado Historical Society)]

[75] Mangan, Terry; letter to Jim Foshee, undated [author's collection]

[76] Thompson, Mark; "Ram Dass: A Life Beyond Labels" *Gay Soul: Finding the Heart of Gay Spirit and Nature with Sixteen Writers, Healers, Teachers, and Visionaries* (New York, NY. Harper San Francisco, A Division of HarperCollins Publishers, 1994) 148-167

[77] Dowling, Colette; "Confessions of an American Guru" *The New York Times*, Dec 4, 1977

[78] Davidson, Sara; "The Ultimate Trip" Tufts University *Tufts Magazine*, Fall 2006

[79] Leighton, Jared E.; "Freedom Indivisible: Gays and Lesbians in the African American Civil Rights Movement 5-2013" University of Nebraska-Lincoln, Dissertations, Theses, & Student Research, Department of History, May 2013 [digitalcommons.unl.edu/historydiss/61, accessed Nov 15, 2017]

[80] Colorado Historical Society later was renamed History Colorado.

[81] Interview of Jim Foshee, *Colorado Gaybreak* recordings, Aug 18, 1977 [Denver Public Library, Central Library, Western History/Genealogy] -and- [ONE National Gay & Lesbian Archives at the USC]

[82] Singular, Stephen; *Talked to Death* (New York, NY: Beech Tree Books William Morris, 1987)

[83] Dukakis, Andrea; "Murder of Colorado Radio Man Alan Berg Still Resonates 30 Years Later," Jun 18, 2014, Colorado Public Radio website [cpr.org], (date of access Mar 11, 2016)

[84] Lee, Michael Adam; "The Politics of Antisemitism in Denver, Colorado, 1898-1984" 2017, History Graduate Theses & Dissertations, University of Colorado, Boulder [https://scholar.colorado.edu/hist_gradetds/37]

[85] "Roar" Rory Poliac

[86] Author signed the contract with KWBZ and was responsible as Executive Producer for collecting the money to pay the station each week for the broadcast time to air *Colorado Gaybreak* and for selling and producing commercials that funded the money paid to KWBZ for the airtime. Also responsible for producing the show and supervising all volunteers.

[87] "Rick" Richard Miller, at that time the author's partner

[88] Elder, Dean; "Around Town," *Dispatch* newsletter of Rocky Mountaineers Motorcycle Club of Colorado, Oct 1977, 2 [author's collection]

[89] "Ken" Kendall Watts

[90] Watts, Ken; letter to Bob Steele, Nov 13, 1977 [author's collection]

[91] "Jan" Janice Grimm

[92] "Jan" Janis Hoegh

[93] "Will" "Bill" William Guthrie

[94] Percy, William A., PhD, Professor of History; "Pre-publication reviews, commentaries, evaluations..." *Rough News—Daring Views*, by Kepner, Jim (Binghamton, NY: The Haworth Press, 1988), first page

[95] Dynes, Wayne R.; "Foreword" *Rough News—Daring Views*, by Kepner, Jim (Binghamton, NYK: The Haworth Press, 1988), *viii*

[96] Survey of Lesbian and Gay Archives and Libraries, circa 1984 [ONE National Gay & Lesbian Archives at the USC Libraries]

[97] *ONE* magazine, 1954-1960 [ONE National Gay & Lesbian Archivers at the USC Libraries]

[98] Kepner, Jim; "Introduction" *Rough News—Daring Views*, by Kepner, Jim (Binghamton, NY: The Haworth Press, 1988), 11

[99] Pride Newsletter, Oct. 24, 1966, Vol.1 No.6, 2 [ONE National Gay & Lesbian Archives at the USC Libraries]

[100] Kepner, Jim; "Epilogue" *Rough News—Daring Views*, by Kepner, Jim (Binghamton, NY: The Haworth Press, 1988), 394-395

[101] Finding Aid of ONE Inc. records 1907-2001, bulk 1952-1994 Coll2011-001 pg. 5, Timeline of People [ONE National Gay & Lesbian Archives at the USC Libraries]

[102] Kepner, Jim; letter "To Whom It May Concern" Nov 8, 1980 [author's collection]

[103] Foshee, Jim; letter to Jim Kepner, Spring 1981 [ONE National Gay & Lesbian Archives at the USC Libraries]

[104] "Did You Know?" *Gaynin'* newsletter of the Gay Community Center of Colorado, Vol.5 Issue1, Jan 1981, 1 [author's collection]

[105] "Did You Know?" *Gaynin'* newsletter of the Gay Community Center of Colorado, Vol.5 Issue1, Jan 1981, 1 [author's collection]

[106] "The Rocky Mountain GLCCC Archives" *Gaynin'* newsletter of the Gay and Lesbian Community Center of Colorado, Vol.5 Issue2, Feb 1981, 2 [author's collection]

[107] Kepner, Jim; letter to Jim Foshee, Spring 1981 [author's collection]

[108] Kepner, Jim; letter to Jim Foshee, Spring 1981 [author's collection]

[109] Foshee, Jim; letter to Jim Kepner, Spring 1981 [ONE National Gay & Lesbian Archives at the USC]

[110] Kepner, Jim; autobiographical diary, June 23, 1982 [ONE National Gay & Lesbian Archives at the USC]

[111] Kepner, Jim; autobiographical diary, June 23, 1982 [ONE National Gay & Lesbian Archives at the USC]

[112] Kepner, Jim; autobiographical diary, June 26, 1982 [ONE National Gay & Lesbian Archives at the USC]

[113] Kepner, Jim; autobiographical diary, June 26, 1982 [ONE National Gay & Lesbian Archives at the USC]

[114] Kepner, Jim; autobiographical diary, June 24, 1982 [ONE National Gay & Lesbian Archives at the USC]

[115] Kepner, Jim; autobiographical diary, June 24, 1982 [ONE National Gay & Lesbian Archives at the USC]

[116] Doell, Sue; "Herizons: Politics of 'Feminist' Business" *Big Mama Rag*, Jan 1984, 3,16

[117] Donalson, Charlie; "Golden Fleece Run" *Out Front*, Jul 9, 1982, 18,19 [Denver Public Library, Central Library, Western History/Genealogy]

[118] "Club Purchases Gay Park," *Dispatch* newsletter of the Rocky Mountaineers Motorcycle Club, Sep 12, 1988, Vol.20 No.2, 1 [Hart Research Library, History Colorado]

[119] Author was producer of *Pink Triangle Radio* and was responsible to KGNU for producing and airing the program.

[120] "Lisa" Elisabeth Miller Morrissey

[121] Foshee, Jim; two-part interview of Jonathan Ned Katz, *Pink Triangle Radio*, May 7, 1983 & May 14, 1983 [Jonathan Ned Katz papers, Series IX Sound Recordings, Katz Interviews, The New York Public Library, Archives & Manuscripts Division] -and- [*Pink Triangle Radio* recordings, ONE National Gay & Lesbian Archives at the USC Libraries]

[122] Foshee, Jim; gay history report of Rae Bourbon, *Pink Triangle Radio*, Oct 22, 1983 [*Pink Triangle Radio* recordings, ONE National Gay & Lesbian Archives at the USC Libraries]

[123] Author's interview of Phil Price, *Pink Triangle Radio*, Apr 9, 1983 [*Pink Triangle Radio* recordings, ONE National Gay & Lesbian Archives at the USC Libraries]

[124] Mass, Dr. Lawrence D.; "Disease Rumors Largely Unfounded" *New York Native*, May 18, 1981, 7

[125] "Use of AIDS Funds Discussed at GLCCC Membership Meeting" *Out Front*, Oct 14, 1983, 1 [Denver Public Library, Central Library, Western History/ Genealogy]

[126] "Quarterly Membership Meeting of GLCC & AIDS Restricted Funds" *Pink Triangle Radio*, Oct 15, 1983 [*Pink Triangle Radio* recordings, ONE National Gay & Lesbian Archives at the USC Libraries]

[127] Lease, Carol; "Lease Resigns as Executive Director" *Colorado Gay and Lesbian News*, Vol.3 Issue4, Jul 1984, 11 [author's collection]

[128] J.Y.; "Board of Governors Disbanded" *Gaynin'* newsletter of the gay Community Center of Colorado, Vol.2 Issue11, May 1979, 2 [author's collection]

[129] Nash, Phil; "Lease Resigns" *Out Front*, May 25, 1984, 6,14 [Denver Public Library, Central Library, Western History/Genealogy]

[130] "Nash, Phil; "To the Bitter End" *Out Front*, July 20, 1984, 1,7,19 [Denver Public Library, Central Library, Western History/Genealogy]

[131] "Denver Tavern Guild Gives Financial Report" *Out Front*, Aug 3, 1984, 6 [Denver Public Library, Central Library, Western History/Genealogy]

[132] "Profile: The Denver Tavern Guild" *Out Front*, Aug 3, 1984, 11 [Denver Public Library, Central Library, Western History/Genealogy]

[133] Kepner, Jim; autobiographical diary, Feb 22, 1984 [ONE National Gay & Lesbian Archives at the USC Libraries]

[134] Friends living in Yuma were "Jeff" Jeffrey Sperano and Robert Steele (author)

[135] Various papers [William Roosen Files, San Francisco GLBT Historical Society]

[136] Roosen, Dr. William; Regents' Professor of History, Northern Arizona University, letter of Apr 4, 1990 [author's collection]

[137] "Archives Expands Its Name to Reflect Growth Trends" *IGLA Bulletin* (publication of International Gay and Lesbian Archives, Natalie Barney/Edward Carpenter Library), Summer 1984, 1 [author's collection]

Index of Photos

Index

About the Author

Robert C. Steele served as a reporter and producer at various radio and television stations in Colorado and Arizona. He was a broadcaster at the Italian National Broadcasting Company (RAI Radiotelevisione Italiana) in Naples, Italy. While on active duty in the U.S. military he was a reporter for Armed Forces Radio and Television along the coast of Vietnam, the Asian Western Pacific and Vicenza, Italy. He was a volunteer and activist in the early gay liberation movement with the Gay Coalition of Denver and with two weekly gay radio shows in Colorado. Later, as a federal government public affairs officer, he served as a government spokesperson and managed media relations with reporters who worked for media outlets from across the USA and around the world.

For more information visit the book's website: BannedCA.com

CPSIA information can be obtained
at www.ICGtesting.com
Printed in the USA
LVHW082042200122
709010LV00002B/62